Watching Baseball

"A masterful work that tells you more about the game, the strategies, the approaches taken by players and by managers, than you'll find anywhere else."

—*Waterbury Republican-American* (Waterbury, CT)

"Get it and be a smarter fan. Five Stars!"

—*Fenway Nation Book Reviews*

Watching Baseball

Discovering the Game within the Game

Fourth Edition

Jerry Remy

with **Corey Sandler**

THE LYONS PRESS
Guilford, Connecticut
An imprint of The Globe Pequot Press

The Lyons Press is an imprint of The Globe Pequot Press.

Text design: Casey Shain

Photos used as spot art courtesy of Boston Red Sox

Library of Congress Cataloging-in-Publication Data is available.

ISBN: 978-0-7627-4801-3

Printed in the United States of America
10 9 8 7 6 5 4 3 2 1

To Phoebe, my best friend and confidante, the backbone in my life and career.

—Jerry Remy

To Janice, my favorite southpaw, who takes baseball (and me) so very seriously.

—Corey Sandler

Contents

“My relationship with Wally is not that good. Wally only talks to Jerry, which is a little tough on the third guy in the booth.”

NESN PLAY-BY-PLAY
ANNOUNCER DON ORSILLO

Before the game Wally relaxes in his Adirondack chair in the booth, turning his back on his home in the Green Monster in left field.

Photo by Corey Sandler

Foreword

It's not easy being a green monster. People talk to me all the time, but I don't really like to answer. I just watch.

I was around here in 1912 when Fenway Park opened; we won the World Series that year, don't ya know? And we did it again in 1915 and 1916 and 1918 . . . and then there was a brief interruption.

For eighty-six years I watched the Red Sox play hard, win a bunch of games, and break a lot of hearts. And then in 2004 there was a change in the air around here. There was a new flag flying from Fenway Park, and I heard the distant echo of what sounded like a Nation full of cheers, tears, and joy.

The next two years were exciting, but in the end . . . no joy. But things were very special in 2007: The cheers started on Opening Day and the joint was rocking all season long. And now there are two new World Championship banners hanging on Yawkey Way.

Like I said, I am a monster of few words. I've traveled with the team, flown on the charters, sat in on clubhouse meetings, and visited the press box buffet in every major league park.

Here's what I know: This Jerry Remy guy is not as dumb as he looks. He knows more about baseball than many managers, coaches, and players. Heck, he even knows more about the game than I do.

Jerry has been part of the Red Sox for thirty years; that's almost a third of the history of Fenway Park.

Born near Fall River, Massachusetts, he was a high school star at Somerset High School. After coming up to the bigs and playing three seasons with the California Angels, Jerry returned home to Red Sox Nation in 1978. He was a dirt dog at second base for seven years, and then someone got the crazy idea of giving him a microphone in 1987. He hasn't stopped talking since.

I know this guy, and he's the real thing. This is not a history of baseball or a locker room confessional; there are more than enough of those. Instead, allow yourself to let Jerry talk to you about how to watch baseball, just like he tells me during every game.

WALLY THE GREEN MONSTER

Acknowledgments

Nothing would have been the same without my wife, Phoebe. We've been married more than thirty years now, and across all of my years in baseball and broadcasting, she's had most of the responsibility for raising the family. She's the strongest person I know.

My parents, Joe and Connie Remy, were my first and foremost supporters. They made it through my playing days, which were tough on their nerves, and now they keep track of me on television.

Going back, I will always remember my high school coach in Somerset, Jim Sullivan, who was one of the most positive people I've ever been around.

Kenny Myers, a great scout for the Angels, believed he could teach me to be a player, and I guess he did.

Dave Garcia, manager of the Double A El Paso team, and for a brief period my manager with the Angels, took me to the next step, making me believe I could be a big leaguer. Grover Resinger, a crusty old baseball lifer, watched me play Triple A ball and helped guide me through.

Dick Williams taught me more in one year than any other manager I ever played for.

Walt Hriniak, hitting coach for Boston and my close, trusted friend for many years, taught me to put the best effort into everything I do.

Thanks to Jeremy Kapstein—without him I wouldn't have had a clue about the business side of baseball. He's as trustworthy as they come, always looking out for my best interests, and still my close friend.

The late, great Ned Martin was my first partner in broadcasting and helped me ease into the job. Mercy.

Sean McDonough brought out the best in me as an analyst.

And I've also been lucky to work with Bob Kurtz and most recently with Don Orsillo and the rest of the NESN broadcast crew, friendly booth and traveling companions.

I had a great relationship with my coauthor, Corey Sandler; he did a wonderful job interviewing me and making me look smart in this book.

And, of course, there's Wally the Green Monster, my alter ego and best friend on the road. He never gives me any back talk.

JERRY REMY

The Oracle of Fenway, answering questions from the NESN studios in a "Triple Play" segment.

Photo by Corey Sandler

Coauthor Corey Sandler in the NESN broadcast booth at Fenway Park.

Photo by Tessa Sandler

I thought I knew a lot about baseball until I heard Jerry Remy on television analyzing the choreography of a double play, and so I went back to school, listening to him across a season.

And then I got the chance to spend much of a hot stove league winter across the table from Jerry, enrolled in a one-on-one graduate course.

The result is this book, a labor of love for me. This is the fourth edition, revised and updated. I hope you'll come away with a new appreciation of the whys and wherefores of baseball, a game that combines athletic ability, ballet, and intellect in a way no other sport does.

Jerry is the real deal: smart, funny, and a great teammate for a book. He is the Rem Dawg.

Thanks, too, to longtime facilitator Gene Brissie. We extend our thanks to editor Tom McCarthy, a guy who knows a good team when he sees one. Thanks, too, to Dan Spinella, Shelley Wolf, Casey Shain, and Melissa Evarts at The Globe Pequot Press. And Janice Keefe converted hours of audiotape to megabytes of words in her inimitable style.

We appreciate the assistance of Eric Kay and the Los Angeles Angels of Anaheim Baseball Club. Thanks, too, to Debbie Matson, Meghan McClure, Brita Meng Outzen, and the Boston Red Sox for research and photographs from their archives.

COREY SANDLER

22

INTRODUCTION

Why Baseball Matters

I love baseball and I will always love it. My favorite time begins when the umpire says "play ball" and ends with the final out.

I have never been a big fan of the politics of the game. I don't particularly care for pregame predictions and postgame comments. I don't care about contracts. I don't care about collective bargaining agreements. I just like the game.

When I first wrote this section, the ground was blanketed with snow, but people were already talking about the beginning of spring training in a few weeks. People here in Red Sox Nation are so much in love with baseball that they'll tune in to the annual spring training exhibition game between the Sox and Boston college students in March. I guess it brings hope at the end of the harsh New England winter that spring has arrived.

One more thing: The first edition of this book was published in the spring of 2004. Since it came out, the Red Sox have been World Series champions twice. Coincidence? I think not.

Baseball is part of the fabric of our lives. It's a love that is handed down from father to son, mother to daughter. Baseball was huge with my father and my grandfather when I was a kid in Somerset, Massachusetts.

All of us cherish the first time we went to a major league ball game. I remember the first time I walked up the ramp inside Fenway Park and stepped out into the grandstand. The first thing that I saw was the wall, a huge green thing. And then there was the beautiful grass and the colors of the players' uniforms. I was stunned. I guess I still am.

It bothers me when people say baseball is a boring game. It's not boring if you learn how to watch the game closely, and that's what this book is all about. If it really were so boring, I don't think you would see 35,000 people at Fenway for every game and millions tuning in on television and radio. People love watching the great players play.

"Jerry Remy is an extraordinary broadcaster. He makes the victories sweeter and soothes me when the Red Sox suffer a defeat. He's a great analyst, but the best part is that you feel like you're having a beer with a friend while you're watching the game."

THOMAS C.WERNER,
CHAIRMAN, BOSTON RED SOX

In recent years they've cheered for pitching stars like Curt Schilling, Daisuke Matsuzaka, Josh Beckett, Tim Wakefield, and Pedro Martínez. Today's fans have been thrilled by stellar players like Manny Ramírez, David Ortiz, Jason Varitek, and Mike Lowell.

And Fenway still echoes with the ovations for Jim Rice, Carl Yazstrzemski, Carlton Fisk, and Ted Williams. And the record books tell the stories of fabled Boston players like Cy Young, Tris Speaker, and Joe Cronin.

When we talk about a place called Red Sox Nation, we're talking more about a state of mind than a set of states; the Red Sox hear the cheers of the faithful almost as much on the road as they do in friendly Fenway. And New England Sports Network (NESN) broadcasts have moved beyond local cable in New England and are carried by satellite signals across the country.

No matter where these fans live, their connection to the Boston Red Sox is deeply embedded in their hearts and minds. It's a wondrous mixture of hope . . . and longing.

There are going to be so many ups and downs over 162 games and six months of playing: wins, losses, injuries, players upset at the manager, the manager upset with the players, superstars who refuse to talk to the press, and superstars who talk too much.

In football you have one game on Sunday and then it is all preparation until the next game a week later. Baseball changes every day.

During the off-season people ask me all the time who's going to be in the lineup on opening day. First of all, I have no idea what kind of trades the team will make and who will look good in spring training. And then three days into the season, the opening day roster could be thrown out the window if a rookie gets hot or a proven star breaks down.

Over the course of a season, we don't know if our star shortstop is going to get hurt or if our superstar pitcher's shoulder is going to fall apart. We don't know if a guy with a great career record as a hitter is inexplicably going to have a terrible season, or if some unheralded rookie is going to tear the cover off the ball for the entire season and take the job of a veteran. These are the days of the baseball soap opera.

While "Hail to the Chief" blasted through the speakers at Fenway Park, I threw out the first pitch before Game 1 of the American League Division Series in 2007. It was my first official act as the first President of Red Sox Nation.

Photo by Brita Meng Outzen

RED SOX

PART ONE

Inside Baseball

Early in the minor leagues, in a flannel uniform . . . with something missing from my upper lip.

Photo courtesy Los Angeles Angels of Anaheim Baseball Club

CHAPTER ONE

We've Got to Think about the Game

Looking Deeper into Baseball

If all you do is follow the ball, you're missing much of the game.

Baseball is much more complex than that. One of the great things about the sport is that, from the first pitch to the final out, it's all presented right in front of you on a beautiful green stage.

Everyone second-guesses the manager; that's a lot of fun for everyone except the manager being second-guessed. That's what you hear all day on the sports talk shows and read in the newspaper columns. But if you're really going to get into the game, start first-guessing.

As you're watching a game, think about what you would do right now if you were in charge. Would you call for a hit-and-run play? Would you instruct the batter to work the count?

Should the first baseman hold the runner? Are the infielders adjusting their positions for each batter and changing them as the count changes?

Watch the pitcher. Is this a good time for a pitchout? Does he have a plan to get the batter out? Is he out of gas? Who's ready in the bull pen? Is it time to bring in a right-hander or a lefty?

Watching a play

Here's the way a casual viewer might see a baseball play:

- The pitcher, who has been showing a blazing fastball all through the game, throws an unexpectedly slow pitch to the plate, completely baffling a right-handed batter.

The view from the Fenway broadcast booth, high up above home plate.

Photo by Corey Sandler

- The batter swings way before the ball is over the plate and hits a sharp ground ball to the left side of the infield.
- The shortstop is standing directly in the path of the oncoming ball.
- The fielder catches the ball and fires it across the infield to the first baseman, with the ball arriving a half step ahead of the runner.

If that's the way you watch baseball, you're seeing the essential action, but you're missing almost all of the game within the game: the strategy, planning, and execution.

In this book you'll learn how to really watch a baseball game. I'll show you how to look at the game through the eyes of a player or a manager . . . or a television color analyst.

On the very simple play outlined earlier, ask yourself the following questions:

- Why did the pitcher throw a changeup?
- Why was it likely that the batter would swing on a 2–0 count?
- Why had the shortstop moved two steps to his right as the pitch was delivered, ending up exactly where the ball was headed?
- Why did the catcher follow the runner up the base path toward first?
- What was the right fielder doing coming in toward the infield on a play at first?

Along with learning how to watch a game, together we'll look at much more complex elements of the game, including the art of pitching, hitting, fielding, and baserunning. I will try to take you inside the minds of the players and the coaches.

This is not a tutorial on how to play baseball or a history of the Boston Red Sox; there are plenty of those already on the bookshelves. Instead, in this book I'll show you how to open your eyes to the inside game of baseball.

Picking a Place to Sit

As much as I love the way television takes you deep inside the game with up close shots, when you watch games on TV, you only see what the cameras show you. When you sit in the stands, you can watch a lot of things that you've missed on TV. You might want to watch the center fielder the whole game or concentrate on the defensive adjustments that the shortstop makes with each pitch.

In general sitting behind home plate is the best place from which to see a baseball game. You are squared up with the pitcher and can see the location, movement, and velocity of pitches. You pretty much see the field the way the hitter does; a good hitter takes note of the positions of the infielders and the outfielders.

Some people like to sit along the first-base line or the third-base line to be close to the players when they go on or come off the field. In most—but not all—parks, the home team's dugout is along the first-base line and the visitors are on the third-base line.

If you're seated along the line, you also can watch for the signs exchanged between the second baseman and shortstop when there's a runner on first base to indicate who's going to cover second base on a throw from the catcher or pitcher.

Although it's a long way from home plate, you can get some idea of the location of pitches when you sit in the outfield bleachers. And if

Rem Dawg Remembers

The Boys from New York

I don't hate the Yankees; I never did. I respect them.

I think more of the rivalry is between fans, although from time to time there were a lot of guys on both teams that did not like each other. In the 1970s there was Carlton Fisk and Thurman Munson, Fisk and Lou Piniella, and a few others.

There were a lot of personal relationships that were not good. But how can you not respect teams that have done what they have done? I really like Hideki Matsui; he showed me a lot in 2004. This guy is an all around solid baseball player. And Derek Jeter is one of the best competitors in the game. You may not like the uniform they are wearing or the city they play in, but you can't argue with success.

you're looking for an overview of the whole field and the positioning of the defense, the bleachers are a great spot to sit.

From the bleachers you can also watch the communication between outfielders about how to defend against the batter at the plate. You may be able to see into the dugout and watch the coach who is in charge of positioning outfielders yelling to get their attention; you can see if they listen to him or not.

Before the pitch, watch the catcher. If he is setting up outside, do you see the infielders moving toward the hitter's opposite field (left field for a right-handed hitter; right field for a lefty batter)? Does the center fielder, right in front of you, make an adjustment?

Another great spot is in the grandstand right above home plate. You see pitches break and had a good look at the positioning of outfielders and infielders.

And then there's my seat, a bit higher over home plate. It's been my view ever since I left the field, and it's a great privilege to watch from there.

PART TWO

It All Begins with a Pitch

I watch the pitches and close plays on the monitors; the screen to my right is the Telestrator, where I can scribble lines, arrows, and the occasional comment.

Photo by Corey Sandler

CHAPTER TWO

Pitchers

The Starting Pitcher

Everything starts with the pitcher.

The three people with the best view of the incoming pitch are the batter, the catcher, and the umpire. All the rest of us have a secondhand view: from above, the side, or far away. From the stands—and from the dugout—it's pretty hard to tell the location and movement of pitches.

Here is where television really shines: You get a great view of the pitch from the camera that looks over the pitcher's shoulder toward home plate. That's the one we watch most closely in the broadcast booth.

If you're at the ballpark, there are other things to watch. Most parks now display the speed of the pitch; you can watch the variations in fastballs and spot breaking balls. And you can learn something about the pitch by the adjustments the infielders make.

Watch the pitcher's body language. Some pitchers lay claim to the mound with a sneer and a swagger. Others seem to dissolve before your eyes, with a deer-in-the-headlights panicked stare when they give up a few runs.

A guy may be on top of his game, and all of a sudden he has a bad inning and his shoulders drop. The man at the plate is so close to the pitcher he can see the look in his eyes and the droop in his shoulders. If the message is, "I don't want to be here," the batter knows he has the advantage.

A good starting pitcher is one of the most valuable commodities in baseball. In today's game most pitching coaches try to keep him healthy by limiting the number of pitches he throws per outing.

The starting pitcher used to be expected to pitch a complete game, unless he was ineffective or got hurt or if a pinch hitter replaced him in the lineup. There are still some pitchers who can go out and pitch nine innings, but complete games are now about as rare as 50-cent hot dogs.

In 2007 the Red Sox had a grand total of four complete games in the regular season. (By way of comparison, the great Cy Young completed forty-one games all by himself in 1902.) One was the heart-breaking one-hitter (he came within one out of a no-hitter) by stalwart veteran Curt Schilling. A second was tossed by Daisuke Matsuzaka, a solid MLB rookie with a proven record in Japan. The third was a gem by Kason Gabbard, a promising rookie who was traded to Texas late in the season for reliever Eric Gagné. The fourth complete game was the extraordinary no-hitter by Clay Buchholz, who became the first Red Sox rookie ever to throw a no-hitter; it came on his second major league start, on September 1.

Today most managers say, "Give me a solid six or seven innings and the bull pen will take over." From there they'll go to the setup man for an inning or two and then to the closer.

During the game, among the pitching coach's principal assignments is paying attention to the pitch count; before the game begins he'll usually decide how many pitches he wants the starter to throw. The magic number for most pitchers is around 115; anything above 100 pitches and most managers are looking for the moment to lift him.

Back in the day, a guy like Luis Tiant would tell the manager, "No, no, no. I am finishing my game." And I played in games with Nolan Ryan when he threw 150 or 160 pitches in completing a game.

But a complete game is now so rare that even if a pitcher is carrying a no-hitter into the seventh or eighth inning, the manager and coach may be secretly hoping for a harmless single to end the zeros in the hit column.

When Buchholz threw his no-hitter, the rookie had not thrown more than 98 pitches in any game all year, and Red Sox general manager Theo Epstein confirmed that he had spoken with manager Terry Francona during the game. They had set a limit of 120 pitches; Buchholz completed his gem with 115 pitches. I think there would have been a riot if they pulled him from the game.

The emphasis on pitch count can sometimes affect the course of the game. The starter might have had a tough first couple of innings, throwing fifty pitches, and then he'll try to economize the rest of the way, which may or may not be the best way for him to pitch.

Is a 100 MPH fastball all you need?

There have been more than a few ballplayers who were capable of throwing a fastball at 100 miles per hour but who had no success as pitchers. These guys are throwers, not pitchers.

If every pitch is 99 miles per hour, a good batter will eventually learn to time his swing; mixing in an off-speed pitch, say at 92 miles per hour, at the proper time can be very effective.

A thrower doesn't know how to set up the hitter this way. And when a thrower becomes a pitcher, it's not all about velocity: It's where he puts the ball.

It's just like real estate: location, location, location. That's pitching.

Control is the most important skill: A pitcher needs to throw strikes, make quality pitches, get ahead of hitters, and expand the strike zone when he gets ahead in the count. You can't pitch successfully in the big leagues from behind in the count.

If you can paint the corners all day long, move the ball in and out and up and down, change speeds, and otherwise keep hitters off balance, you are going to be a good pitcher. I think of a guy like Greg Maddux, who is not a hard thrower but is headed for the Hall of Fame.

Pitchers also have to make adjustments. In any particular game only two of his pitches might be working, and sometimes everything deserts him but one pitch, and he's got to be able to win with that.

And then you have great pitchers who once were fireballers but continue having success late in their career because of their ability to put a good pitch in a good place, even if it no longer scorches the air on the way to the plate. Over the course of the 2007 season, Curt Schilling moved into that group.

The expressway to the majors

Today a guy who can pitch well often does not spend much time in the minors; the parent club will rush him up to the majors as quickly as possible. There simply are not enough quality pitchers at the major-league level.

But sometimes a great pitcher takes a long time to reach his peak. Nolan Ryan is the perfect example. When Ryan came up to the Mets at age nineteen, he could throw the ball through the wall but sometimes couldn't find the strike zone with a map. His effectiveness as a pitcher developed through experience, and part of that came from realizing that he didn't have to throw every ball that hard.

Opening the Door to the Bull Pen

Most teams have a well-defined routine for use of the bull pen. If the starter gets in trouble early, the manager is going to bring in a new arm; if he's doing well, the starter may last until the seventh or eighth inning before the door to the bull pen is opened. In today's game, though, there is no such thing as an all-purpose reliever; they're all specialists in the bull pen.

The **long reliever** has to be ready from the beginning of the game; if the starting pitcher gets in trouble, the long reliever may come in during the first inning and pitch a large piece of the game. The **middle reliever** is called on for three or four innings of help if the starter falters a little later on.

Then there is the **setup pitcher,** who is typically expected to keep things under control during the seventh and eighth innings of a close game. And finally there is the **closer,** who will watch the game in the clubhouse and walk out to the bull pen around the seventh inning only if it looks like a game in which he is going to be used.

The middle reliever

Most pitchers would like to be a starter or a great closer. I don't think anybody says, "I want to be a middle reliever." The pitcher in this role usually is a starter who has been bumped out of the rotation. The middle reliever's job is to eat up the middle innings of the game, keeping his team close. He may pick up a couple of runs on his earned run average (ERA) but not a win.

The setup man

Late in a close game, the manager may bring in a setup man. These are specialists who come in for just an inning or two, or sometimes just for a

Remy Says: Watch This

The Rules of the Bull Pen

Pitchers sitting out in the bull pen are sometimes in a world of their own, which may explain some of the strange things that go on out there. Most of these guys spend a couple of hours not directly involved in the game, and I guess they have to keep occupied doing something.

It is their little sanctuary, their home away from the clubhouse. They talk a lot. They tell jokes. In some places they watch for fights in the stands. You don't see anybody going out to the bull pen with a lunch box, but I am sure plenty of hot dogs have changed hands between fans and players. Some players have been known to send out for food.

It can also get a little weird. In 2007 Boston's excellent relief corps—mostly young arms like those of Papelbon, Okajima, and Manny Delcarmen—were taken under the wing of veteran Mike Timlin. With a lot of time on their hands, these guys chose to reenvision themselves as the crew of a pirate ship, complete with secret names, handshakes, and a stuffed parrot as a mascot. And they put together a powerful rhythm section in the bullpen, pounding away during rallies and in crucial pitching situations with water bottles, fungo bats, and anything else they could scavenge from their kit. Obviously it worked: In the playoffs, the Angels, Indians, and Rockies were robbed on a regular basis.

few batters, to shut down the opposition. Managers like to have two setup men; if lefties are coming up, they may bring in the left-handed pitcher first and perhaps follow with the righty. The goal is to keep the other team off the board until they can get to their stud closer to pitch the ninth inning.

There is a theory now, and I think it is mostly true, that some of the most important outs in the game may come in the seventh inning. But the problem with that is if the manager uses his best guy then, who does he use in the ninth? Someone not as effective?

In 2007 the Red Sox received the most pleasant of surprises from Hideki Okajima . . . the *other* Japanese pitcher they signed. Not all that much was expected of the thirty-one-year-old veteran from the Yomiuri Giants and the Hokkaido Nippon Ham Fighters; all eyes were on the much-heralded Daisuke Matsuzaka. But Okajima made his presence known early in the season shutting down the Yankees in a game when Jonathan Papelbon was not available.

Then he went on to establish a remarkable streak as the eighth- (or seventh-) inning setup man who kept the game in control until Papelbon could close.

Okajima doesn't have a blazing fastball, but there's something about his windup, including the fact that he looks away from the plate at a critical moment in his delivery, and a few wrinkles in his "Okey-Dokey" pitch that make him very effective. He called himself the "hero in the shadows."

The mind of the closer

The perfect closer is Mr. Lights Out: a pitcher who can come in and mow down three batters in the ninth inning before the other side can even think about putting on its rally caps. He almost never comes in when his team is behind and rarely when it is tied. His job is to close the door when the win is on the line.

The best closers are usually strikeout pitchers: The less contact a batter makes, the less chance you have of getting beat. Most closers have a trick pitch, like a splitter or a cut fastball. Or they have overpowering velocity.

A closer has to be able to take the mound knowing there's nobody else warming up. It's his game to hold . . . or blow . . . the lead.

Intimidation is a big part of being a closer. Troy Percival, in his prime, squinted at the batter like Mr. Magoo, put a frightening scowl on his face, and then threw a 100 MPH fastball.

The closer also needs a short memory. He is not going to save every game, but he has to be able to forget what happened last night and go back out there the next day. As a hitter, if I went 0 for 5 in a game, I would

Schilling Talks

Curt Schilling lays it all out there on his blog. He talks about his contract, his life, and everything else. I could never have done that sort of thing. Schilling pitches once every five days so he has the time, and more to the point he loves it. Check it out at 38pitches.com.

"You don't always make an out. Sometimes the pitcher gets you out."

RED SOX GREAT CARL YASTRZEMSKI

go to bed tossing and turning. I am sure closers do the same thing after they blow a game. But while a hitter hopes for a .300 average, if a pitcher is .500 as a closer, he is not going to be working very long.

The manager doesn't have to hold back the closer for the last innings; some are brought in for sticky situations in the eighth. Let's say there is one out and the other team has runners on second and third. The manager really needs an out, and the safest way would be to keep the ball out of play and get a strikeout. In that instance the manager might go to the closer and ask him to give the team five outs instead of three.

In 2006 we saw the emergence of a great closer in Jonathan Papelbon, but by the end of the season he was shut down because of strain on his arm from near-daily throwing. As the 2007 season approached, Paps was supposed to be changing over to a starting pitcher—and he probably would have been a good one—but at spring training he solved a critical need on the Red Sox by asking to go back to the bull pen.

Papelbon had a spectacular year in 2007, in the class of Mariano Rivera. He finished with a postseason in which he was almost untouchable: 4 saves, 1 win, and no runs in seven appearances. And his victory dance, a Texas version of an Irish jig, earned him a spot on the *Late Show with David Letterman* and the thanks of a grateful Red Sox Nation.

Distractions from the Mound

You've got pitchers who windmill their arms, kick their legs above their shoulders, turn their backs, and do just about anything you can imagine in their windup. Hitters will tell themselves they've got to pick up the baseball when the pitcher releases it from his hand; they've got to put all of the windup theatrics aside because none of it means anything.

A pitcher's delivery is like a hitter's stance before he swings: You can

Now pitching, Terry Francona

Red Sox manager Terry Francona played for parts of ten seasons in the Major Leagues, coming up with the Montreal Expos in 1981 and later playing for the Chicago Cubs and the Cincinnati Reds in the National League and then the Cleveland Indians and the Milwaukee Brewers of the American League.

A lefthander, he began as an outfielder but shifted to first base for the latter half of his career. He finished with a career batting average of .274 in 1,731 at bats. He hit a total of 16 home runs and drove in 143 runs. Oh, and he pitched one perfect inning.

On May 15, 1989 the Milwaukee Brewers were being pounded by the Oakland Athletics on the road, behind 12–2 after seven innings. Francona volunteered to give the bullpen a rest, and came in to pitch the bottom of the eighth inning. Three up, three down: 12 pitches, no hits, no walks, and one strikeout. Stan Javier, not a bad hitter, went down swinging on three pitches thrown by Francona.

have any stance you want at the start. It's how you finish that matters, how you make contact. A pitcher can do three flips and a handstand and then throw the pitch. Regardless of what the windup looks like, at some point the pitcher has to release the baseball and that's what the hitter is supposed to focus on.

Today pitchers are not supposed to wear jewelry and other things that might distract the batter. When I played, I faced guys with chains and pendants and other stuff. We had Oil Can Boyd pitching for Boston in the 1980s. Let me put this carefully: He was a bit excitable. He used to wear all these chains and some opposing managers would let him start the game, and if he got himself in a pretty good groove, they would try to disrupt him by asking umpires to make him take the stuff off.

Curt Schilling wears a necklace and various emblems and slogans for causes that are important to him. Josh Beckett also hangs a collar-like "sports necklace" around his neck.

In recent years there have been some funny incidents regarding fashion statements by players. In 2001 Seattle's Arthur Rhodes came in to face Omar Vizquel, then with Cleveland, in the ninth inning. It was a sunny day and Vizquel asked the umpire to tell Rhodes to take off a big jeweled earring he was wearing.

Now it is quite possible that the glare from that earring really was bothering Vizquel. Or it might have been an attempt to aggravate the pitcher and get him out of his rhythm. In any case Rhodes absolutely lost his composure and started yelling at Vizquel, and there was a bench-clearing tussle that ended up with Rhodes thrown out of the game. All for an earring.

Pedro Martínez got called on the carpet a few times, too. Once the home-plate umpire made him change his glove because it had red stitching that was distracting. He also used to cut his sleeves, and they would be flapping with his delivery. I don't think he was trying to bother the hitter with it; he just felt comfortable that way. But the rules say you can't do that.

When you're up against a guy as good as Pedro, you look for any kind of edge. But with him, it probably works the other way. I don't know that I would want to get Martínez ticked off at me when I was up at the plate.

And in 2003 Roger Clemens—before he retired, unretired, retired, unretired, and retired—took to the mound for the Yankees against the Red Sox with hopes of winning his 300th game in front of his traveling troupe of friends and family. Right at the start of the game, manager Grady Little complained to the umpires about a flashy "300" patch Clemens had attached to his glove. He had to change gloves, and he was sent to the showers in the sixth inning. The glove escapade just may have nudged the Rocket off course.

Men at work midgame in the broadcast booth. Don Orsillo calls the plays while I study the monitors for details and Wally keeps an eye on the wall.

Photo by Corey Sandler

CHAPTER THREE

Pitches

Four-tenths of a Second

It takes just four-tenths of a second or so for a baseball to travel from the pitcher's hand to the plate. In that time a good hitter tries to figure out what kind of pitch is coming, where it's going, and whether it's worth a swing.

One key to recognizing the pitch is to focus on the pitcher's hand as it comes through to the release point. Attentive hitters also pay attention to the arm slot, which is the angle of the arm as the ball is released. A pitcher can have an over-the-top, three-quarter, sidearm, submarine, or any other arm slot.

When he throws a curveball, his arm may be more on top. When his wrist is facing home plate, the pitch is probably going to be something straight like a fastball. When the wrist is turned in a position like pulling down a shade, that's going to be a breaking ball or a curve.

Pitching coaches try to encourage pitchers to have the same release point for every pitch, but that is a very difficult thing to do. There are so many tiny differences in the way the pitcher might throw the ball or release it. One sinker might drop more than the other. One splitter might break down and away, while the next pitch might be straight down.

A good slider is supposed to be hard, breaking down and away. If the pitcher changes his arm angle to drop more to the side, that slider is going to stay flat in the zone, and those go a long, long way when a batter makes contact with them.

Seeing the spin

If it's a slider, the rotation of the ball is around the seams, and it looks like a dot coming at the hitter. A slider breaks the opposite direction from a curveball—from a left-handed pitcher that's down and in to a right-handed hitter. A right-handed pitcher's slider breaks down and in to a lefty at the plate.

When a pitcher throws a curve, the release is more over the top and the rotation of the spin is from twelve o'clock to six o'clock, as if it were tumbling toward the hitter. A right-handed pitcher's curve breaks down and away from a righty at the plate; a left-handed pitcher's curve moves in the opposite way.

There's very little spin on a fastball, which comes in a straight line, although some pitchers' fastballs rise or sink. With a changeup or splitter, hitters don't see any flow to the rotation of the ball. Many players can pick up the lack of pattern pretty easily.

Hitters see the spin on a ball better in day games than at night. And some stadium lights are better than others.

Submariners

Submarine pitchers who throw from the ground up are pretty rare in baseball, and that is one of the reasons some of them have success. Byung-Hyun Kim, who passed through Boston in 2003 and 2004, had uneven success; Mike Venafro had a similar career.

Batters are accustomed to pitchers throwing three-quarter, sidearm, or over the top, and all of a sudden there's this guy scraping his knuckles against the mound. To hit a submariner the hitter has to look down toward the rubber instead of looking up high for the release point.

When submarine pitchers throw a sinker the ball darts down and away from a left-handed hitter and down and in to a right-handed hitter. And their breaking balls usually seem like Frisbees, like they are going uphill; if they don't hit the right spot with it, the ball is going to go back the other direction a long way.

Dan Quisenberry was one of the best, a very good closer for Kansas City. He would bury the ball down and in on right-handed hitters.

My approach as a left-handed hitter was to try and hit him the other way because I figured most of the time the ball would be down and away. So I'd be leaning out over the plate and trying to make contact, and Quisenberry would bust a pitch inside because that was the last place I was looking for it.

Remy Says: Watch This

Pitching Mechanics

See if you can spot differences in the pitcher's delivery. Does he use a different arm slot when he throws a curveball? If you're sitting behind the plate—or watching on TV—can you see the spin on the ball?

The pitching rubber—the white rubber slab a pitcher must keep contact with as he starts his windup—is twenty-four inches wide. Watch where the pitcher plants his back foot; some start from the first-base side, some toward third, and some right in the middle.

The pitcher's position on the rubber affects the angle of the ball coming in toward the plate. You'll sometimes see a pitcher who has always thrown from the first-base side of the rubber move to the right side because the pitching coach has noticed something in his delivery or because he wants to show the hitter a different angle.

The Fastball

The fastball—the *heat, cheese, smoke*—is the basic pitch in baseball and the easiest to put in a particular location. A typical major league pitcher throws the fastball at about 90 miles per hour. Some reach the upper 90s and a few cross over 100 MPH on some pitches.

There are three different types of fastballs, and they vary by how the pitcher grips the seams.

The *cross-seam fastball* (or *four-seam fastball*) is a straight pitch with very little movement. Thrown hard and flat, the ball rotates bottom to top, from six o'clock to twelve o'clock. When it is thrown hard, it almost looks as if it rises as it comes to home plate. Truth is, a rising fastball doesn't jump up as it nears the plate. It's just going uphill. You'll see batters swinging underneath a rising fastball because a high pitch always looks better to hit than a low pitch.

The *two-seam fastball* is a *sinking fastball,* or a *sinker,* or a *heavy fastball.* Released the same way as a four-seam fastball and thrown just as hard, the wrist is turned just slightly. As a result the ball rotates off-center; it still spins bottom to top, but it might come in more like one o'clock to seven o'clock. It is also a little more difficult for the pitcher to hit a precise location in the strike zone with this pitch.

A two-seam fastball has good velocity—in the vicinity of 90 MPH for most pitchers—but it takes a hard dip at the end because of the rotation of the seams. If a batter makes contact, it feels like he's hitting a shot put. This was Derek Lowe's specialty, a ball that moves down and in to right-handers or down and away to a lefty.

And then there is the *cutter* or *cut fastball,* which is somewhere between a fastball and a slider. To throw a cut fastball, the pitcher holds it a little off-center from his normal grip. It looks like a fastball coming in, and at the last moment it cuts a little bit; thrown by a righty, it goes in on the hands of a left-handed hitter or toward the outside of the plate against a righty.

This is Mariano Rivera's bread and butter. You would think that after batters see it a few times, they would be able to hit it, but most can't. It is so deceptive.

A right-handed batter is likely to swing as a cut fastball moves away. With luck the batter hopes to at least be able to hit a cut fastball off the end of the bat, going to the opposite field. When he hits a ball off the

Remy Says: Watch This

Eight Feet off the Ground

Another factor that comes into play is the height of the pitcher. As good as he was, Pedro Martínez is only of average height, about 5'11". Curt Schilling and Josh Beckett each stand 6'5". In 2007 the tallest pitcher for Boston was reliever and spot starter Kyle Snyder at 6'8".

And then remember Randy Johnson at 6'10". Standing on top of the mound, which is ten inches higher than home plate, and whipping his arm over his head, Johnson released the ball about 8 feet in the air.

Even the tallest batters were looking up at Johnson at an unusual angle. By the time he finished his stride, he might be just over 50 feet away from the batter. And oh, by the way, he's a lefty and when he was right he threw the ball at something close to 98 miles per hour.

end of the bat, he generally gets less power on the ball, and the bat often breaks.

Or the hitter can hope the pitcher misses over the plate.

It's just the opposite for a left-hander. When it cuts, it moves toward the label of the bat. He gets jammed and probably breaks the bat.

Either way, when a hitter faces a guy like Rivera, he had better have a good supply of bats.

The mystery of the Gyroball

Does he or doesn't he? We're not talking about whether Daisuke Matsuzaka colors his hair. The question is: Does he throw a *gyroball?* Or maybe, does such a pitch exist?

The answer, thus far, is a definite maybe.

It appears to me that among his wide arsenal of pitches there is one that may—sometimes—act a bit differently. I'm not convinced that it is a completely new pitch. I think it may be a slightly different spin on a slider or a cutter; some says it's a tight screwball.

In any case it's a hard-thrown breaking ball with late movement that moves down and away from a right-handed batter. It's thrown so hard that you could also think of it as a fastball with movement.

Or maybe not.

More variations of the fastball

A *running fastball* is almost like a cut fastball, but it is usually a mistake. The pitcher may have held the ball just a little bit off-center. The result is that at the last minute it runs in on a hitter.

Most cross-seam fastballs are thrown right over the top to three-quarters. And a lot of cut fastball pitchers are right over the top, too. Most sinker-ball pitchers release the ball down a little bit lower, still well above the shoulder.

A fastball is a good strikeout pitch for a pitcher who can get some velocity on the ball. There's a baseball saying: "Climb the ladder." The pitcher climbs the ladder with each successive pitch—throwing each pitch a little higher, at times out of the strike zone—hoping that the batter will chase as the ball goes upstairs.

A pitcher will sometimes throw what they call a *batting practice fastball,* sometimes when the count is 2-0. The batter is all geared up for the pitcher to throw something hard, and instead the pitcher will just take a little bit off his fastball and get the batter swinging out front a little bit.

The Curveball

The *hook,* the *deuce,* the *hammer,* the *knee buckler,* the *yakker:* whatever you call it, this is the basic breaking ball or *curveball.*

Instead of being released in a natural manner, in the direction the fingers point at the batter, a curveball is thrown with the wrist cocked so that the thumb is on top. When the ball is released, it rolls over the outside of the index finger. The ball rotates from top to bottom, the opposite of a fastball. A typical major leaguer's curveball is about 7 to 10 miles per hour slower than his fastball.

A curveball thrown by a right-hander breaks down and away from a right-handed hitter, which makes it difficult to hit; a curve by the same pitcher will break down and in to a lefty, which is a location most batters prefer.

A curveball thrown by a left-handed pitcher breaks in the opposite way, which is tougher on a lefty at the plate and easier for a righty.

When a pitcher has a good breaking ball, you'll see what I call a *jelly leg curve.* That happens when the pitcher throws the ball directly at the hitter and it curves back out over the plate. The hitter thinks he's going to get hit, his legs buckle, and all of a sudden the ball is by him over the plate. That's a nasty pitch.

A bad curve—*hanging breaking ball*—stays belt high and is often redeposited over the fence by a power hitter.

The break of the pitch depends on arm angle. If the pitcher releases the ball straight over the top, the break is going to be twelve o'clock to six o'clock. If he drops down a little bit more to the side, it's going to be two to eight. The basic definition of a curveball calls for it to start inside and finish away, but there are very effective pitchers like Mike Mussina, whose successful curves break almost straight down.

A right-handed pitcher can also throw a backdoor curve to a left-handed hitter. That's a pitch that starts outside and breaks in to pick up the outside corner. Many lefties quit on that pitch because they expect it to be outside.

"[Satchel Paige] threw the ball as far from the bat and as close to the plate as possible."

CASEY STENGEL

The *screwball* is a pitch we don't see very often any more because it is so demanding on the arm and the elbow, and it is difficult to throw. It breaks in the opposite direction of the curve. It also doesn't have the arc of a curve. A screwball from a right-hander goes into a righty at the plate and down and away from the left-hander.

The Slider

A *slider* has a bigger break than the cut fastball but less than a curveball. It is thrown harder than a curveball, perhaps 4 or 5 miles per hour slower than a fastball. Today you see more sliders than curveballs, probably because it is an easier pitch to throw and control.

The pitcher holds his first two fingers close together, off-center, down the length of the seam on the ball. The late break in the pitch is caused by its off-center spin.

Sliders can be nasty because they look like a fastball out of the hand. Left-handers are generally good low-ball hitters, but if the slider arrives down and in off the plate, it is almost a blind spot.

If a pitcher makes a mistake with a slider, it goes a long way in the other direction. A slider has good velocity, and if the movement brings it out over the plate, the batter gets a good fastball-like swing on a pitch that is not thrown as hard.

The Split-Finger Fastball

To me the *split-finger fastball* or the *splitter* is the most difficult pitch to hit. It's thrown like a fastball and the bottom just falls out. The pitcher is trying to get the batter to swing at a pitch that usually ends up out of the strike zone. He thinks he is swinging at a knee-high fastball and it is not there.

Remy's Top Dawgs

Ever wonder what it's like to face a tough pitcher? I played with **Nolan Ryan** on the Angels and then against him with the Red Sox. I saw him change more opposing lineups than any pitcher on a team I played on. If he was pitching, you would see guys ask for days off or report in with bad backs, the flu, a headache . . . whatever. Guys just didn't want to face him.

When I was playing with him, every fastball was 99 or 100 miles per hour, and he had a hard curveball. As he matured in his career, he continued to intimidate but also learned how to pitch. He developed a changeup and turned the ball over now and then.

He had seven no-hitters; I can't imagine that record ever being broken.

The grip for a splitter has the fingers spread very wide on the ball. A similar pitch is the *forkball,* but with the forkball the pitcher actually sticks the ball between his fingers. The splitter can be thrown harder. The result is a weird rotation that picks up some drag on the way to the plate, usually about 4 or 5 miles per hour slower than a fastball.

A good splitter goes down to drop out of the strike zone, but some may go down and in or down and away. When a pitcher has a good splitter going, he is going to keep his catcher real busy throughout the game, blocking a lot of balls on one hop. The pitcher needs to have confidence that his catcher can block a pitch when he throws it with a man on third base.

When I was playing, I thought this was the worst pitch ever invented; the only chance I had was when the pitcher made a mistake and it ended up belt high.

The Changeup

A good changeup—also known as an *off-speed pitch,* a *dead fish,* a *circle change*—is a very effective pitch. Done right, the arm action, the speed of the arm, and the angle of release are exactly the same as for a fastball.

The fastball is the fastest pitch; a slider is not quite as hard, but it is still moving. And a curveball is slower. But for most pitchers, the changeup is the slowest of all.

Hitting is timing, and batters generally gear themselves for fastballs. The changeup is designed to keep hitters off-balance with a pitch that looks like a fastball and has fastball movement but arrives at the plate just late enough to throw off their swing. And a smart pitcher makes it even more difficult by throwing an off-speed pitch on counts when batters think they are going to get a fastball.

The ideal changeup is low, about knee high or lower.

The pitcher holds the ball back in the palm of his hand and squeezes it tight, often with the thumb and forefinger touching in a "circle" on the side of the ball. While a fastball uses the full leverage of the arm to give it speed and picks up its spin from the first two fingers, the changeup grip spreads the force around more of the ball.

A good major league changeup may be 10 or 15 miles per hour slower than the same pitcher's fastball, but it looks the same at the point of release. In theory a changeup is not as tough to hit as a splitter because it is off-speed and straight, while the splitter has that downward action. But for most batters, a changeup is a very tough pitch to hit.

When Pedro Martínez was king of the hill, he had a very effective changeup that acted almost like a screwball. He was the kind of pitcher who could walk up to home plate and tell the batter, "I am going to throw you three changeups and you won't hit them."

You would think that if a batter knew a changeup was coming, he could adjust his timing. But if a pitcher like Martínez throws a good one down and away, the batter may hit it, but not well.

There's got to be a good spread between the fastball and the changeup to make the off-speed pitch effective. If Martínez is throwing the heat at 95 miles per hour, his changeup might be 78 MPH. That's a pretty good ratio. If there's a guy who's throwing 87 miles per hour and his changeup is 83 MPH, that is not going to be good enough.

The Knuckleball

The *knuckleball* is not necessarily the most difficult to hit, but it is certainly the most unusual pitch a batter is ever going to see. It is a freak pitch, different from any other pitch. It's slow—it can flutter in there as slow as 50 or 60 miles per hour—but there's no predicting where it'll go. Knuckleball pitchers themselves don't always know.

I hope all Red Sox fans recognize the privilege we have in seeing Tim Wakefield throw the knuckler. He is among just a few of the great pitchers of modern baseball to be able to win with the pitch. I was going to say "master" the pitch, but I'm not sure that even Wakefield would use that word.

When Wakefield is having success, some of the best hitters in the game look like Little Leaguers swinging with their eyes closed at a curve ball. But when his knuckler flattens out, it sometimes looks like batting practice.

I've always wondered what a pitching coach can say to Wakefield when he starts to lose the ability to throw strikes or if the pitch stops knuckling. The ordinary bits of advice for a pitcher don't apply.

But there is no arguing with success. As of the end of the 2007 season, Wakefield had 154 wins as a member of the Red Sox (plus 14 more from the beginning of his career with the Pittsburgh Pirates.) That puts him into second place on the all-time wins list for Boston, behind Cy Young and Roger Clemens who each recorded 192 wins for the Red Sox. (Mel Parnell is in fourth place with 123 wins, Luis Tiant won 122 games, and Pedro Martínez and Smoky Joe Wood are tied for sixth with 117 wins.)

To throw a knuckleball, the pitcher grips the ball with the tips of his first two fingers on top and the thumb anchoring it from below. The ball is pushed out toward the plate rather than thrown. (Contrary to what you might have thought, the knuckles are not involved in the pitch as it is thrown today; the name of the pitch comes from an old baseball term about the ball *knuckling* on the way to the plate.) A well-thrown knuckleball has no spin at all, and its movement on the way to the plate is affected by wind currents.

There have been a thousand theories on how to hit them: move up toward the pitcher, get closer to the plate, swing at the early pitches in the count because the pitcher is just trying to get one over for a strike. Or try to get hit by the pitch to get on base; it doesn't hurt much.

There's a baseball saying: If it's high, let it fly. The theory is that if a knuckleball stays up high, that's a good one to hit. If it is down low, it is probably going to dart all over the place. I'm not sure either theory works.

But knuckleball games can turn into disasters in a hurry if the pitcher loses control of the pitch and starts making wild pitches. Or the catcher may simply be unable to grab the ball or block it. Either way you've got guys running all over the bases.

And if the knuckleball stops knuckling—if it comes in flat—it goes back the other way a long distance. I have seen knuckleball pitchers start off great and all of a sudden the magic is gone. I have seen guys go through one inning when they can't control the thing, and then they have a great one.

There's not a lot a batter can do to prepare for a knuckler. Even if there's someone who can throw a knuckleball in batting practice, many hitters say, "Why waste my time practicing against a pitch that is going to screw up my regular swing? I would rather take my normal batting practice against fastballs, feel good about my swing, and then take a chance in the game."

Most pitchers would love to have the wind behind them; it helps their pitches move around and it bothers hitters to have the wind in their face. Knuckleballers want the wind against them because it seems to make the ball dance more. But for some reason Boston's Wakefield has always seemed to do well in indoor stadiums, where there is no wind current to play with the ball as it comes in.

For most knuckleball pitchers their fastball becomes very effective when they throw it at a time when the batter is expecting a slow knuckler. Just like a change-up from a guy who throws heat, a change from a knuckleball to a fastball throws off the hitter's timing.

A knuckleball pitcher may have a very ordinary fastball, maybe 80 MPH, but it can look like it is coming in at 90 MPH if the batter is looking for the knuckler.

If a knuckleball pitcher gets into a 2–0 or 3–0 count and he worries he might walk someone, he might sneak in a curveball or a fastball to try to get a strike. As a batter, that may be the last thing you're expecting. So the fastball and the curveball become his trick pitches.

The Spitball

Years ago, we used to hear about pitchers who threw *spitballs* or *Vaseline balls* or who cut the ball in some way; you don't hear much about that anymore. I am sure that still goes on, though. If a pitcher is throwing a fastball that is doctored with a foreign substance, the batter sees a different rotation, maybe one similar to that of a splitter. If the pitcher cuts into the hide, that may make the ball sail or make it dart away, depending on where the cut is. I don't think the pitcher knows where it is going to go, but he knows it is going to do something different.

Of course, if a pitcher is caught doctoring the ball, he is gone from the game and probably due for a visit to the league office. But some guys are pretty crafty at their trade.

Sometimes a pitcher may just get lucky and receive a baseball with a cut in it from the last play. He'd be crazy to ask the umpire for a fresh ball. That's why when a batter hits a foul ball that bounces around a bit, the umpire will take it out of play because there could be a cut on it. Or the batter might ask the ump to check it.

Is doctoring rampant? No. Are there certain guys who I think do it consistently? Yes. There always will be players trying to gain the advantage in some way.

Pitchers who throw illegal pitches can really mess with the mind of a hitter. He'll keep stepping out and asking the umpire to check the ball and end up psyching himself out.

Joe Niekro had a file fall out of his back pocket on the mound. There are guys who have had tacks in their gloves. Some have had stuff sewn into their glove. In 1999 Brian Moehler, pitching for Detroit at the time, got caught with a small piece of sandpaper taped to his thumb and was suspended for a few starts.

I don't know if it is true or not, but they used to say that Gaylord Perry would soak himself in baby oil prior to a game; when he started to sweat, he could get oil anywhere he wanted. Toward the end of his career, he used to throw a puffball; he would take the rosin bag and get a bunch of

Checking my swing on a lunge for a bad pitch.

Photo courtesy Boston Red Sox

it in his hand, and when he threw the ball, it would seem to explode out of a cloud of rosin.

He didn't mind being accused of all that stuff. The more he got batters thinking about it, the more it was to his advantage. He wanted them to think he was going to do something crazy.

I'm not making this stuff up, you know; Perry even wrote an autobiography about his life . . . and oils.

CHAPTER FOUR

Pitching Strategies

Who Owns the Inside of the Plate?

Pitchers have to be able to throw to the inside part of the plate. If that is taken away, hitters will lean out over the plate to hit nasty pitches on the outside corner.

A pitcher who doesn't have the ability to work inside or is afraid to do it is not going to have great success.

One of the keys to pitching is intimidation of the batter; if the batter is not a little nervous at the plate, the pitcher has not done his job. A great pitcher wants batters to be worrying: Is this next pitch going to be inside or away?

Many of the great power pitchers achieved their success by establishing the inside of the plate; if they can make the batter move back a bit, that allows them to paint the outside corner with pitches that are harder to hit or harder to drive with power.

You can start with some of the all-time greats: Nolan Ryan and Roger Clemens among them. In today's game some of the pitchers who owe at least some of their success to throwing inside include Justin Verlander of Detroit and Boston's own Josh Beckett.

At the same time batters seem to be getting more and more upset about pitches inside: *jamming, handcuffs, brushbacks,* whatever you call them. Today it is almost to the point where anytime a pitcher throws inside, he gets at least a hard stare from the batter, and sometimes more.

It's absurd because that's the way the game is supposed to be played. If a pitcher is going to pitch inside, occasionally batters are going to get hit; that doesn't mean it was intentional. If a batter gets hit because the pitcher is working inside, he should be happy to get on base.

The use of aluminum bats in high school and college may be one reason why some pitchers are reluctant to throw inside, and why some batters coming into professional baseball are not used to seeing pitches in on their fists. With an aluminum bat, many batters can still hit the ball well if they're jammed, and an aluminum bat is not going to break with a swing on an inside pitch.

Another reason pitchers can't claim to own the inside of the plate is the body armor that some batters now wear. They've got all this junk on and they are not afraid to get hit.

A warning from the umpire

There are, of course, situations in which some pitchers will purposely throw at a batter; often it is in retaliation for something done to a player on their team. Sometimes, though, a batter gets hit because the pitcher loses command of a pitch. The batter, the fans, and the umpire have to know the situation.

Players used to police themselves; a pitcher who hit a batter knew that a guy on his side was likely to get plunked later in the game. Or in the National League, the pitcher himself would have to come up to bat sooner or later.

But now umpires have been instructed by Major League Baseball to get more involved. Today any time an umpire believes a pitcher has intentionally thrown at a batter, he can immediately eject the pitcher. Or he can warn both managers that the next time either side hits a batter or even comes close, the pitcher and the manager will be out of the game.

Look, I'm not saying that pitchers should be throwing at guy's heads. That is dangerous.

But when he was at his peak, many managers were quite happy to see a pitcher like Pedro Martínez issued a warning by the umpire against throwing inside.

The fact is that a pitcher like Martínez doesn't care about warnings; he still has the control to be able to pitch inside. At this point we've got to trust the umpire. He has to have a knowledge of what's going on in the game. Is this guy trying to hit somebody, or is he just pitching inside?

A warning to Martínez or Clemens made no difference. They were not going to stop throwing inside. That's why Martínez and perhaps Clemens are going to go to the Hall of Fame.

The Rem Dawg Remembers

I'm Coming In

Batters coming to the plate against Roger Clemens or Pedro Martínez at their peak never got too comfortable in the box.

Just before the 2003 All-Star Game, the Red Sox came into Yankee Stadium with their bats blazing, bashing David Wells and Clemens in back-to-back games. Clemens hit Kevin Millar with a high-and-inside pitch—perhaps because the Sox had hit seven home runs the day before, or maybe just because he wanted to establish his ownership of the inside of the plate.

Millar was angry, but it was Clemens who was upset. "Guys don't get out of the way anymore," Clemens told reporters after the loss. "If you're throwing a ball 85 or 88, you've got a chance. But I rush it. When I'm coming in, I'm coming in hard."

Former Boston dirt dog Trot Nixon had a great response, depositing Clemens's next pitch over the fence. And David Ortiz hit two more out.

All that said, when Clemens faced Martínez in Game 3 of the ALCS in 2003, Pedro did not cover himself in glory in the third inning with his pitching to Karim García and his taunts to Yankee catcher Jorge Posada.

And then the next inning, when Manny Ramírez overreacted to a high pitch from Clemens, the benches cleared and out came Yankees coach Don Zimmer, charging at Martínez. Here was a seventy-two-year-old guy still thinking like a twenty-year-old. But Zim's a baseball lifer. He forgets sometimes, and his competitiveness takes over.

Here Comes the Heat

Baseball lore includes stories about a pitcher announcing to the batter that he's going to throw a fastball, daring him to hit it. It's not all fiction.

I remember an episode between Bernie Williams of the Yankees and Pedro Martínez on the Red Sox. Bernie had this thing where he would step out of the box and just stand there; it drove Pedro crazy. And so Martínez starts yelling at Bernie, "Let's go."

In that situation everyone knew he was coming with his fastball because he was angry. Pedro did throw a fastball, and of course, he struck Williams out.

There have also been situations where great players are up for their final at bat in the big leagues, and the catcher will tell them—as a sign of respect for a player headed to the Hall of Fame—"Here comes a fastball." I think that happened to Yastrzemski. But the problem was that the pitcher threw it a little too soft, and Yaz popped it up in his last at bat.

Intentional Walks

There are some top-notch pitchers who feel they are giving in to a hitter if they are asked to issue an intentional walk. The great pitchers are hungry for a test; that's why they are great pitchers. They have the ability and they don't feel there is anybody in the world who can hit them. They have no fear of an awesome matchup.

I remember one game when the manager came out and told Nolan Ryan to walk the next batter, and he said, "No." Ryan told the catcher to get back behind the plate, and then he struck out the batter. He was a superstar player and he was not going to be embarrassed by issuing a walk to this guy. It was: "I am Nolan Ryan, and you are who you are, and I am going to get you out."

And what do you think the manager had to say about it? Something like: "Nice going, Nolan." What else was he going to say to him?

But most pitchers go along with the program. If the manager puts up four fingers—the signal for an intentional walk—they're okay with it. They know the manager is trying to set up a double play, or pitch around a really tough hitter.

And of course there was the 2002 World Series during which Barry Bonds was walked nearly every time he came up to bat in a meaningful situation. In all the time that I have been in baseball, I have never seen anything like that. For the record he was walked thirteen times in seven games. He still managed to hit four home runs, but it was the Angels who won the Series. And in 2003 Bonds was given six more intentional walks and the Giants fell to the Florida Marlins in the divisional series.

There are obvious situations when a pitcher should walk a great hitter, places where a walk will hurt a lot less than a hit. But I had never seen the game being played around one player. Actually, I don't blame the manager, Mike Scioscia; I would have done the same thing. But as a pure baseball fan I would have loved to see Bonds swing the bat; he is one of the greatest home-run hitters of all time.

In 1998 Buck Showalter of the Arizona Diamondbacks ordered Bonds walked with the bases loaded; the D-Backs had an 8–6 lead, and they walked him to make it 8–7 to get to the next guy. It worked; the D-Backs won the game.

In July of 2007, just before the All-Star break, the Red Sox were facing the Detroit Tigers in a tight game. David Ortiz started off the game with a two-run homer, and Manny Ramírez was scuffling. And so, Detroit's wily manager Jim Leyland had slugger Big Papi intentionally walked three times, and Ortiz earned a fourth free pass on his own. Oh, and the Tigers won the game 3–2 in the bottom of the thirteenth inning.

The pitch-around

Not all intentional walks are as obvious as the catcher standing up and moving outside of the batter's box to receive four pitches. Sometimes the way it works is that the pitcher is instructed to throw nothing hittable; if the batter chases a bad pitch, that's fine because he's likely to pop it up or hit it weakly. But if the batter refuses to swing at bad stuff, so be it. Let him walk instead of putting the ball over the fence. The manager is saying: It wouldn't kill us if we walked him, but let's see if he will swing at something bad. We call that a *pitch-around.*

In the 2007 postseason, Boston's two big boppers, David Ortiz and Manny Ramírez, received fourteen and sixteen walks respectively over fourteen games. Only a handful were intentional, but you can bet that most of the others were the result of a pitcher and manager saying, "I'm not going to let you beat us with one swing." Of course, there was also Mike Lowell and five or six other good bats in the lineup and the Red Sox got the flashy rings once again.

Good hitters know when pitchers are doing that, and don't get fooled. On the other hand, an impatient hitter might be tricked into swinging. He is not a disciplined hitter, or he may be young and inexperienced.

PART THREE

The Batter Swings!

Not a particularly good follow-through, probably a swing that resulted in a weak ground ball or a soft fly to the opposite field. When I got to Boston, Walt Hriniak changed my swing more downward to get the ball on the ground and on the line.

Photo courtesy Los Angeles Angels of Anaheim Baseball Club

CHAPTER FIVE

The Primary Skill

Hitting the Ball

The primary skill in baseball is hitting. That's the toughest thing in baseball, and it may be the most difficult thing to do in any sport. Every player who goes to the plate wants to hit. Great defensive players take pride in their fielding, but even they want to go up and hit. That's the fun of the game.

Over the history of organized baseball, a .300 batting average has always been the mark of a good hitter. It hasn't changed all that much over the years; I guess that has to do with the skills of the guy throwing the ball and also the fact that there are eight other players out there trying to get the batter out.

Now consider someone hitting .406, like Ted Williams did for the Red Sox in 1941. That's an incredible number. That's why he always had the great respect of players, because they know how difficult that is to do: a little better than 2 for 5 across an entire season.

Batting for average

One of the most telling things about baseball is that a superstar batting .300 is someone who fails to get a hit at least seven out of ten times to the plate.

Over the history of modern baseball, team batting averages have remained pretty consistent: A successful team usually bats somewhere in the range of .260 to .280. Let's take a look at a few notable years in Boston Red Sox history.

Year	Red Sox batting avg.	Comments
1918	.249	First place . . . and winner of the World Series.
1941	.283	Ted Williams batted .406 all by himself, but Boston finished seventeen games behind the Yankees.
1950	.302	The team batting average record, but the Red Sox ended four games behind the Yankees.
1967	.255	The "Impossible Dream" included a ticket to the World Series but no ring.
1975	.275	Another trip to the World Series, but still no ring.
1978	.267	My first year with the Red Sox; I batted .278, went to the All-Star Game, and Boston finished one game behind the Yankees.
1986	.271	First place, five and one-half games above the Yankees. Second place in the World Series, losing to the Mets in seven games.
1993–2003	.275	The team batting average during a decade of chasing the Yankees.
2003	.289	A record-breaking offense included the highest slugging percentage in MLB history, but only good enough for second place, six games behind the Yankees.
2004	.282	222 home runs, including 43 from Ramirez and 41 from Ortiz, good enough for second place to the Yankees once again. But once October was over, the World Series Championship flag would fly over Fenway Park for the first time since 1918.
2005	.281	The highest team batting average in the major leagues. The Red Sox also had the highest number of runs scored and RBIs in all of baseball. The Sox won ninety-five games, same as the Yankees, but they did not win the division title because New York won one more game in the series between the teams. Neither Boston nor the Yankees advanced past the divisional series in postseason.
2006	.269	192 home runs (including 54 by David Ortiz) but only 86 wins to finish a dismal third in the standings behind Toronto and the Yankees.
2007	.279	The Red Sox had fewer hits and home runs (only 166) than the previous year. But solid hitting and very strong pitching allowed Boston to win 96 games, which was worth a two-game lead over the Yankees and sole possession of first place in the American League East. Oh, and they won their second World Series in four seasons.

When I played, the great hitters were batting .320 or .330. Now they are hitting .360 or .370. Why? I'd start with better training. There are smaller ballparks. And great pitching is spread pretty thin.

At the same time that the averages of the better batters have inched up slightly, there continue to be players who reside at or near the "Mendoza Line." (Mario Mendoza, a pretty good defensive shortstop for the Pirates, Mariners, and Rangers from 1974 to 1982, batted as low as .180 for a season and ended up with a career batting average of .215. Many sportscasters, writers, and fans look to see who is at or below .200, which has become known as the Mendoza Line.)

It doesn't take that many hits to improve a so-so average to a notable one. Calculating a batting average over the course of a season with 500 at bats, the difference between batting .290 and .310 is just ten hits:one more hit every sixteen games.

I was a pretty good bunter, and coaches used to tell me all the time that if I got twenty-five extra bunt hits a year, I would hit forty points higher.

If I had a couple of hits and went 2 for 5, I figured I had done pretty well. If I was 1 for 4, I figured I had survived. Players hope the occasional 2 for 2s and 3 for 3s will keep them afloat.

A man with a plan

Being a hitting coach is not an easy job. The coach may have a philosophy, but he's the coach for fifteen position players, and they all have different hitting styles. Anyway, players have a tendency to go to anyone they think can help them, whether it is the coach or the clubhouse guy.

Some hitting coaches say their goal is to have every player come to the plate with a plan. That means knowing the opposing pitcher, knowing how he pitches to you, and knowing how he adjusts with men in scoring position. And it means learning how to work the count to increase your chances of getting a pitch you can hit.

One common goal is to try to get to a hitter's count. The problem, though, is that many players get in a hitter's count, let's say 2–0, and then fail to swing at their pitch.

Even with a plan there are players who are very set in their ways and well known for their habits. There are some batters who almost always swing at the first pitch. If pitchers know someone is a first-pitch hitter, they'll usually try not to throw something hittable to open the at bat.

That's not to say that there haven't been a lot of great first-ball hitters in the history of this game: Paul Molitor, Kirby Puckett, and Nomar Garciaparra among them. Everybody in the world knew they were going to swing at the first pitch if it was a strike. But the big difference: If it wasn't a strike, they would let it go.

At the other end of the spectrum, you have some batters who never swing at the first pitch, preferring to get some sense of the pattern and speed of the pitches. In his rookie season of 2007, Dustin Pedroia took the first pitch 84.8 percent of the time.

And Manny Ramírez has gone entire seasons without swinging at a 3–0 pitch; some coach somewhere must have drilled that into him. It hurts sometimes to see a pitcher lay one right down the middle of the plate on that count and watch Manny take it.

On many teams today it all comes down to an increased emphasis on boosting a batter's on-base percentage. Let me define that: *On-base percentage* is a recalculated batting average that includes hits, walks, and times hit by a pitch. It gives a better sense of how often a player gets on base and sets up a chance for a run.

Preparing for the at bat

A batter, with the assistance of the hitting coach, makes a plan based on his past history with a pitcher. It is much easier today because of videotape and computers. Most teams have a library of at bats, pitches, and plays that can be consulted before, during, and after the game.

Before the game, or at least at the start of a series, most teams will have a hitter's meeting, led by the hitting coach. They will go over the starting pitchers and the bull pen. For each pitcher they want to know the velocity of his pitches. Does his ball sink or is it straight? What are his off-speed pitches? Does he throw a curveball, a slider, or both? What is his changeup? Does it run away from right-handers? Does he throw a split-finger fastball? What is his percentage of first-pitch strikes? Does this guy start everybody off with a breaking ball?

There are some pitchers who won't throw fastballs when they are

"I'm impressed with this kid. He really swings a bat. A left-handed hitter who hits to the opposite field as he does is going to help himself at Fenway Park. Some of those opposite-field fly balls will reach the screen or at least be off the wall."

TED WILLIAMS, SPEAKING ABOUT JERRY REMY IN HIS FIRST SPRING TRAINING SEASON WITH THE RED SOX IN 1978. OF REMY'S SEVEN CAREER HOME RUNS, NONE CAME AT FENWAY PARK.

behind in the count: 1–0, 2–0, 3–0, and 3–1. Instead they will throw a breaking ball.

If there's an unknown pitcher on the mound—a rookie or someone who just came over from the other league—when the leadoff hitter gets back to the dugout, many of the guys will go up to him and ask, "What's he got?" But that doesn't always tell you much because a good pitcher throws differently to each batter. A pitcher would attack me differently than he would attack hitters behind me.

A player might go up to bat a couple of times when the pitcher has nothing on his fastball. On the third at bat, all of a sudden it's really moving. Or a pitcher might have been getting the curve over early in the game and then lost it in the sixth inning.

These are the sorts of things that will spread around quickly on the bench.

But when you are hitting well, you don't think about any of this. It's when you're not swinging well that most of this stuff comes into play, and there are times when you think way too much.

There's a baseball saying that goes like this: When you're hitting well, the ball looks like a beach ball, and when you're not hitting well, it looks like a golf ball.

Player Rituals

Curt Schilling is an extraordinary athlete, but he has some pretty ordinary superstitions and rituals. He won't step on the foul line when walking to or from the pitching mound. For your basic 7:05 p.m. night game, he starts his warm-up routine at 6:45 p.m., not 6:44 and not 6:46. And he kisses his necklace before throwing the first pitch.

Old favorite Nomar Garciaparra used to drive some people nuts with his apparent inability to find batting gloves that fit. Garciaparra who, when he was at his peak, was one of the best hitters in baseball, tugged on his batting gloves over and over, tapped his helmet, and kicked his feet before he settled in for a pitch. If he didn't get a pitch to hit, he'd do it all over again before the next pitch. You have to wonder if he is going to have to medicate himself for obsessive-compulsive disorder when he is out of the game.

Watch the players run on and off the field: How many won't step on the foul line, touch a bag, or take a particular route to the dugout?

If you went to every game and you focused on one player, you would see that he does the same things over and over again through spring training and 162 games a year. Players get into a routine and find a set way of doing things that works for them. Sometimes they get to a point that if they forget to do something, it throws them way out of whack.

At least Nomar went through his routine quickly. Manny Ramírez used to walk all over the place before he got in the box; he's cut down on that now.

If the batter takes way too long, the umpire might say, "Let's get going here." The catcher, though, is not likely to squawk too much because he probably has his own routine when he comes up to bat.

Understanding Batting Practice

If you get to the park early enough, go to your seats and watch batting practice. There's a lot more to it than a couple of swings at easy tosses from a coach.

A good hitter has a plan for every batting practice. First might be a couple bunts. Then, he might try moving the ball to the opposite field, up the middle, and attempt to pull some balls.

A batter with a plan may work on hitting situations. He may begin with a hit-and-run swing, when he has to make contact because the runner on first is going to take off. Next, he'll try to hit the ball to the right side to move a man over from second to third. Then, he'll try to loft a fly ball to get a runner in from third.

Some players are very finicky about batting practice. The batting practice pitcher gets to know the spots where these guys want the ball. Some hitters call their own at bats, telling the pitcher to give them something down the middle of the plate, outside, or inside, so they can work on particular swings.

While all of this is going on, you'll see infielders taking ground balls, working on their throws to first, and practicing double plays.

Outfielders may have a coach hitting fly balls to help them with their timing. If you are in a ballpark with some unusual features, you'll probably see a coach working on that; at Fenway Park with the Green Monster, you'll see coaches hitting balls off the wall so that left fielders can practice playing the rebound.

During batting practice you'll usually see pitchers shagging fly balls in the outfield, and then they do whatever running program the pitching coach asks.

The visiting team takes batting practice

When some hitters come to a park like Fenway with the Green Monster in left or Yankee Stadium with the short porch in right, they feel compelled to make adjustments to their swings to try to take advantage of the park.

When you watch batting practice in New York, you'll see some left-handed power hitters trying to hit one up on the second deck. When right-handers come to Fenway, you'll see great shows during BP, with power hitters parking one after another on Lansdowne Street behind the Green Monster. That may not be the proper way to take batting practice, but some players can't help themselves. They put on a show, and fans love to see it, but they may also be taking themselves out of their normal routine, possibly putting themselves off their game.

How to Swing the Bat

Let's say that there are two different kinds of hitters—those who have their *hands inside the ball* and those who *surround the ball.*

When I say a hitter has his hands inside the ball, I mean that his hands are coming in closer to his body, and the barrel of the bat is pulled through the swing. This type of hitter is able to use the whole field.

A good example of this kind of player is Manny Ramírez, a power hitter who keeps his hands inside the ball and doesn't surround it. The same thing goes for Barry Bonds. Wade Boggs, another great hitter, was like that, too. A-Rod has his hands inside the ball and has great power to all fields. He's a bit like Ramírez with his leg kick and his smooth, controlled swing.

In general, though, a big power hitter surrounds the ball with his swing. By surrounding, I mean that instead of the hands starting in close to the hitter's body, the hands are held out and away before the swing. A ball thrown inside can jam him; a batter who has his hands inside the ball gets to foul off the pitch.

Remy's Top Dawgs

Ichiro Suzuki does things I have never seen before. He has the ability to hit any pitch in any part of the strike zone—and out of the strike zone—and hit it hard. I've seen him take two steps toward the pitcher, swing at a ball down near his shin, and foul it off the other way. I sit there and say, "How can he do that?"

In 2004 he broke George Sisler's eighty-four-year-old record by collecting 262 hits in a single season. And he is also a very good outfielder with a strong arm.

In the 2007 All-Star Game, Ichiro put the American League ahead with an inside-the-park home run that skipped away from Ken Griffey Jr.

(You can thank Ichiro, and All-Star Game's winning pitcher Josh Beckett, for giving Boston the home-field advantage in the World Series in 2007, although the Sox didn't need to go past four games.)

Guys who surround the ball break a lot of bats because they get jammed, and they usually don't have a high batting average, although they may hit more home runs.

From the pitcher's point of view, a guy who surrounds the ball usually has more holes they can throw to. In a bases-loaded situation, I think most pitchers would rather have a power hitter up there. If he has some weaknesses they can exploit, they've got a chance to strike him out.

A contact hitter is a bigger problem for pitchers in a tough situation because he is going to put the ball into play. When he makes contact, something is going to happen—it could be a hit, an error, or an out that will drive in a run.

Good bad-ball hitters

There are some players who are excellent at hitting bad balls: pitches out of the strike zone or strikes that most other hitters would not swing at unless they were in a two-strike count. A lot of these good bad-ball hitters keep their hands inside the ball.

When a pitcher with an above-average fastball throws that ball around the letters or higher, very few batters can hit the ball. Those few good high-ball hitters may be able to make contact, but you don't see many high fastballs hit for home runs.

For most batters a high fastball is a pitch to stay away from. If it's a high, hanging breaking ball, that's a different story. Those are the ones that can go a long way in the other direction.

It used to be that left-handed hitters were considered low-ball hitters, while right-handed hitters were better at high pitches. That's no longer necessarily true; all pitchers now work low, and most batters try (not always successfully) to not swing at a pitch above the belt unless it is a high breaking ball.

To hit a high pitch, you have to be able to get on top of it. One way to do that is to bring your hands up and in. Most players hold the bat higher. The swing is like chopping down a tree.

Fouling off a pitch

There are some batters who regularly have long at bats, fouling off pitch after pitch. You'll hear some announcers and coaches say they are intentionally fouling off the pitch.

I can't say that I have ever run into a player who has said, "I purposely fouled that off." The reaction time for an incoming pitch is less than half a second, and we're expecting a batter to decide whether to take a pitch, swing for a hit, or foul it off?

Does it look like guys do that? Yes, with extraordinary hitters like Ichiro Suzuki or Wade Boggs. You may see a guy like Ichiro foul off ten pitches. But I don't think that Ichiro is saying to himself, "I am just going to flick at this one and foul it off."

Most of these superior batters are contact hitters, hands-inside-the-baseball hitters who don't strike out a lot. They swing and try to get the ball in play and get a hit. The best hitters can see a tough pitch and make contact, when most others would miss it. Such a hitter is spoiling a great pitch by making contact and not striking out.

Because of the angle of the bat, the location of the pitch, and his own hand–eye coordination, an exceptional hitter is able to foul that ball off and stay alive instead of swinging and missing it. He is able to get to pitches other guys can't get to.

And I thought that one of the best performances of the 2007 regular season was Dustin Pedroia's epic at bat against Eric Gagné (then with the Texas Rangers) on May 27. With a one-run lead going into the top of the ninth, Pedroia got to a 2–2 count and then fouled off seven consecutive pitches before finding one that he liked: a fastball over the heart of the plate that he drove 368 feet to left for a home run. It turned out to be the winning run, too, because the Rangers got one back in the bottom of the inning.

Checking the swing

One judgment call for the umpire is whether a batter has checked his swing: started to swing and then changed his mind.

At what point has the swing become a strike? I look at it as mostly a judgment about whether the batter had control of the head of the bat. If it looks like the batter had control, I say it wasn't a swing. Some people say it's a strike when a batter "breaks his wrists." To me that's the same thing as losing control of the head of the bat. When a batter does that, his wrists roll over.

It is much easier for a batter who gets his hands inside the baseball to check his swing than it is for a guy who surrounds the ball. It is very hard for power hitters to check because they get so much whip into their swing. I once saw Jim Rice check his swing and have the bat snap right in his hands—that's how strong he was.

Choking up on the bat

It used to be that certain batters would choke up on the bat—move their hands up a bit from the handle toward the barrel—to get a little more control and a quicker swing. Some batters would choke up when they had two strikes against them and they just wanted to make contact, at the cost of some power.

Barry Bonds, who had tremendous power, choked up on the bat and still put balls out of the park.

How to Hit a Home Run

What makes a great home-run hitter? Physically, he has to be big and strong—you don't see many 5'9", 165-pound home-run hitters—but, more than size, it comes down to bat speed and the pitches he chooses to swing at.

It is amazing how much fear players like Bonds put in the opposition. Players like him have the ability to change the complexion of the game with one swing.

Mark McGwire had that amazing home-run stare. He was a huge man with a slight uppercut swing, and he hit very high, very long monster home runs. When he made solid contact, you'd think: "Forget about it. Where's this thing going?"

And we've all seen old movies of Babe Ruth coming up to the plate, looking just like the guy selling beer in the stands. That is, until he swung. Ruth was big and strong, especially compared with players of his time, and he had great bat speed. And the Yankees built a ballpark tailored to him.

David Ortiz is big and strong and has learned to fill the few holes in his left-handed swing. Manny Ramírez, when he is fully in gear, has strength and the ability to stay back behind the ball, which allows him to use nearly the entire field.

Why Would They Hit Me?

Over the course of my ten seasons in the major leagues, across more than 4,800 appearances at the plate, I was hit by a pitch only four times. Just for comparison's sake, in the first fifteen seasons played by slugger Manny Ramírez (through 2007), he came to the plate about 8,200 times and was hit eighty-five times.

The reason why my number is so low is this: Why would they want to hit me? I was not likely to hit a long ball. And when I was hitting in front of guys like Freddie Lynn, Jim Rice, Carlton Fisk, or Carl Yastrzemski, they didn't want me on base because those other guys could hurt them with a two-run home run.

The other reason I was rarely hit was that I was mostly pitched away, being an opposite-field hitter. I wasn't a patient hitter, and if the count got to 3–1, pitchers were not going to try to trick me. They'd come with a fastball, and I would swing to try to get on base.

I wasn't an ideal leadoff hitter because I didn't walk to get on base a lot. (I averaged 1 walk for each 13.5 plate appearances. Leaving aside David Ortiz and Manny Ramírez, who get intentionally walked or are pitched around, consider the cautious and successful approach of Kevin Youkilis who averages 1 walk for each 7.4 times at the plate.)

Me, I was up there hacking.

Taking one for the team

When a pitcher throws too far inside or throws right at a batter, the natural inclination is to get out of the way. Some players, though, are willing to get hit to get on base. Done right, they can have an inside pitch just graze the shoulder or the forearm, and the worst they are going to take is one on the backside, where there's plenty of meat. It is kind of an art; guys practice this.

Ron Hunt, then with Montreal, holds the one-season National League record for being hit by a pitch, with fifty in the 1971 season. Don Baylor of Boston got nicked thirty-five times in 1986 for the American League record; a big, strong guy, he would be right on top of the plate and just turn into an inside pitch.

Derek Jeter of the Yankees has been plunked 129 times in thirteen seasons through the end of 2007. Alex Rodriguez is close behind with 127 hit-by-pitch markers across fourteen seasons. The reason is pretty apparent when you look at their batting stance; they both stand close to the plate and in Jeter's case he holds his hands out in the zone.

The most dangerous pitch is one that's coming at the batter's head. But that's also the easiest pitch to get out of the way of, as long as the batter sees it, because all he needs to do is duck.

The pitch that's almost impossible to get away from is one that is right at the batter's side because it is not always clear which way to jump.

Toothpicks or Tree Trunks?

Many players today are using bats with big barrels and skinny little handles. The thinking is that the bigger barrel gives more area to make contact, while the thin handle gives a better whip. Of course, this sort of bat is more likely to snap.

And many players have switched to lighter bats, again to increase the bat speed. You might see a 34-inch bat, but it might only be thirty-one ounces in weight.

The choice of a bat is another matter of individual preference. I have seen home-run hitters who have used 34-inch, thirty-four-ounce bats, and some who swing 35-inch, thirty-two-ounce bats. Some players will go to a lighter bat as they go through the course of a season to give them better bat speed as they tire. And a player might change to a lighter bat against a hard thrower.

Here are a few choice cuts: Ken Griffey Jr. and Derek Jeter generally use a 34-inch thirty-ounce ash bat. Alex Rodriguez uses a similar bat, but an ounce heavier. Manny Ramírez also waves a 34-inch bat, but his weapon is made of maple and weighs thirty-two ounces. Prince Fielder, a rising star for the Milwaukee Brewers and a large man at 6' and 260 pounds, uses a 33.5-inch-long ash bat that weighs thirty-four ounces. And Babe Ruth used bats like this: 35 to 36 inches long, and forty-two to forty-six ounces in weight.

Dressing up the tools

Players get their order of a dozen bats and they work on them, dress them up, and put them in the batting rack, and most expect nobody else to touch them.

When I say "dress them up," I mean that some—not all—players can be a bit obsessive about their bats. They'll reject some bats if they don't like the width of the grain, and they will shave the handles if the bat doesn't quite feel right. Some will put tape on the handle for a better grip. Players will also "bone" their bat, rubbing the barrel with a bone to make it harder.

Some players are a lot more picky than others; they might get a dozen bats and only three of them will feel good enough to use in a game. They will pick out the best ones, and those will be their game bats. The rest will become batting practice bats. And there are some players who get an order of bats and just use them as they are.

Many players use pine tar on the handle to get a better grip, although most players these days use batting gloves. There are guys who put gobs of tar on the handle, and others who will just dab a little. It's not supposed to go more than 18 inches from the handle of the bat, which was the cause of the famous "Pine Tar Incident" in 1983, when George Brett of Kansas City lost a game-winning home run against the Yankees because he apparently violated the rule; the home run was later allowed.

Cheating with the tools

And then there are cheaters who might "cork" a bat. I don't think it is widespread, but it has always been in the game and probably always will be. Players are forever trying to get some kind of an edge, and inserting some cork may make the ball jump off the bat a bit more.

There are many ways to doctor a bat, besides putting cork into the barrel. I'm told there were players who have had golf balls and other things in their bats. When I was playing, I remember hearing some batters make contact, and it sounded like a thud instead of a crack. We had a pretty good idea that something was unusual about their bats.

It is awfully embarrassing when a guy gets caught—unless you're Albert Belle, who got caught and suspended by the league but still denied it. Or Sammy Sosa, who got caught and accepted responsibility, sort of.

NESN play-by-play announcer Don Orsillo and I face the camera for the pregame show. Orsillo has a great voice for exciting plays.

Photo by Corey Sandler

CHAPTER SIX

Hitting It Where They Ain't

Opposite-Field and Pull Hitters

When a hitter "pulls" a ball, he is hitting it to the field that is on the same side of the plate as his feet. (Think of it as "pulling" the ball to his side of the plate.) A right-handed hitter pulls the ball to the shortstop side of the infield or left of center in the outfield; a lefty pulls toward second base and right of center.

An "opposite-field" hit is to the side of the plate across from the batter. A right-handed batter goes the opposite way toward the right side of the infield or outfield; a lefty goes away toward the shortstop or left field.

The ideal hitter uses the whole field; many players get into trouble when they try too hard to pull the ball. For example, a player may try to pull an outside fastball when he would be better off shooting the ball the other way. But that's not an easy thing for a pull hitter to learn to do, because it is not his natural swing.

Most opposite-field hitters probably didn't learn to hit that way, either; it's just their natural style.

You will see more coaches try to teach pull hitters to use the whole field than you will see coaches trying to get opposite-field hitters to pull the ball. Many pull hitters surround the ball, something I talked about earlier. These guys break a lot of bats.

Converting from opposite field to pull

I was an opposite-field hitter, batting from the left side of the plate; most of my hits went up the middle or to the opposite field, which to me was the left side of the infield and outfield. For me to be able to pull the ball, I had to open my stance a little (that is, pull my right foot slightly back from the plate) and look for a pitch from the middle of the plate in. And then I would have to be quicker on the trigger than I normally would be.

In other words most hitters tell themselves: "Wait, wait, wait for as long as you can." Players who are natural pull hitters can do that. But an opposite-field hitter or up-the-middle hitter can't do that.

Then hitters look for a pitch in a certain zone to pull, perhaps hoping for a breaking ball or something off-speed. Batters shouldn't try to pull an outside pitch; they've got to look from the middle of the plate in.

It's not easy to remake an opposite-field hitter into a full-time pull hitter. He's generally not quick or strong enough.

Going from pull to opposite field

Changing a swing from a natural pull to hitting to the opposite field is more difficult for a player. When a pull hitter tries to use the whole field, a lot of it comes down to the position of the hands. A hitter who gets his hands inside the ball can do it. Ichiro Suzuki can take an inside fastball and still hit it the other way. But a batter who surrounds the ball could never do that; he would break the bat.

The other part of it is pitch selection. If the ball is from the middle of the plate to away, a hitter has a better chance to hit the ball the other way. If it is middle to inside, most pull hitters are going to do what is natural to them and pull the ball.

And then when it comes time to swing, players have to tell themselves to wait longer than would be normal for them, as pull hitters.

Many dead-pull hitters are so programmed to hit in a certain way that the only time they go to the opposite field is when they make a mistake. As an example, consider Jason Giambi when he was at his peak with the Yankees. Most teams defended against him by shifting the infield, putting three infielders on the right side. He didn't try to change his swing, and the only time he seemed to hit a ball on the ground to the opposite field or in the left-center gap was when he swung late on a fastball. When he put the ball in the air, though, his hits usually went to the opposite field, so the defense in the outfield did not put on a shift.

Standing in the Box

A hitter is allowed to stand anywhere in the batter's box, a rectangle that is about 6 feet long and 4 feet wide, with its nearest point 6 inches away from the plate. The rules say the batter has to be in the box, and if he makes contact with one foot out of the box, the umpire is supposed to call him out. That happens rarely; you might see it sometimes when the batter lays down a drag bunt.

Kevin Youkilis, a right-handed hitter, parks his right foot as far back in the box as is legal, earning a few precious extra fractions of a second as he times his swing for a fastball.

The relatively few batters who position themselves near the front of the box are contact hitters. These are hitters who bunt, put the ball in play, and have good speed.

In most cases a hitter doesn't intentionally stand outside the box, but there are a few batters who will rub out the back line to get closer to the catcher. That gives them a bit more distance from the pitcher and a few milliseconds extra to react to the pitch. The catcher will often object when a batter does this because it gives him a bit of an advantage and also throws off the positioning of fielders.

It used to be that hitters would make adjustments depending on the pitcher. If a guy threw hard, they would stand deep in the box to give themselves a little more time to see the ball. If a sinker ball or curveball pitcher was on the mound, they would move up in the box to try to get to the ball before it sank too much. But you don't see players doing that much anymore. Most players take the same position with every at bat, with most of them deep in the box.

Inside or outside in the box

You can assume that a player who is way inside in the box—on top of the plate—has had trouble with outside pitches and is trying to cover the outside corner. He also has to be very quick on inside pitches.

Players who stand away from the plate have probably had trouble with inside pitches but have the ability to cover the outside corner.

When Carl Everett played in Boston, he had an extreme position in the box; his front foot was almost touching home plate. I guess that means he wasn't in the box. Everett was exceptionally quick on pitches that were down and in. From a pitcher's point of view, that left no room to throw inside without hitting him.

It's a game of adjustments all the time. If a hitter stands on top of the plate and pitchers keep pounding the inside of the plate, he might back off a bit to better get to the ball. If they keep pitching away, away, away, the hitter may move up a little bit closer.

But the catcher is also watching the hitter's position in the box. If he sees the hitter move one way or another in the box, he and the pitcher will make adjustments of their own. It's fun to watch Jason Varitek studying the position of the batter in the box before setting up to receive a pitch; that's one reason why he's one of the best in the game.

Switch-Hitters

Switch-hitting is a mystery to me; it seems like double the trouble. I have a lot of respect for players who can do it because I know how difficult it is for a player to hit from one side of the plate.

I've mentioned some of the things that can go wrong in swings: Your hands are not right, your footwork is off, you're jumping at the ball, or you're not seeing the ball well. Can you imagine having to deal with that from both sides of the plate?

The reason to switch-hit is so that most pitches are coming in to the batter, where most have greater success. Switch-hitting is something that should start very early in life, at the high school level or even before then. To try to learn to do it as a professional is very, very difficult.

There have been some great switch-hitters, though. Hall of Fame players like Mickey Mantle and Eddie Murray had power from both sides.

And let's not forget former Red Sox third baseman Bill Mueller. In 2003 he blasted back-to-back grand slams against Texas in the seventh and eighth innings of a game—the first from the right side and the second from the left. He had started the game with a solo homer in the third inning. I don't know how you can sleep after a game like that. I used to toss and turn after I got a pair of singles. Mueller went on to win the 2003 American League batting title, with a .326 average.

"Jerry Remy has grown into an immense talent in the broadcast booth. He's always thinking about situations, about what could happen, just like he did when he was a player."

RUSS KENN, PRODUCER OF BOSTON RED SOX TELECASTS

Mueller, who helped lead the comeback against the Yankees in the 2004 ALCS, retired as a player in 2006. He made a cameo appearance at Fenway when the Red Sox returned to play Game 6 of the ALCS in 2007, their backs against the wall down three games to two. He threw out the ceremonial first pitch and Boston went on to win the game 12–2.

But not all switch-hitters are equally capable from both sides of the plate. For some of them you've got to wonder why they even bother—they are so much better from one side than the other. Most switch-hitters have a great difference in batting average between the left and right sides. For example, over the course of his long career, Omar Vizquel was a contact hitter from the left side, while from the right he has a little bit more pop. (Perhaps some of that might be credited to coaching from Eddie Murray.)

Red Sox captain Jason Varitek is an accomplished switch-hitter, although his stats are different from each side. Across his career he has made 3,205 plate appearances from the left side of the plate against right-handed pitchers and 1,351 appearances the other way around.

Through the end of the 2007 season, consider these Varitek stats:

Left-handed against right-handed pitchers: .260 batting average, 102 home runs, and 663 strikeouts

Right-handed against left-handed pitchers: .284 batting average, 46 home runs, and 239 strikeouts

So, Varitek has a bit more power swinging the bat from his unnatural side, but a lower batting average and a slightly higher percentage of strikeouts. (Overall, his career batting average is .267.)

If a hitter is naturally left-handed, there is really not much point to switch to the other side because most of the pitchers he is going to see are right-handers. And a left-handed hitter is a step and a half closer to first base, so if he has any kind of speed, it is almost ridiculous to move to the other side of the plate.

Another thing to consider is that some left-handed pitchers give right-handed hitters problems. Righties generally don't throw right-handed batters a lot of changeups. But lefties may do just that, and the changeup becomes a very difficult pitch for them to hit. As an example, Tom Glavine works the outside of the plate, changing speeds, giving right-handed hitters a totally different look than they are getting from right-handed pitchers.

Batting from the "wrong" side

I am right-handed. I throw with my right hand, and I'll sign your baseball with my right hand. But when it came to hitting, I came to the plate as a lefty. That's just how it happened. When I was a kid, I just started swinging left-handed and that was where I was comfortable. I never even gave it a thought.

It was an advantage for me because I could run.

When I swung, I was trying to hit the ball flush, but I wanted my hands on top of the ball. My dominant hand was my right hand, and that's also my throwing arm. So, for me swinging left-handed was much more comfortable because my dominant hand was my bottom hand on the bat. I always said my right hand led me to the ball and my left hand was just going along for the ride. (We are getting into hitting technique and philosophies here; my dog, Rajj, could give you one and the cat around the corner could give another.)

You'll always see a few right-handed throwers who choose to go up to the plate as a lefty. More unusual is a guy who throws left-handed and hits right-handed, like Rickey Henderson.

Taking a Stance

There are three basic batting stances: straightaway (also called neutral or even), closed, and open.

In a *straightaway stance,* the hitter's feet are equally distant from the

"When you play this game twenty years, go to bat 10,000 times, and get 3,000 hits, do you know what that means? You've gone zero for 7,000."

PETE ROSE

plate, at a right angle to a line between the pitcher and the catcher. This is the most common stance in baseball.

The second most common position is the *closed stance.* Here the foot closest to the pitcher is moved a bit closer to home plate than the back foot. For a right-handed batter, the front foot is pointed more directly toward first base; for a left-handed batter, the front foot is headed in the general direction of third. A closed stance brings the shoulder in. Many players who come to the plate this way are vulnerable to pitches inside, but they can handle the ball away a little bit better.

Players who have a tendency to let their shoulder fly too soon will sometimes use a closed stance. When a batter swings, he wants to go directly back toward the pitcher with his front shoulder. When coaches say a player is leaving too soon, that means the front shoulder is flying out; this makes the bat drag, opening up a lot of the plate for the pitcher.

Less common is an *open stance.* Here the foot closest to the pitcher is pulled slightly back from the plate. A righty would have his front foot angled toward third; a lefty's front foot is turned slightly toward first. An open stance helps the batter see the pitch a little bit better. When he opens up, he is clearing his shoulder slightly so that he is facing the pitcher better.

An open stance helps him to be a little quicker on an inside pitch, but at the same time, he is usually vulnerable to pitches away because he has to reach across the plate. To cover the outside of the strike zone, he'll close up the stance with a step back toward the plate as he swings.

Holding hands

If you see a batter holding the bat up high above his shoulders, he is probably a good high-ball hitter. Most hitters who hold the bat low are going to be low-ball hitters—it's pretty much impossible for a guy who starts out low to get back on top.

It's all a matter of comfort for each hitter, and it is really not where he starts, it's how he gets to the pitch. He can start from just about anywhere. He can stand on his hands. It doesn't matter. It is what position he gets into that will determine how good a hitter he is.

Wiggling and waggling

Some players go through a whole routine of wiggling and waggling before they settle in for a pitch, and I'm not just talking about Nomar and his batting gloves.

I don't really concern myself with anything that goes on before the hitter is ready to swing. That's just his routine; every guy's got one. That's just how he gets ready to hit. There are guys who are relaxed and laid-back. And then you'll see players who have everything going one way or another. But when it comes to the trigger time—the swing—most players do the same thing.

Hitting the Ball on the Ground

Sometimes a batter will intentionally try to put the ball on the ground. This is something that players with speed will do, especially left-handed hitters, who are already closer to first base and are ready to fly. A batter puts the ball on the ground by getting his hands above the ball to hit the top.

Remy Says: Watch This

Spreading the Wealth

Players who use most of the ballpark are generally the best hitters in the game and usually have the highest batting averages. Manny Ramírez is a perfect example of a guy who can hit from right-center field to the leftfield line because of his swing.

Ramírez has the ability to make the decision to go to the opposite field, and he has the ability to look for a certain pitch and pull it.

Remy Says: Watch This

The Hitter and the Defense

Watch the batter's swing and see if you can figure out what he is trying to do: Is he trying to pull the ball, or is he trying to move it the other way? Check the defense: How are they positioning themselves? The way they set up against a particular batter the first time he came up to bat may be different from the way they play him later in the game. Fielders may be trying to counter adjustments the batter has made in his swing, or the team may have made a change in pitching strategy against him.

Are the outfielders moving to different locations based on the count? When the pitcher has two strikes, look at the outfielders to see if they are moving more toward the opposite field because they expect the batter to cut down his swing to try to make contact and avoid striking out.

Some players used to try the Baltimore Chop, hitting a ball intentionally into the ground near home plate so it bounced high enough to allow the runner to reach first base before a play is made. It got its name in the 1890s when it was a favorite of legendary Baltimore players like John McGraw and Willie Keeler.

I can't think of anybody who does this regularly today. There are those who have a downward plane to their swing, but they are still trying to hit line drives.

Hitting the Ball in the Air: Sacrifice Flies

There are times in the game when a batter tries to bring home a runner by hitting a sacrifice fly—a ball hit in the air deep enough to allow a runner to tag up and score from third base. Like most things in baseball, it's not as easy as it sounds.

The batter begins by looking for a pitch he can lift in the air, perhaps a hanging breaking ball or something else that is up in the zone. He'll try to stay away from a sinker ball; he's more likely to hit it on the ground. Some players without a natural uppercut will try to adjust their swings to hit a fly ball. For example, a ground ball, line-drive hitter may drop his hands a little bit to try to get underneath the ball.

The catcher's glove is closed and my mouth is open, which means I probably swung and missed.

Photo courtesy Boston Red Sox

CHAPTER SEVEN

Hitter's Counts

Working the Count

Not every hitter can hit every type of pitch, thrown to any location in the strike zone. And not every pitcher cooperates by throwing a hittable pitch on any particular count in an at bat.

But a smart batter can increase the chances of getting a pitch he can hit by working the count to situations in which the pitcher really needs to throw a strike. The goal is to try to get into a hitter's count, giving the batter the luxury of being able to look for a particular pitch in a particular location.

There are some batters who may see only a few pitches per at bat; they come out of the dugout swinging. And then there are guys who average six or seven pitches each time they're up to bat. Batters who see a lot of pitches tend to receive many walks and have good on-base percentages.

In order to work a count, a batter is going to be down in a lot of counts. These hitters are not afraid to take strikes, and they're not afraid to be up there with two strikes on them.

Many of the hitting mistakes made by players come when they are in a hitter's count, but they don't narrow down their zone enough. In other words they are swinging at a strike, but it is not their strike. It is not where their strength is.

The hitter's advantage

Across the course of a season or a career, a hitter will almost always be more successful when he manages to work the count to his advantage. A hitter is "ahead" in the count when the pitcher has thrown more balls than strikes: 1–0, 2–0, 2–1, 3–0, and 3–1.

Conversely, the batter is "behind" in the count in 0–1, 0–2, 1–2, and 2–2 counts. There's a lot to be learned—and admired—in looking at Boston's two most successful hitters for the 2007 season, David Ortiz and Mike Lowell.

Big Papi led the Red Sox in the regular season with a .332 batting average and 35 home runs; he drove in 117 runs. Mike Lowell was close behind for the season, batting .324 and clubbing 21 homers; he led the team with 120 RBIs.

Let's look inside those numbers:

	Ortiz	**Lowell**
Season batting average	.332	.324
BA with RISP	.362	.356
BA ahead in the count	.358	.356
BA ahead in the count with RISP	.392	.385
BA behind in the count	.246	.235
BA behind in the count with RISP	.206	.298
BA with no outs	.317	.308
BA with one out	.352	.348
BA with two outs	.332	.312

BA: batting average; RISP: runners in scoring position.

What can we learn from these two exceptional hitters? First of all, we can see their value in the lineup. These guys make the most of their opportunities to drive in runs.

Both Ortiz and Lowell bat about thirty points higher when they come up to the plate with runners in scoring position, and both are even more successful when they get ahead in the count. Both are also quite good at maintaining their batting average even with two outs against them; the count matters more to them than the number of outs.

Finally, we can see how important it is—for the opposing pitcher—to try to get ahead of Ortiz or Lowell. The numbers drop off for both, but Lowell shows solid numbers even when he is in the hole.

What's the Count?

From the pitcher's point of view, there's a story line behind each pitch in an at bat. One pitch is often thrown to try to set up the batter for another. When the pitcher is ahead in the count—at 0–2, for example—his goal may be to get the batter to chase something way out of the strike zone; in another situation, such as 3–2, in most cases the pitcher is going to throw something he's pretty sure he can get into the strike zone.

Across a five- or six-pitch at bat, the seesaw battle between the pitcher and batter offers counts where one or the other may have a bit of an advantage. A smart pitcher—and his catcher—knows the story line that goes with each count. A smart batter turns around the pitcher's mind-set to try to choose the counts when he may get the pitch he wants to swing at.

The pitcher's advantage

Here's a tour through each of the possible pitcher's counts in an at bat, starting with "neutral" counts, **0–0** and **1–1**.

Pitchers are urged to stay ahead in the count and try to get a strike with the first pitch; for some pitchers that means throwing a fastball, while others with good breaking pitches may try to throw something out of the zone that a batter will chase.

Some batters are ready to go on the first pitch. On **0–0** Nomar Garciaparra was looking for something over the plate, whether it be a fastball or a breaking ball. Wade Boggs was known for taking the first pitch, but every now and then he would let it fly, especially if the pitcher believed too much in the scouting report and threw a batting-practice fastball to open the at bat.

Kevin Youkilis and Dustin Pedroia share the same trait: neither is likely to swing at the first pitch, doing so only about 10 percent of the time.

But, in general, it all comes down to the individual batter and the pitcher he is facing. For example, if the man on the mound is wild and has a tendency to walk a lot of opponents, a hitter probably shouldn't plan on swinging at the first pitch. The idea is to give him a chance to be wild.

Now, let's say the pitcher has thrown eight balls in a row, walking the last two batters. A coach might want to put the take sign on: Make the pitcher throw a strike, don't help him out. But in the back of the hitter's mind he is saying: "This guy just threw eight balls. He is going to try to throw a strike here and there's going to be nothing on it." So the batter may be ready to swing.

When I was facing a pitcher struggling with control and the pitching coach made a visit to the mound, I felt that I pretty much knew what he was being told: "Just throw strikes. Make him swing the bat, and we've got guys ready out there to catch the ball for you." So as a hitter, I could reasonably expect he was coming right down the middle with his next pitch.

The first pitch came in, and the batter either swung at it unsuccessfully or couldn't get to a tough strike. The count is now **0–1.** The batter doesn't want to fall behind **0–2,** so if the pitch is on one of the corners, he is probably going to swing at it.

Now the pitcher's strike zone expands a little bit; that doesn't mean that the umpire's calls will change, but instead that the batter may be a little less selective.

To me an even count of **1–1** is the same as **0–1.** The batter wants to avoid ending up with two strikes on him.

This is a situation in which the hitter doesn't have the same flexibility he has with a **1–0** count. He's got to cover a little bit more of the plate, but again he doesn't want to swing at a nasty strike because he still has a chance at **1–2.**

Let's say the pitcher throws a changeup on this count to a fastball hitter; in that situation the batter should not swing. But if he gets a fastball in the strike zone, he should take a hack because nobody wants to be down two strikes.

A batter deep in the hole at **0–2** or **1–2** is living on borrowed time. He's got to cover the plate and swing at anything close to try to make contact. He doesn't want to leave it in the hands of the umpire on a close pitch.

For a batter who doesn't strike out much, an **0–2** or **1–2** count may

> **"Hitting is 50 percent above the shoulders."**
>
> TED WILLIAMS

not be that bad. But a two-strike count is not good for a power hitter or a player who chases bad pitches.

These counts offer the pitcher the opportunity purposely to throw something off the plate, trying to get the batter to chase a pitch out of the strike zone. With a count of **0–2** or **1–2,** a pitcher usually considers wasting a pitch to see if the batter will cooperate and get himself out.

Once again, on a **2–2** count the pitcher doesn't have to throw a strike; he still has some room to work with. You may see the pitcher come in with his best strikeout pitch, or he may throw a waste pitch out of the strike zone.

In this situation the batter is a little more sure in the box because he's already seen at least four pitches, and he may have fouled off a few more. But he still has to protect the plate to avoid striking out.

Taking a Good Rip

Now here are the counts that favor the batter. The pitcher has either missed with his first pitch or intentionally wasted a pitch to try to get the batter to swing at something outside the strike zone. At **1–0** the count favors the hitter. The pitcher does not want to fall behind **2–0,** so the batter is expecting him to try to throw a strike. He is ready to swing.

What the batter gets, of course, depends on the pitcher. Is it going to be a fastball? Or will it be a curveball, a changeup, or a slider? That's why pitchers like Pedro Martínez are so great. The batter never knows what they are going to throw on any count. With many pitchers, on a **1–0** count it would be reasonable to expect a fastball. But Martínez might throw a changeup.

From the pitcher's point of view, if he just missed a strike with the first pitch, sometimes he'll try to nibble at the strike zone with the same pitch, hoping the batter will lay off.

Now comes the question: take a strike or swing? If the batter is leading off the inning, he might want to take a pitch here and hope to draw a walk. On the other hand, if the batter has power, this pitch might be a good one to take a rip at.

If the pitcher misses again and falls behind **2–0,** this is a real hitter's count. Here's where a batter can get real choosey, based on his knowledge of his own strengths and weaknesses. On this count the hitter's goal should be to narrow his zone to a location and a pitch he has a good chance of hitting well. For most batters that means a pitch they can pull.

Let's say he is a power hitter, strong from the middle of the plate in, and he can get the most on a ball that is just below the belt. And let's say he prefers a fastball to a breaking ball. The batter picks a zone and looks for the pitch he wants. If the pitch is in the zone and something he can catch up with, he swings; if it is away or too high or too low, he lets it go by.

If a batter doesn't see *his pitch,* he should not swing because he is almost as good with a **2–1** count as he is at **2–0.**

When the pitcher is all the way in the hole, with a **3–0** count, you might think this is the perfect hitter's count, but that's not always the way it works. When some batters are given the green light on a **3–0** count, they get so anxious and excited at the prospect of a fat pitch over the plate that they don't know how to handle it. They will swing at anything.

For that reason, and because the manager may be just as happy getting a base runner with a walk, most hitters are instructed to take a pitch on **3–0.** Guys like me were never told to swing on **3–0.**

There's not really a "green light" in this situation; it is more a matter of taking away the red light. The manager has to learn which guys he can trust hitting **3–0.** It is almost always power hitters—guys who have the ability to hit home runs—who are allowed to swing on this count. The batter should be one who has the ability to identify his zone; if the pitch is not in that zone, he doesn't even think about swinging.

Depending on the game situation and the batter, a pitcher with a **3–0** count may just lay in a fat, hittable pitch. A guy who ordinarily throws at

Knowing the Count

Count	Hitter's count	Pitcher's count	The batter expects	Batting average[a]	On-base percentage[a]
0–0			**Neutral count.** High percentage of fastballs. Some batters, like Ted Williams, argued that batters should take the first pitch. Tell that to Nomar Garciaparra.	.340	.345
0–1		✔	**Pitcher's choice.** Batter is in a defensive situation and may be less aggressive	.325	.335
0–2		✔	**Protect the plate.** The pitcher often throws a breaking ball or a waste pitch.	.165	.180
1–0	✔		**Expect a fastball.** Focus on favorite zone.	.345	.345
1–1			**Neutral count.** Pitcher can throw any pitch.	.330	.335
1–2		✔	**Protect the plate.** Often a breaking ball count.	.185	.190
2–0	✔		**Expect a fastball.** Focus on favorite zone. Excellent hitter's count.	.370	.370
2–1			**Expect a fastball.** Excellent hit-and-run count.	.345	.345
2–2		✔	**Protect the plate.** Expect pitcher's best strikeout pitch, often a breaking ball.	.200	.200
3–0	✔[b]		**Expect a fastball.** Focus on favorite zone.	.430[b]	.960[b]
3–1	✔		**Expect a fastball.** Focus on favorite zone. Excellent hitter's count and run-and-hit count.	.345	.690
3–2			**Pitcher wants a strike.** Expect a fastball if the pitcher does not have command of breaking ball.	.240	.240

[a] Based on analysis of 2000–2002 MLB seasons

[b] Usually only the best hitters are given a green light with a 3–0 count, while most batters are told to take a pitch in hopes of receiving a walk. The expected highest batting average for most batters comes with a 2–0 count, followed closely by a 1–0 situation. The highest on-base percentage for most batters is the 3–0 count, because the chances of getting a fat pitch to hit or one outside the strike zone for a walk are high.

95 miles per hour may step it down to 90 or 91. That's still moving, but it is nothing like his strikeout pitch.

To a batter being ahead **2–1** is similar to a **1–1** count. He's protecting the plate to try to avoid ending up behind in the count with two strikes. At the same time the pitcher is trying not to fall behind **3–1,** so the batter is probably going to get a pretty good pitch to hit.

This is what I call an *action count.* It's a good pitch for the manager to call a hit-and-run or a squeeze. The pitcher is likely to throw a strike; he is not likely to pitch out or throw an unhittable waste pitch.

The hitter may or may not get a fastball here, but the pitcher does want to try to get the pitch over the plate on this count.

A **3–1** count is another hitter's count, and also an action count. Once again, the hitter wants to narrow his zone and not swing at a pitch out of the strike zone or one he can't drive well.

The manager might want to call for a *run-and-hit* play here. With a **3–1** count, he is not going to put on a *hit-and-run* because he doesn't want the batter to be forced to swing at a pitch that is a ball. With a run-and-hit play, the batter is given the option of not swinging if the pitch is not a strike.

On a run-and-hit, the base runner takes off on the pitch, and it is up to the batter whether or not to swing. If it is a strike, the coaches want the batter to swing; if it is ball four, the hitter should take the pitch and not chase a ball.

On a **3–2** count the batter is probably going to see a pretty good pitch because the pitcher doesn't want to issue a walk. He is likely to throw whatever he thinks he can get over the plate. In this situation the pitcher is battling as much as the hitter is.

You are likely to see a pitcher's nastiest stuff on a **1–2** or **2–2** count. When the count is full, at **3-2,** he wants to make sure he throws a strike. So that makes this a much better hitting count than the others.

Protecting the Plate

When a batter is in the hole—with two strikes against him—he'll usually adjust his swing to try to avoid striking out; coaches call it protecting the plate. It's mostly a matter of cutting down on the swing to try to improve the chances of making contact.

In other words a batter's swing should be different with two strikes than if he is ahead in the count. Players who don't protect the plate are usually guys who strike out more than a hundred times a year.

A good two-strike hitter has excellent hand–eye coordination. He has the ability to lay off a tough pitch, put it in play, or foul it off. The best at this are probably inside-the-baseball hitters.

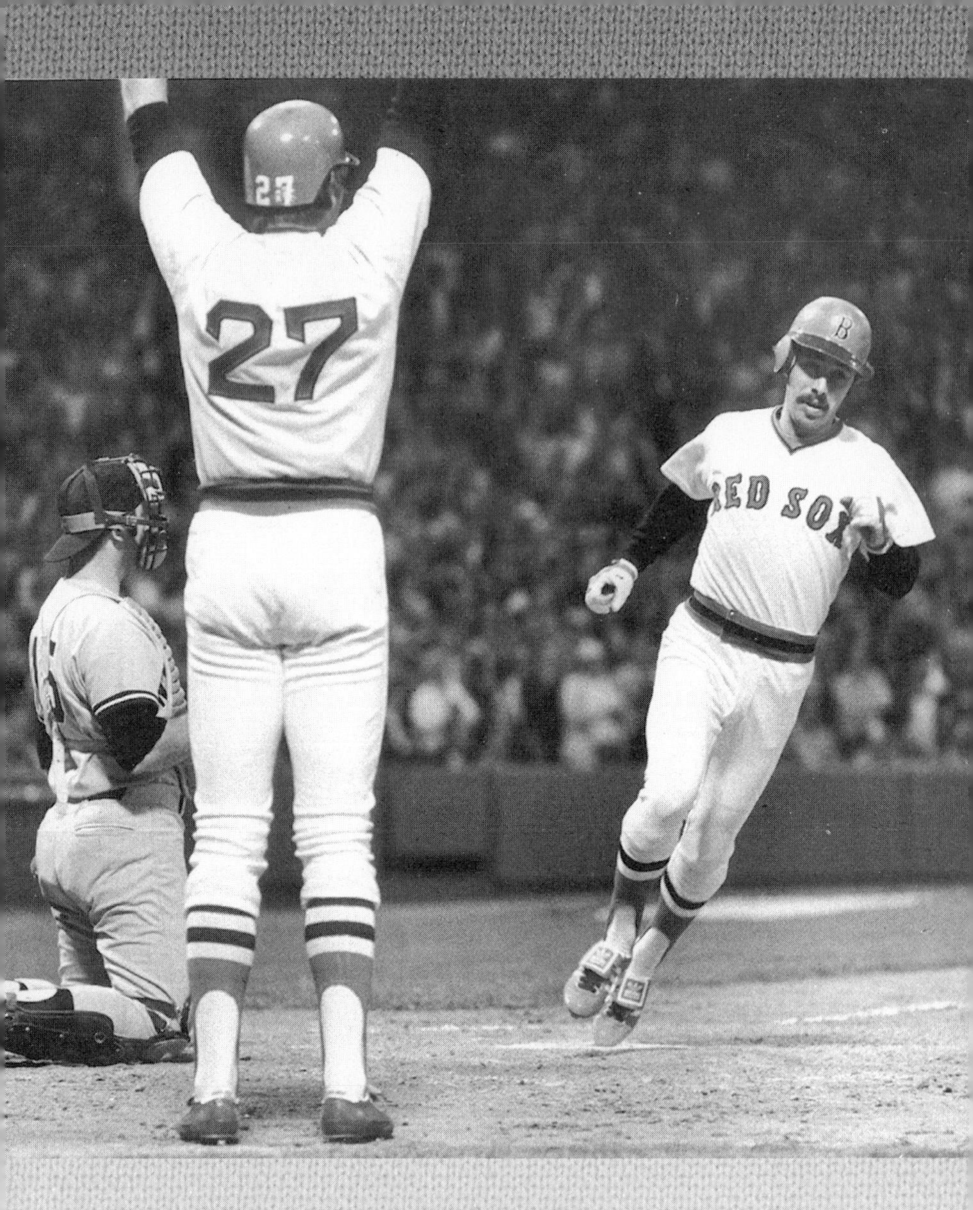

Carlton Fisk gives me the stand-up signal as I cross the plate at Fenway.

Photo courtesy Boston Red Sox

CHAPTER EIGHT

Bunt, Squeeze, and Hit-and-Run

The Beauty of a Bunt

Big guys who have power can bite with one swing of the bat. Little guys who are able to bunt can sting like a bee.

I couldn't hurt pitchers with home runs. The only way I could aggravate them was by doing anything—including bunting—to get on base. I had more than twenty bunt hits per season a few times, and every one of them counted just as much as a line drive in my batting average. Today, though, there are not many great bunters. The game has become such a power game that even guys who have the ability to bunt don't do it much.

One of the advantages of being known as a bunter is that the other side expects an attempt on almost every at bat. They bring the third baseman and the first baseman in close, and they may move the shortstop and second baseman to double-play positions. So before he even steps into the batter's box, the hitter has cut down the range of the infielders. If he ends up swinging away, the ground ball that infielders might have caught if they were playing their normal positions may go through.

Causing disruption

A bunt is a disruptive thing. It takes the pitcher out of his normal sequence, and it creates havoc in the infield. For example, if I was drag bunting as a left-handed hitter, I'd want to get three guys moving: the first baseman, the pitcher, and the second baseman. If I made a good bunt, first base would be wide open. Most batters would expect a fastball on a 2–0 or a 3–1 count, and that would be their pitch to wiggle on and hit one out of the ballpark. For me those were great counts to bunt, because I used to time everything off fastballs.

To bunt a ball, a hitter starts with the same stance he would have if he were swinging, because he doesn't want to give anything away. He times his steps for a fastball; anything off-speed generally throws off the timing of his footwork.

As a left-handed batter, if I planned to drag the ball down the first-base line, my lead foot would angle toward the pitcher instead of down the line. Then I would swing my back leg around in a crossover step. In order for me to cover the plate, my first step would have to be toward the pitcher or toward the plate. And I would try to take the ball with me and make those three infielders move.

For a drag bunt I used to have a tight bottom hand and a loose top hand. And then I'd like a high fastball that I could push. On a drag bunt I didn't want to deaden the ball. I wanted to hit it hard enough to get by the pitcher but soft enough that the second baseman or first baseman had to charge it.

Bunting to third base is a different story. The hitter has to wait a little longer to go into his bunting stance because he is trying to fool the third baseman and hold him back at his position. The third baseman watches the head of the bat. Once he sees the bat move into a bunt position, he is going to charge hard at the plate.

Actually, there's a bit more finesse involved in deadening a ball down the third-base line than there is with dragging a ball to the first-base side. The batter bunts off his lead foot instead of the crossover.

For a right-handed hitter, the ideal ball to bunt down the third-base line would probably be an off-speed pitch. Once he gets his pitch, the hitter tries to deaden the ball; think of it as almost catching the baseball with the bat—as if there were a glove at the top of the bat.

A push bunt from a right-handed hitter toward second base would be the equivalent of a left-hander's drag bunt. Again, the idea is to try to get the pitcher, first baseman, and second baseman all moving.

Laying down a bunt

The key to laying down a good bunt is technique. I used to work on my bunting as much as I worked on my hitting. It was one of the things I did best, but it is the hardest for me to explain.

I would always try to drag bunt. My goal was to send the ball toward second base and have the pitcher, the second baseman, and the first baseman all moving. And eight out of ten times, with a good bunt, I could beat the pitcher to the bag. It was very rewarding to see three guys falling all over themselves trying to make a play, and it aggravated the pitcher, as a bonus.

As I've pointed out, with a drag bunt the batter takes a crossover step toward the pitcher and is on the move; he's really got to get the momentum going toward first base. It's not really like taking a swing.

I was terrible at bunting to third base. I never had the patience to stay back and deaden the ball. I always wanted to be on the move with a good jump toward first.

But I did learn to compensate later on in my career. For some reason other teams always played me in shallow at third base, even though I never bunted in that direction. So I used to try to slap the ball by the third baseman; it would go all the way to the shortstop, who was playing deep.

The disappearing art of bunting

One reason bunting is a lot less common today is the introduction of many new, smaller ballparks. They're home-run friendly and have accelerated the emphasis on power hitters. Another is that nobody gets a raise in his contract for being a good bunter. And many of today's managers don't like to give up outs with a bunt, especially early in the game.

Another of my theories involves the use of aluminum bats: Guys coming up through college and high school have played mostly with aluminum bats, and those bats are much harder to bunt with than wooden ones.

Players don't devote much time to working on bunts during spring training and in pregame batting practice. If you watch batting practice, a player might see twelve pitches, putting down two bunts and taking ten swings. Most players treat bunts as a joke; it's just not a part of their game.

It's a real loss to the game, especially when a player comes up in the eighth inning in a situation where a sacrifice bunt would be appropriate, but the manager doesn't put on the play because he knows the player can't execute a bunt. To me that's inexcusable. It's a failure on the part of managers and coaches to stress that bunting is important and have the players practice it.

In today's game there aren't many good bunters. Ichiro Suzuki is very good, and at his peak, so was Kenny Lofton. The best I ever saw was Rod Carew. The rules say if a batter bunts foul with two strikes, he's out, and for that reason the infield usually drops back to normal position. Carew had the ability to drop a ball down the third-base line on two strikes. He could put underspin on the ball like he was playing pool. He'd get just enough under the ball but not enough to pop it up.

Carlton Fisk would get something like ten bunt hits a year because they played him deep at third base. He dropped balls down the third-base line and totally surprised everybody. That's ten extra hits.

Sacrifice bunts

If a batter is bunting for a hit, he tries to hide his intentions by waiting as long as he can before moving into a bunting stance. If he gives away the bunt too soon, infielders can react quicker. I used to try to wait until I saw the ball leave the pitcher's hand before I started to make my move.

But a sacrifice to move a runner along is a whole different animal. Everybody in the park knows the batter is trying to lay down a bunt. With a man on first base, the hitter tries to bunt down the first-base line; the first baseman can't react as quickly or charge hard after the bunt because he has to hold the runner on. If there is a man on second base, most of the time the bunt goes to third base to pull the third baseman off the bag to field the bunt, leaving an open base for the runner.

Squeeze Plays

A squeeze play—a sacrifice bunt by the batter with a runner on third base—is one of the most exciting offensive plays in baseball and a lot of fun if you can execute it. A squeeze play's supposed to be a surprise, or else it's less likely to work.

As an analyst I especially enjoy calling squeeze plays. I look at how many outs there are, the score of the game, who is hitting, and who is on base. And when it feels right, I take a shot at predicting it: "There's a good chance you may see a squeeze here." When I get it right, I love it, because it is a play you don't see but four or five times a season.

"Watching a situation in the game, Remy thinks of four or five different things that would never even occur to me. He's right 95 percent of the time. The 5 percent wrong is when the manager is not aggressive enough. Jerry would be an outstanding manager."

NESN PLAY-BY-PLAY
ANNOUNCER DON ORSILLO

You will almost never see a squeeze play when there is nobody out in the inning, because there's still a chance to have a big inning, and in any case all that is needed is a deep fly ball to bring the runner home. You're most likely to see a squeeze with one out, because the chances of having the big inning are diminished by having an out.

There's an important difference between a *safety squeeze* and a *suicide squeeze.* With a suicide squeeze the man on third takes off for home as soon as the pitcher's front foot hits the ground. With a safety squeeze the batter makes the bunt and then the runner on third determines whether the bunt is good enough to get him home; if not, he stays on the base.

A good time to call a squeeze play is after a lot of action on the field in the previous at bat—when the other team may be distracted. A lot of bad stuff has happened to them, and the other side has been running and balls have been thrown all over the place. For example, after a throw comes in from the outfield and gets by the catcher, the next at bat is a perfect time to surprise the other side; nobody is thinking about a squeeze. Bing, another run.

And it makes more sense to call a squeeze not so much to tie the game but to take a one-run lead or to add another run.

Despite what I just said about not often seeing a squeeze play with no outs, in the 2007 season we saw a well-executed surprise bunt by Alex Cora in a Fourth of July game against Tampa Bay. Coco Crisp had just startled the Devil Rays with a triple to lead off the game, and Cora took advantage by laying down a safety squeeze on the first pitch he saw. Bing, bang, a run on the board and the start of a winning game.

Red Sox manager Terry Francona's take on the Crisp-Cora one-two punch: "If it gets by the pitcher we have a rally, and [if] it doesn't, we get a run."

The right guy to bunt

There are few scenes more sickening than seeing the batter miss the pitch on a suicide squeeze. It is deflating because it results in an easy out, removing a runner from scoring position at third base.

Managers generally use the play with a player who knows how to bunt and in a count where the batter is pretty sure he is going to get a strike. You don't ask a guy who can't bunt to squeeze; coaches have to have confidence that the batter can make contact, even on a bad pitch. He has to get the ball on the ground or he has got to foul it off.

In a suicide squeeze, the hitter's intention is to just get the ball on the ground. It doesn't have to go to third or first. There's nothing wrong with trying to bunt it right back at the pitcher; the most important thing is to make contact.

Advancing the Runner

One of the common mistakes fans make involves a situation with a man on second base. If there is nobody out and the batter hits a fly ball to right field to advance him to third, the batter is giving himself up with a productive out.

If he does the same thing with one out, it's not much of a good thing; in that situation he is trying to get a hit to drive the runner in. But you still hear the fans give him an ovation for moving the runner along.

The difference between a steal and a hit-and-run

The difference between a straight-out steal and a hit-and-run play is this: On a steal, the hitter is not swinging.

The manager would like whoever is hitting behind a base stealer to be someone not afraid to go to two strikes. If I was up to bat and there was a speedster in front of me on first base and I saw him get the steal sign, I was not going to swing unless the count went to two strikes. Until then I would give him the chance to steal.

After the batter gets to two strikes, the batter has to be ready to swing. It drives me nuts when I hear announcers or fans say that there was a hit-and-run on a 3–2 count.

Watch the counts: 1–0, 1–1, and 2–1 are hit-and-run counts. If the count goes to 2–0, the manager is probably not going to call for a hit-and-run because that's where he wants the batter to try to hit one out of the ballpark.

Another way to spot the difference between a hit-and-run and a straight steal is to watch the runner carefully. When a player takes off on a hit-and-run he usually will take a peek back toward home plate while he runs to see if contact was made and where the ball was hit. If you watch base runners on a straight steal, you'll see most won't even look at home plate. Or at least they shouldn't.

You also need to pay attention to the situation in the game. If a team is down by three or four runs, they're not likely to put on a hit-and-run. It's a bad idea because the manager might be forcing that hitter to swing at a bad pitch and make an out. A manager generally calls the play when his side is ahead or down by one or two runs. But some managers will put on a hit-and-run just for the hell of it because their team has really been struggling and they're trying to open up a hole and get something going.

Looks like I just faked a bunt to see which way the infielders are going to be moving. If I got a reaction that I liked, I would probably try to bunt for real on the next pitch.

Photo courtesy Los Angeles Angels of Anaheim Baseball Club

CHAPTER NINE

Pinch Hitters, DHs, and BP

The Pinch Hitter

Being a pinch hitter is the most difficult offensive job. This player has to go from sitting on his tail for most of the game to coming up to the plate at a pivotal moment. I have seen some pinch hitters whose natural instinct is to go up and whack the first good pitch they see. Other guys are more patient and work the count.

A good pinch hitter is a key member of the team. This is a guy who can start a rally, keep one going, or provide the big hit to take the lead. It takes a special temperament for this job. Ted Williams could have been a lousy pinch hitter. You cannot merely say, "This guy is a career .350 batter so he should make a good pinch hitter."

Remy Says: Watch This

Go Figure

Bobby Kielty batted .218 in 2007, with a total of 87 at bats split between Oakland and Boston. As a pinch hitter, he was 0 for 33 for the season, and for his entire career he had 53 regular-season home runs—about one every 34 at bats.

And though he had recorded a few hits here and there against Colorado pitching in interleague play, he was 0 for 2 against reliever Brian Fuentes. So, of course, the following happened in the eighth inning of the final game of the 2007 World Series: Sent up to the plate as a pinch hitter for Mike Timlin with the Red Sox clinging to precarious 3–1 lead, Kielty swung at the first pitch he saw and sent it over the leftfield wall. The run turned out to be the winning margin in the 4–3 clincher.

Bursting out of the box on a base hit to left.

Photo courtesy Boston Red Sox

In the American League, you usually don't see a pinch hitter until late in the game. In the National League, managers may use a pinch hitter to bat for the pitcher earlier in the game. Sometimes the manager is able to give a little bit of advance notice. He might tell the pinch hitter that if a certain situation happens, he will be hitting for the second guy up in the next inning. In that case the player might go into the clubhouse and stretch, perhaps run a bit to get some blood flowing.

But often he will have almost no warning at all; there may be two outs and someone gets on base in scoring position and the manager decides to bat for the next man in the lineup. The pinch hitter is placed into the most important moment of the game and he doesn't even have a sweat going.

The Designated Hitter

The designated hitter (DH)—a position in the American League only—is also a difficult assignment for many athletes who made it to the major leagues on the basis of their overall ability as a ballplayer. Such a player is accustomed to having his plate appearance and then taking his spot in the field; when he is in the field he is concentrating on defense. For most players baseball is similar to football in that they know that if they screw up one play, they'll get a chance to make the next one right. But if they're the DH and all they are doing is hitting, that's the only thing on their mind until their next at bat. Some guys adjust very well, but other guys hate it because they don't get a chance to go out in the field.

A single at bat might last a minute or a minute and a half, and the DH might not get up again for another forty-five minutes. So he might be involved for seven or eight minutes out of a three-hour game.

Some DHs sit on the bench, but most go to the clubhouse to watch the game on television and videotapes of their last at bat. Some will swing at tape balls, ride a bike, and do anything to stay loose. Then they need to get back out to the bench a few minutes before they're due up; it takes a few minutes for eyes to adjust to the light, especially in a night game.

Remy's Top Dawgs

One of the best pinch hitters in the history of the American League was **Joe Cronin,** whose number 4 is one of five retired by the Red Sox (along with Ted Williams 9, Bobby Doerr 1, Carl Yastrzemski 8, and Carlton Fisk 27).

As a player-manager he seemed to know when to put himself into the game: He still holds the American League record for most pinch-hit home runs in a season with five, and the most pinch-hit RBIs in a season with twenty-five. Both marks were made in 1943.

He also became the first player to hit pinch-hit home runs in both games of a doubleheader, on June 17, 1943, in a stretch when he hit three 3-run pinch-hit homers in four at bats.

Defensive substitutes and pinch runners

Going into the ninth inning with a lead, a manager might bring in a weaker-hitting defensive replacement in hopes of improving the team's chances on the field. (Or he might take a star hitter out of the lineup to insert a pinch runner late in the game, but he'd try not to do that if he thought the hitter might have a chance to come up to the plate one more time.)

It could backfire if somehow the game gets tied and the defensive

Remy's Top Dawgs

David Ortiz was the best designated hitter in baseball in 2005 and again in 2006. In 2005 he batted .300 for the season with 47 home runs and 148 RBIs, almost all as the DH. He appeared at first base for all or part of just ten games, mostly against National League teams when the DH rule did not apply.

In 2006 his batting average and RBIs declined slightly, to .287 and 137, but his home run total went up to 54, setting a new Boston Red Sox record for long balls, eclipsing the previous record of 50 set by Jimmie Foxx. He was also responsible for five walk-off base hits (including three home runs) during the season.

For 2007 Ortiz saw his power numbers decline a bit, but he was still a force to be reckoned with in the Red Sox lineup. He posted the highest batting average of his career, at .332. But his home run and RBI numbers were "only" 35 and 117. He had the most hits of any season in his career, with 182, and the most doubles, with 52. Big Papi battled problems with his right knee and his shoulder, and Manny Ramírez's very slow start to the season might have allowed some opposing pitchers to work around Ortiz . . . just a little bit.

Since the inception of the DH rule in 1973, the Red Sox have had a few of the best designated hitters. **Orlando (Cha Cha) Cepeda** won the Associated Press Outstanding DH Award in 1973, batting .289 with 20 home runs and 86 runs batted in, at age thirty-five. He came over from the Atlanta Braves in the National League and never took the field again, appearing in 142 games as a DH in 1973 and 26 games in 1974 for Kansas City before retiring.

Jim Rice won the AP award in 1977, batting .320 with 39 home runs and 114 runs batted in. That year, he played 116 games at DH and 44 in the outfield. And **Don Baylor** won in 1986, batting just .238, but hitting 31 home runs and driving in 94 runs at age thirty-seven.

"How can you hit and think at the same time?"

YOGI BERRA

player has to come to the plate. But in close games managers will generally go for their best defensive team in the field in hopes of picking up an out they would not have otherwise gotten. If the game goes to extra innings, well you have to go with the lineup you have.

I hate to see managers second-guessed when they make a substitution because most of the time they are doing the right thing. The manager is trying to get the best players on the field at the right time. If the team can't hold the lead, it is probably not going to be the manager's fault.

Batting Practice

There are some players who almost never take batting practice. And there are great hitters who will be out there every day. I remember seeing Ken Griffey Jr. taking extra batting practice every day before the rest of the team started batting practice, and then he would take his normal turn with them.

A player can get as much batting practice as he wants, including live batting practice with somebody throwing to him, or flips in the batting cage. Some batters hit off a tee, trying to perfect certain things in their swing. Other guys prefer to have the ball flipped to them because it is moving toward them like a regular pitch.

If the team is on the road, the regularly scheduled time for batting practice for that night's game might be 5:30 p.m. But there will be guys out on the field at 3:00 who want to get in some extra swings. Most teams will work with the visitors to make the field available. At home it's your home park and you can pretty much do what you want.

All the new stadiums—and many old ones like Fenway Park—have indoor cages. So even if there's a rainout, there are ways to take some batting practice. In many of the newer ballparks, the cages are just steps from the dugout or the clubhouse. Some designated hitters or pinch hitters go into the indoor cages in the middle of the game.

PART FOUR

Around the Horn

Looking the ball into my glove as I prepare to turn the double play; once again, I've got my mouth open, too.

Photo courtesy Boston Red Sox

CHAPTER TEN

The Infield

Thinking about the Infield

When we talk about a good infielder, we might say he has "good hands." There are some fielders who jab at balls and others who look so smooth. There are some who attack balls and those who let the ball come to them.

Watch players take ground balls during infield workouts; what you see in practice is probably what you'll see in the game.

Good infielders always seem to play the right hop. They don't get fooled by bad hops. They get themselves in good position to make that smooth play. You can clearly see how some players funnel the ball from the ground up to their body, and it's so smooth: good hands. Other guys seem to be fighting it all the time. In Boston I played for a couple of years with Rick Burleson, who was not the classic smooth shortstop. He jabbed at balls, but he got the job done.

The feet are the base for everything in baseball; if a fielder doesn't get his feet in the proper position, his hands are going to be all over the place. A guy like Derek Jeter is smooth; he always seems to have his feet in the right spot. The same thing goes for Alex Rodriguez.

A lot of an infielder's work, especially at second base and shortstop, is anticipating where the ball is going to be hit. He's got to know the difference between a sinker-ball pitcher and a power pitcher. He's got to know who is at the plate and how the batter deals with different types of pitches. And he needs to pay attention to the count. There are certain hitters who are probably going to pull the ball in a hitter's count.

Then there's the choice of pitch. Many right-handed hitters tend to pull a curveball; an alert fielder knows that and takes a few steps to his right. Similarly a left-handed hitter will often try to pull a sinker ball, so that should take an infielder a couple of steps to his left.

In general, when there is a right-hander at the plate, infielders might shade toward first—not a huge adjustment, maybe a step. But it all depends on that hitter: Does he change his swing with two strikes? Does he cut down on his swing to try to make contact?

Rookies in the infield

You can usually spot the difference between a seasoned veteran and a rookie, even a very talented one. In a word, this is a matter of experience. A kid may come up to the major leagues as an outstanding fielder, looking beautiful taking ground balls and showing a great throwing arm. But he doesn't know the hitters and he doesn't really know his own pitching staff. And he's got to learn it on the job.

When I look at an inexperienced infielder, I usually find a guy who seems to be just missing ground balls by inches. It may just be a matter of not being in the proper position.

The infield stance

If you're watching the replay of an error on the stadium screen or at home, see if the fielder jabbed at the ball or played it smoothly. You can't be a good infielder if your glove is hanging around your stomach and you are reaching for balls. If that's the way you play, you become a jabber.

A good infielder tries to work from the ground up. He holds his glove low, with knees bent and butt down toward the ground. He squares up to the ball, keeps his eyes on the ball, and tries to follow it right into his glove.

At shortstop and second base, fielders try to get in a rhythm, so that when the ball is delivered to home plate, they've got a little momentum going either toward first base or back and forth between their normal position and one of those bases. It helps them get a good jump on the ball.

First basemen also try to be on the move, unless they are holding a runner on.

Third base is a reaction position. A lot of third basemen do not make any side-to-side movements or take a step in. Balls are usually hit so hard to third, and they are so close to the hitter, that their most important step is the first step, a reaction step.

The Marriage in the Infield

I've always thought that the idea of a "marriage" between the second baseman and the shortstop is a bit overrated. People like to say, "There's such a comfort level there because they've worked together for such a long time."

The two fielders have to know each other's abilities and habits. Where is this guy going to give me the ball as I am trying to turn a double play? And at what velocity is it coming? That's all either really needs to know to make the "marriage" work.

Obviously, it is much easier to be out there with someone you play with every day because you know where the throw is going to be. On the other hand, I don't think it takes all that long to get to know somebody, at least when it comes to baseball. I could go out with anyone and take ground balls for five minutes, and I would have a pretty good idea where I'm going to get the ball. For example, if a shortstop is going toward the bag, as a second baseman I would expect him to give me an underhand flip. In that case I know that I can come across the bag.

If the ball is going to be right at him, does he go with the underhand flip or does he like to make the throw sidearm? If he throws sidearm, as the second baseman I'll have to be a little bit more defensive around the bag because I don't know where the ball is going to go.

The plays that are tough are the ones where the shortstop has to go to his right toward third base, backhand the ball, and throw off-balance. He is going to try to give it to the second baseman in front of the bag, but if he is off-balance, the throw could be behind the bag.

As a second baseman, I always found it more difficult reading my third baseman than reading my shortstop. The third baseman has a longer throw, so there is more chance for an error or a bad throw.

With a throw from third, you've really got to be patient. You've almost got to straddle the bag, and always anticipate a bad throw.

Playing Back

There are three basic positions for infielders: infield back (near the outfield grass), double-play depth, and infield in (on the infield grass).

In the best of all possible worlds, an infielder likes to play as far back from the plate as he can get away with; this gives him extra time to play a ground ball or grab a line drive. Of course, he can't play too far back or he won't be able to throw the runner out at first base. And if he plays too far back against a good bunter, the batter can make him look foolish by dropping a dribbler in the infield.

Double-Play Depth

To turn most double plays in the infield, a fielder has to get to the ball as quickly as possible and get it to the other middle infielder in enough time to allow him to throw on to first base to get the batter. If they play back, they often can't do that; it would just take too long.

Double-play depth moves the infielders somewhere between the infield-back and infield-in positions, a little bit deeper than halfway between the edge of the infield and the outfield. The second baseman and shortstop also move a step or two closer to second base than usual. This repositioning comes with a risk: A fielder will not get to a ball he could have reached if he was in the normal infield position.

As always, it's important to know the opposing players. If the runner on first can motor, you might see the fielders place themselves directly in the middle of the infield, so the shortstop or second baseman doesn't get killed on a relay. If there's a guy at bat who can really run, like Ichiro Suzuki, a team might not go to double-play depth at all, because they figure they're probably not going to double him up.

On the Infield Grass

With a runner on third and fewer than two outs in a close game, most teams will bring the infield in to increase the chances of making a play at the plate. As with double-play depth, a drawn-in infield limits the range of the infielders. A ground ball two steps to the right or left is probably going to get through.

The decision to gamble on playing the infield in should depend on who is hitting, who is pitching, and who is running at third base. If there is a slow runner, infielders don't have to play all the way in and instead can play back four or five steps. Even if the infielders take just a step or so

"Jerry Remy was a scrappy little ballplayer who didn't think he had played the game unless he got his uniform dirty. He was not the best second baseman who ever played, but he tried to be."

DAVE NIEHAUS, VOICE OF THE CALIFORNIA ANGELS FROM 1969 TO 1976 AND THE SEATTLE MARINERS FROM 1977 TO THE PRESENT DAY

in toward the plate, the third-base coach will probably tell a slow runner not to go home unless the ball gets through to the outfield.

The manager will also look at where the other team is in its lineup. If it is toward the bottom of the lineup—presumably with weaker hitters—you're liable to see the infield in. If the power hitters in the middle of the lineup are up, the infielders may stay back.

Sometimes a manager will draw in the infield early in the game, even in the first inning. He might do this when there is a great pitching matchup, for example. The manager may figure in that game there are not going to be a lot of runs scored, so he would try to cut down runs as early as possible. One run may be the difference in the game.

I remember as a player going up against teams managed by Gene Mauch; he always brought the infield in early in the game, no matter who was pitching. Mauch always wanted to be ahead in the game.

The Yankees lose, the Yankees lose!

Let me take you back to the seventh game of the 2001 World Series, not just because the Yankees lost but because it was a perfect example of the difficult situation faced by managers when the winning run is in scoring position.

Luis González of the Arizona Diamondbacks came up to the plate with bases loaded and one out in the bottom of the ninth inning against the New York Yankees. He was facing Mariano Rivera and his almost-unhittable cut fastball.

Remy Says: Watch This

The Making of an All-Star Shortstop

What separates an All-Star from an average player? Arm strength, the ability to make backhanded plays, range going to his left and his right, and positioning.

A shortstop doesn't need to have great speed, but he does need quickness, which creates some range. He needs a strong throwing arm, or a very quick release, and good hands. There are a lot of infielders who have some of those weapons, but there are very few who have all of them.

You would certainly include Cal Ripken among great shortstops, but he did not have all the tools that Alex Rodriguez had when he played short, or that Derek Jeter or Orlando Cabrera have. But Ripken made it look easy because he always seemed to be in the right position.

With a sinker-ball pitcher in the game, a manager could reasonably expect the hitter to hit a ground ball, and so it's an easy decision to bring the infield in. However, Rivera doesn't get a lot of ground balls; he is a strikeout/fly ball pitcher. With that kind of pitcher, the manager might not ordinarily draw in the infield. But in a World Series, if there was ever a ground ball hit by accident and the manager had the infield back, he wouldn't be able to live with himself. He's just got to try to cut down that run.

Former Yankee manager Joe Torre pulled the infield in, drawing shortstop Derek Jeter out of position. González choked up on the bat—something he hadn't done all season—and flared a single right over Jeter's head. If Jeter had been in his normal position, he probably would have caught the ball for the second out, and the Yankees would have had a good chance of surviving the inning and taking the Series into extra innings.

It always looks bad when the infield is pulled in and a guy drops a hit a few feet behind the infield, which is exactly what happened.

Managers are second-guessed all the time. He makes his decision. If it works, great; if it doesn't, he's still got to do the same thing next time. Joe Torre never backed down from his decision, and I agree with him.

Guarding the line

Late in the game when their team has the lead—usually from the seventh inning on—managers will often have the first baseman and third baseman guard the baselines. They move closer to the lines to try to prevent an extra base hit that goes down the line and into a corner of the outfield. This is a manager's call, a flip of the coin. Certain managers will even do it with two outs right from the start of the game to try to keep a man out of scoring position at second base.

It's always been a weird concept to me because you are penalizing yourself for being ahead in the game. You are moving one or two players out of position because you have a one-run lead.

Some managers feel the same way I do. They'd rather take away the base hit, because the double is harder to get than the single. And you'll see this situation come up when there is a great base stealer up to bat. Why play the line? If he gets on first, he's going to steal second anyway.

Now there is another situation when a team might want to play the lines: if there is a man on first who represents the tying or winning run. In that situation you may see infielders playing the lines and outfielders playing the gaps and standing deeper. They're trying to prevent the extra base hit that might score the man on first.

Once again, though, it depends on the hitters. If there's an opposite-field hitter at the plate, like I was or like Wade Boggs was, why play the first baseman on the line? An opposite-field hitter would never pull the ball down there. But a team might take the third baseman and put him on the line to try to prevent a double.

Positioning also depends on the ballpark. At Fenway Park, for example, a ball down the third-base line is not guaranteed to be a double because of the way the wall comes out. Many times you'll see a ball hit off that wall and come back out onto the field, and the fielders can hold the batter to a single. Some managers won't play the third-base line at Fenway.

Guys You Can't Defend Against

The toughest guys to defend against are hitters who use the whole ballpark. When you see one of the better batters come to the plate, you'll probably see the infield and the outfield straight up, not shading one way or the other.

If one of the best batters is down in the count, he'll move the ball to the opposite field. If he gets a certain pitch, he'll pull it. If he's thrown a high fastball, he'll go the other way or up the middle.

I think of a guy like Rod Carew, who was impossible to defend against. We used to go over him in pregame meetings and ask, "How are we going to pitch this guy?" Nobody had an answer. So the pitcher would throw Carew breaking balls and hope that he got himself out.

There was no way to set up a defense against Carew because he would go line to line. He'd hit a ball down the leftfield line on the chalk and the next time he hit down the rightfield line on the chalk. Then he'd bunt with two strikes.

Defensive shifts

Some batters are so predominately pull hitters or opposite-field hitters that it makes sense to put on a defensive shift in the infield. For example, against a right-handed opposite-field hitter or a left-handed pull hitter, a team might move the shortstop behind second base or even put both the shortstop and the second baseman on the right side of the infield.

The manager is hoping either that the shift will improve the chances of making a play, or that it will convince the batter to go against his natural style and give up some power or ability to hit the ball.

The most famous such alignment was the "Williams Shift," first employed by the Cleveland Indians against Boston's Ted Williams. The defensive alignment was designed by Cleveland's Hall of Fame player-manager Lou Boudreau; interestingly Boudreau ended up his career playing for Boston in 1951, and then managing Williams and the Red Sox from 1952 to 1954.

On the Red Sox the guy who most often is greeted with an extreme shift is David Ortiz, a left-handed hitter who tends to pull the ball to the right side of the infield when he hits it on the ground or on a line; when he puts it up in the air he can tattoo the Green Monster in left field or put it out of the park almost anywhere else, but there's no defending against that.

Some opposing managers bring the shortstop to the right of second base and the second baseman into a midway location at the lip of the outfield grass. Ortiz hasn't made much of an adjustment and that's probably good because it has not screwed up his swing. He still gets his share of hard-hit balls that get past infielders wherever they are.

I remember one series the Red Sox played against Seattle when Ken Griffey Jr. was with them, and he was hitting a lot of home runs. Red Sox manager Jimy Williams put the shift on him. It got to Griffey and took him out of his game. He was thinking, "I'm going to bunt to third because I've got nobody over there. I'm going to get a base hit." The Red Sox were perfectly happy; they'd rather have Griffey get a base hit than a home run.

Most players say "to heck with the shift, I'm just going to take my at bat. I'm going to have the same swing." And that is what you should do.

Charting the Pitches

At the start of a new series, most teams have a meeting to discuss their new opponent. Some managers are very focused on detail, using charts. Others rely strictly on an advanced scouting report or what they saw the last time they played against the team.

Dick Williams, my first manager at the major league level, was very much into the details. He had everything charted: every single pitch against every hitter. In those days that was unusual.

When I came to Boston a few years later, Ralph Houk basically planned his game based on what the other team had done against us before and what the advance scout might have seen in the last three games they played.

Today it is very different. Every team has an electronic library and hitters can study every at bat against a particular pitcher over the last five years if that's what they want to do. They can do it before the first pitch, or even duck into the clubhouse during the game.

And the same goes on defense. There will be a coach who handles the infield and a guy who is in charge of the outfielders. They'll have a plan prior to a series, and they will make adjustments as they go along. Watch the dugout and you'll often see a coach on the top step moving an outfielder or signaling to the infield.

Right-handed pitcher, left-handed batter

As with most everything else in baseball, there is no one-size-fits-all rule for how to set up the infield when a right-handed pitcher is throwing to a left-handed batter, or any other pitcher-batter combination. It depends whether this left-handed batter is a pull hitter, an opposite-field hitter, or a straightaway hitter. And it is also affected by the game situation.

Let's say there is nobody on base and there's a left-handed pull hitter facing a pitcher who is not overpowering. In that instance you can expect the batter to pull. So obviously the whole infield can shift around toward first base—a step or so left. Or let's say a batter has faced Josh Beckett twenty times in his career. The Red Sox would have a pretty good chart that the coaches can consult to see where he has hit the ball, and the team can set up a defense based on his history.

And things may be quite different with the same batter against a different pitcher. When knuckleballer Tim Wakefield is throwing, for example, the Red Sox play everyone to pull because the pitch is coming in at about 60 miles per hour and most guys are going to swing early and pull the ball.

Pay attention, too, to the outfield. You'll see quite a few situations when the infield might be shading a batter to pull, while the outfield will be shading him to the opposite field. That's because the charts say that when he hits the ball in the air, he usually hits the other way, but when he hits it on the ground, he pulls it.

Left-handed pitcher, right-handed batter

Left-handers tend to have more movement on their pitches than right-handers. And right-handed hitters, going back to when they were kids, mostly saw right-handed pitchers. Even going through pro ball, they don't see that many left-handers. So let's start with the fact that many right-handers hit right-handers better or are least more comfortable against right-handed pitching than they are against lefties.

Obviously there are different styles. Take a guy like Randy Johnson; when he was at his peak, he was a power left-hander: A smart hitter's approach to him will be different than when he is facing another successful veteran like Jamie Moyer, who relies not on power but instead on control. When right-handers try to pull Moyer, that's exactly what he wants them to do.

Tom Glavine is another example of a control pitcher, a likely Hall of Famer who played for Atlanta for sixteen seasons and was still winning for the New York Mets at age forty-one in 2007 and probably has a few more seasons in his arm. He stays away from right-handers and changes speeds from fastball to changeup. His goal is to keep the batter off balance and make him try to pull the ball. If the pitch is down and away and a right-hander tries to pull it, most of the time anything he hits is going to be on the ground and to the shortstop. If you see a lot of ground balls to shortstop and third base when Glavine is pitching to a right-hander, he is doing his job and the hitter is not. The hitter should be thinking about going up the middle.

Moving on the Count

One of the best indicators of a good defensive team is whether fielders change their position depending on the count. If they don't move, they're probably not a very good defensive club. But if you look out as the count changes and see the center fielder move a couple steps to his right, the right fielder come in a couple of steps, and the third baseman come off the line, you know that the team is pretty well prepared defensively. They may not be the best defensive team, but they know what they want to do.

Moving on the count is important, because batters adjust their swing when they are behind in the count. For example, if a good hitter has two strikes against him, he'll cut down his swing in hopes of making contact with the ball. That makes it more likely that he'll hit the other way and the ball won't travel as far. And so, with a good right-hander at the plate, you'll see the right fielder move in a little bit or stand closer to the line.

If the batter is not a great hitter, a guy who strikes out a hundred times a year and is a dead-pull hitter, he's not going to cut down on his swing with two strikes. He's going for it, so fielders wouldn't make that adjustment.

Some players know enough about the game and the other team to position themselves properly. You expect the veteran player to move more on counts than you would a younger player. But others let the coaches think for them. That's why you see the coach at the top step of the dugout, getting their attention. Some teams have even placed scouts in the press box or on an upper level with a radio so they can report if a fielder is out of position.

Adjusting Position for the Pitch

The second baseman and the shortstop have the advantage of being able to see the signs flashed by the catcher to the pitcher, and they can adjust their position to try to anticipate the type of swing the batter will make. They can, in turn, give some kind of an indication to the first baseman and third baseman about the coming pitch.

Of course that means that the infielders have to know the sequence of signs used between catcher and pitcher, including any changes made during the game. Now here's where the scouting report on the hitter comes into play. What has this guy done on curveballs from this pitcher before? Has he pulled them all? Will he pull this one, or will he try to take it to the opposite field? When a fielder knows what his pitcher is about to throw, he can adjust his position accordingly.

Giving it away

An infielder can't make a move too soon or he's going to give the pitch away to the hitter. A smart hitter can figure out the type of pitch if he sees the infielders shift. At times in his younger days Cal Ripken was too obvious about his positioning.

If a right-handed hitter sees the second baseman take a couple of steps to his left, he's got a pretty good idea he's going to see a fastball away. If the second baseman is standing where he is, it might be a fastball in, or it could be a slider or something that may fool him a little bit. If he sees the fielder take a step to his right, he can be pretty sure he's going to see a changeup or a big curveball, depending on what the pitcher can throw.

Rem Dawg Remembers

The Splendid Splinter

You don't see many great hitters that are strictly pull hitters. There have been some: Ted Williams, for example, and Barry Bonds.

Adjusting defensive alignment

An infielder will sometimes see a batter make an adjustment in the box. This could make him change his defensive position. For example, if he sees the batter change to an open stance instead of a straightaway stance or a closed stance, that means he's probably trying to pull the ball. If he closes his stance up more, he's trying to go up the middle or the other way.

On rare occasions you'll see a guy choke up on the bat a little bit; this is less common today than it was in the past. This is another instance when fielders have to know the hitter. A good infielder (or the defensive coach in the dugout) will know that certain hitters change their swing when they're down two strikes and try to poke the ball somewhere and beat the throw for a hit.

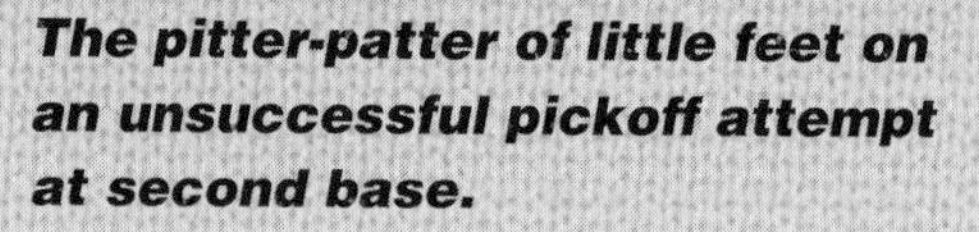

The pitter-patter of little feet on an unsuccessful pickoff attempt at second base.

Photo courtesy Boston Red Sox

CHAPTER ELEVEN

Defensive Strategies in the Infield

Holding the Runner

When there is a runner on second base, the shortstop and the second baseman have to agree who is responsible for keeping him close to the bag. As a rule, if a right-handed hitter is up to bat, the second baseman has that job, and if a left-handed hitter is at the plate, the assignment goes to the shortstop.

But that assumes the batter is a pull hitter: a right-hander who is likely to hit to the left side of the field, or a left-hander likely to hit to the right. If instead a right-handed batter is an opposite-field hitter, the second baseman should move more toward first base and the shortstop should step toward second to hold the runner; they'd step the other way for a left-handed opposite-field hitter.

It doesn't matter so much what pitch is thrown. What matters is where the batter typically hits the ball.

The second baseman has to communicate with the shortstop: You keep him close or I'll keep him close. It's usually done pretty openly because it's obvious to the base runner. If the runner looks at the second baseman and sees him way over toward first base, he knows that fielder is not responsible for holding him. He knows the shortstop is right behind him.

If it's a hit-and-run situation and the catcher has called for a curveball, the second baseman might tell the shortstop to stay at his regular position with a right-hander at the plate because the hitter may pull the ball.

Teams try to guess based on the percentages, the pitcher, and the hitter . . . and they hope they guess right.

Infield Pop-Ups and Short Flies

Sometimes the best drama in a ball game is the result of an infield pop-up near the mound; it's not supposed to be that way, but things can easily fall apart if players forget their assignments.

The basic rule is that on the left side of the infield, the shortstop has priority over the third baseman; on the right side the second baseman has priority over the first baseman. The first baseman and third baseman have priority over the catcher.

Generally the pitcher is not even in the play. That seems foolish to me; some pitchers can catch fly balls as well as any other infielder. But they are almost always called off.

On a pop-up behind first base, the second baseman usually can make the play. He is deeper than the first baseman to begin with, and he has a better angle on a pop-up and an easier chance. The same applies on the left side of the infield, where the shortstop is usually better able to make a play behind third base than the third baseman. The shortstop is coming toward the ball, while the third baseman would have to back pedal or turn around and run toward the outfield.

If the ball is popped up between home plate and one of the bases, the first baseman or third baseman has an easier play because he is coming in on the ball. It's more difficult for the catcher because the ball is going away from him; when a catcher goes out into the infield to make a play, he usually turns his back to the infield so the ball comes to him.

When a pop-up makes it to the outfield, the center fielder has priority over the right fielder and left fielder. And any outfielder has priority over an infielder, if they can get to the ball. Again, the outfielder has an easier play because he is coming in on the ball instead of chasing it toward the fences.

Defending against a Bunt

We've looked at bunts from the point of view of the hitter; now let's look at the defense. There are three types of bunts:

- **Sacrifice bunt**—The purpose here is to give up an out to advance a runner into scoring position, typically from first to second.

"He does everything well. He has tremendous speed, he hits to all fields, he throws well, he makes the pivot perfectly, and he's not afraid of the pitter-patter of little feet."

CALIFORNIA ANGELS MANAGER DICK WILLIAMS SPEAKING ABOUT JERRY REMY IN 1975

- **Squeeze bunt**—The batter tries to score a runner from third base.
- **Drag bunt**—This is an attempt at a base hit using a bunted ball.

Sacrifice bunts

The basic sacrifice bunt is put on when there is a man on first and fewer than two outs. The strategy on defense is like this:

- The **first baseman** holds the runner on; his timing with the pitcher has to be perfect because if he starts charging too soon, the runner at first just takes off for second. That's why you'll sometimes see the first baseman fake a couple of steps in and then come back to the bag for a pickoff attempt. Normally, the first baseman will wait until the pitcher starts to deliver to home before he charges. That's why most hitters try to bunt down the first-base line.
- The **second baseman** is supposed to take a couple of steps in so that he doesn't leave a wide-open hole. Then he has to cut over to first base to cover the bag, while the first baseman charges toward home.
- The **shortstop** holds his position as long as possible. Because a lot of guys will fake—squaring around as if to bunt and then swinging—he's got to protect against that. When the shortstop does move, his job is to cover second base because the second baseman has moved to first base.
- The **third baseman** is drawn in, well in front of the bag on the grass. As soon as he sees the batter square around to bunt, he can charge in toward the plate because he doesn't have to hold anybody on.
- And the **pitcher** can come straight in as soon as he has thrown the ball.

Remy Says: Watch This

Fair or Foul?

Among the oddities of baseball is the fact that first base (like third base) is on the fair side of the baseline, but the base path from home plate to first is in foul territory. So, when a batter makes contact and takes off toward first base, he starts out on the wrong side of the baseline. Ordinarily, this is not a problem unless there is going to be a ball thrown from the catcher or the pitcher. If the runner is in the way of the throw, the umpire is supposed to call him out.

You will very seldom see the umpire call a runner out for being on the wrong side of the baseline on a throw from any infield position other than the catcher and occasionally the pitcher. But it is almost automatic that if he gets hit in the back with the ball, he is going to be out.

On a close play at first, the runner is taught to run through the bag in a straight line; of course, if he does that, he's going to be on the wrong side of the baseline. He's running as hard as he can to beat the throw, and it is usually stunning if the umpire calls him out.

It is very important that an infielder doesn't give up his position too soon on a sacrifice bunt. If he moves too soon, he'll leave a wide-open gap in the infield. A smart hitter, a guy who can handle the bat, will just turn around and try to punch one through the hole.

There are situations when the defense against the bunt may be different. Let's say a team has a two-run lead late in the game, and the other side has runners on first and second. Here it is likely the team at bat is going to bunt. But in this situation, the runner going to third is not as important. So you might see the shortstop go to second base and the third baseman field the ball and throw to the shortstop to get the runner out at second base, erasing the potential tying run.

Squeeze plays

If the batter attempts a squeeze play with a runner on third base, the third baseman's basic assignment is to yell out that the runner is going. But even before that happens, if there's a man on with some speed, the third baseman should be thinking about the possibility of a squeeze.

Before the play, the third baseman should be also paying attention to the other team's third-base coach and the runner. He yells to the pitcher and catcher, though it's usually too late to alert the pitcher, who can see the batter squared to bunt, anyway.

As far as the team that's up at bat, on a squeeze play the coach gives a sign to the hitter, and the hitter usually flashes a return sign to the coach to acknowledge that he's got it. Then there's usually a vocal signal to the runner.

Drag bunt

To defend against a bunt for a base hit, infielders have to know if the hitter is likely to try a drag bunt, or if he likes to bunt down to third base. The basic idea of a drag bunt is to push the ball by the pitcher and get the pitcher, the first baseman, and the second baseman all trying to make a play on that ball, leaving nobody to cover the bag.

Some teams have the first baseman stay near the base while the second baseman charges to make the play. If they get it, they get it. If not, it's no big deal. But at least they have somebody covering the bag.

Backing up the plays

When there is nobody on base, on any play being made to first base, the second baseman's responsibility is to go over there and at least be in the vicinity. If the ball gets by the first baseman, that gives the second baseman a chance to track it down. The second baseman determines his angle to the ball based on where the ball is being thrown from.

Anytime there is a man on base, the second baseman or the shortstop should take a couple of steps behind the pitcher when the catcher throws the ball back. It almost never happens, but there's a chance that the ball can get away from the pitcher. You've got to be there to make the play. If there is a right-handed hitter at the plate, the second baseman usually backs up the pitcher; with a left-handed hitter at bat, it is usually the shortstop who steps toward the mound.

You don't see this as much as you used to, but you should always see the throw backed up when there is a man on third because an error could mean a run.

Despite my campaigning in this 1977 publicity shot for the Angels, I didn't quite get enough votes to make the All-Star team that year. But I was chosen in 1978 in my first year with the Red Sox.

Photo courtesy Los Angeles Angels of Anaheim Baseball Club

CHAPTER TWELVE

The First Baseman

Down in the Dirt

The first baseman's most important skill is the ability to make plays in the dirt. A good first baseman can save infielders many errors if he can handle bad hops and bad throws. If the infielders know they've got a good first baseman, they know every throw does not have to be perfect; this guy is going to bail them out. It's almost like the confidence the pitcher has in his catcher.

A good first baseman can also dive and knock down a ball hit down the line, preventing an extra base hit: Keith Hernandez was good. George Scott was terrific.

Don Mattingly was so pretty to watch when he played first base; he had tremendous range to his left and right. He could make the 3–6–3 double play (first baseman to the shortstop covering second and then back to the first baseman) look beautiful. More recently, John Olerud and Travis Lee were among the game's best first basemen. Olerud, who retired after the 2005 season, was great on balls in the dirt. Former Red Sox Doug Mientkiewicz, was also one of the best; in 2007 he was defensive specialists for that American League team in New York. From 2003 through 2005 the most-used Red Sox first baseman was Kevin Millar, who is right-handed, instead of David Ortiz, a lefty who was used primarily as the designated hitter. First base is sometimes difficult for really big guys like Ortiz, although he does a more-than-adequate job in the field. Ortiz can catch the ball well and can save you on high throws, but it is tough for him to get down on ground balls.

Kevin Youkilis took over at first base in 2006 and quickly showed he had exceptional talent for the position. On June 25, 2007, he played in his 120th game at first without an error, breaking the Red Sox record set in

1921 by Stuffy McInnis. On September 7, he played in his 179th consecutive errorless game, breaking Mike Hegan's 1973 American League record.

His streak continued to the end of the season, reaching 190 games, and will resume with the start of 2008; he could break the major league record of 193 games held by Steve Garvey. (Youkilis was charged with a tough fielding error on a foul popup in the ALCS against the Cleveland Indians, but postseason errors are a separate category.)

Youkilis's streak is even more amazing considering that he did not come up to the majors as a first baseman. He was primarily a third baseman, and had also played second base and left field. And he made his professional debut as a catcher for the Lowell Spinners. (He is unofficially the emergency third catcher for the Red Sox but has never had to put on the tools in the majors.)

Made for a lefty

First base is made for a left-hander. With the glove on the right hand, he can better cover the hole between first and second. On tag plays and pickoff attempts, he just grabs the ball and slaps it down. On bunt plays he doesn't have to spin around to make the play, something right-handers have to do.

The only play that is especially difficult for a left-hander at first base is a backhanded play right down the line.

Nevertheless you'll see mostly right-handers playing first; there are simply more of them. The forehand play for a lefty in the hole between first and second becomes a much more difficult backhanded play for a righty. On a throw to second base, for example a 3–6–3 double play, a right-hander has to field the ball and make a jump pivot; a left hander just makes the catch, takes a step, and throws. On bunt plays a right-hander has to spin or turn all the way around to make a play at second or third base, while the left-hander is in position as he fields it.

The one place where it is an advantage to be a right-hander is a shot down the rightfield line, because his glove is on his left hand.

Giving up defense for offense

On some teams first base is a place to park a so-so fielder with good power or a star who has lost range but can still hit. This may not be the most popular thing with other infielders, but it is a way to get a good bat into the lineup.

"People say I don't have great tools. I make up for it in other ways, by putting out a little bit more. That's my theory, to go through life hustling. In the big leagues hustle usually means being in the right place at the right time. It means backing up a base. It means backing up your teammate. It means taking that headfirst slide. It means doing everything you can do to win a baseball game."

PETE ROSE

A team will almost always sacrifice defense for offense at first base. If there's a big bomber over there—Jim Thome is an example, a guy who can hit 50 home runs a year and drive in 140 runs—most teams will accept some bad first-base play. (Thome was injured for most of the 2005 season, and he has played mostly as a DH for the White Sox in 2006 and 2007.)

An advantage for the first baseman is that he uses a big glove. He doesn't have to be perfect on the fundamentals, and he doesn't have to be the prettiest or the smoothest fielder. If the first baseman can knock the ball down, he still has a chance to get an out. The pitcher should be covering, and he can take a little underhand flip.

The first baseman also doesn't need to make many throws. If he's got a bad arm, he can hide it most of the time. There are some first basemen who will not make a throw on a bunt. Batters can bunt on them all day long because they're not going to try to get the lead runner at second base. In the 2002 All-Star Game, Jason Giambi dove and tagged first base on a bunt when he had all kinds of time to throw to second base. He just didn't want to throw there.

You've still got to be smart

There are, though, a lot of things that can go wrong around first base that can cost runs. You've got to be smart.

For example, let's say there is a ball hit to the infield with a runner on second base and a bad throw is made to first base. Does the fielder try to make the great play and pick the throw out of the dirt—and maybe not get it—or does he come off the bag and block the ball, giving up the out?

By blocking it, at least that run is not going to score from second base. If the first baseman tries to make a pick on a bad throw and doesn't make it, it's a gift run.

The gabby spot

First base is probably the gabbiest position. There is a lot of activity there: The first baseman has the first-base coach, runners on the other team, and his very own umpire to chat with.

Many of the conversations are about the batter's last at bat or about the pitcher or the weather. It's usually not very significant stuff.

Most of the time when I got a hit, I was so happy to be on base I didn't even hear what the first baseman had to say. I do, though, remember early in my career I was struggling and got to first, where Dick Allen was playing the bag; he was with Oakland at the time, at the end of his career. He said to me, "How are you doing?" I said, "Struggling." He told me, "Kid, a slump is only as long as your last time at bat." Words of wisdom.

Anyhow, most players are pretty good about knowing when to chatter. Once the play starts, there is no talk. Of course, if there's a base stealer at the bag, the first baseman might want to chitchat a bit more to try to distract the runner.

The First Baseman's Most Difficult Play

The most difficult play for a first baseman is probably the 3–6–3 double play. In that play he begins by fielding the ground ball. Then he's got to line himself up with the shortstop so he doesn't drill the runner in the back with his throw. The shortstop has to get in position where the first baseman can see him.

Then the first baseman has to get back to the bag, and while he's on the run, watch for a *seed*—a bullet—coming from the shortstop back to first base. Sometimes he's fighting with the pitcher who is also coming over to cover first base.

I say that the ball coming across the diamond is a seed because the shortstop has got to fire that ball back to first base to try to get the runner coming from home plate. When infielders make that play, it looks so nice.

The best I saw at the 3–6–3 was Don Mattingly. Keith Hernandez was also very good and so was George Scott. This play requires quick feet; it is a complicated process and a lot of things have to go right.

The other difficult play is bunt coverage, which is especially tough for right-handed first basemen because they've got to spin to make a throw to second or third base. Getting the lead runner on a bunt is a critical part of the game. Having the ability to scoop up a bunt and make a quick release and a strong throw to second base to get the lead runner is huge.

Pickoff plays at first base

Most pickoff plays at first base are pretty routine. There may be a signal exchanged between the pitcher or catcher and the first baseman, or the pitcher may just throw over there on his own. If the first baseman is holding the runner on base, he's already in position to take a throw.

If there's a concern that the batter may bunt, the first baseman may signal the pitcher to indicate to him that he plans to leave the bag toward second and break in toward the plate.

The first baseman also has to be ready to take a pickoff throw from the catcher. This play is often tried when there is a left-handed hitter at the plate, even though the batter stands between the plate and first base, making it more difficult for the catcher to make a snap throw. At the same time, though, the runner's view of the catcher is blocked by the batter at the plate. The catcher will throw behind the batter.

The first baseman tries to make a swipe tag, catching the ball and bringing it down on the runner in one motion. You'll see good base runners dive to the outfield side of the bag to require a longer tag.

Whether the pitcher makes a pickoff attempt or not, it's important for the first baseman to get off the bag, giving him more range to field a batted ball. He doesn't have to use a crossover step to get into position to make the play; he's already there.

A few years ago, the Mets used a play with left-handed pitchers: The first baseman would play off the bag, and then he would break to the bag to receive the ball. It was a little confusing for a base runner because his view of the pitcher was blocked by the first baseman. Today many teams use this play.

Reaching up to take the throw from the catcher on a close play at second base.

Photo courtesy Boston Red Sox

CHAPTER THIRTEEN

The Second Baseman

Not for Cowards

Good defensive teams have "strength up the middle." That's where most of the action is; it starts with the pitcher, the catcher, the second baseman, the shortstop, and the center fielder.

The job requirements for a second baseman are courage, intelligence, quick feet, and quick hands. He doesn't have to have a strong arm, but it helps to be acrobatic, a tap dancer. I came out of high school as a shortstop, and then on my first day at professional camp, they said, "Go learn how to play second base. You don't have the arm strength to play shortstop."

The second baseman needs courage because he's going to get wiped out regularly on force plays at second base. His back is to the runner, so he's going to be blindsided most of the time when he gets hit. And his left knee is vulnerable every time he makes a double play.

He needs intelligence because many times he's the guy making the calls in the infield: You got it, I got it. He needs to have a good grasp on what the batter and the runner are capable of doing, and he has to know the pitcher and the other infielders.

He needs quick hands to turn a double play and quick feet to cover ground to his right and left and to get out of the way of the runners.

There is no single personality type for a second baseman. When I played I was pretty intense. I never felt calm or relaxed. It didn't happen smoothly for me.

Either way, the second baseman has to be someone who doesn't take his bad at bats to the field. There's a lot of action up the middle of the field, and he's involved in just about everything. He's got to quickly leave his offense in the dugout and take his defensive game onto the field. If he doesn't, he's going to get burned quickly.

What to look for in a second baseman

The most important question is: "Can this guy turn a double play?" That's the biggest job defensively. The more fearless he is, the better chance he has to make a double play. And then you hope for a guy who can make the great plays, like charging in on a slow roller.

Most of the good second basemen have very quick hands, and they'll catch the ball out front of them with two hands. It's almost as if the ball never touches the glove. And while it's happening, they are getting themselves into a good position to make the throw to first base.

It's a position where managers would like to see fewer than twelve errors per year.

It is almost impossible to be a left-handed second baseman, because of the difficulty of turning a double play. If he came across the bag, he'd have to spin all the way around to throw to first.

A Second Baseman's Most Difficult Play

A team can't hide a weak fielder at second because there's too much action up the middle. He's got to make plays on grounders, make the double play, and handle relays from the outfield. If he's a bad fielder, it's not going to take long to expose him.

The most difficult play for any infielder is the backhanded play, and it's particularly tough for second basemen, most of whom don't have the arm strength of the shortstop. When they're on their backhand, they're going up the middle toward center field, and it's tough to plant and throw. It's hard to be accurate and get much on it.

Another reason why the backhanded play is difficult for a second baseman is that he wears the smallest glove in the infield. The reason it's small is to make it easier to get the ball out of the glove when he's executing a double play.

Turning the Double Play

As a second baseman, when you come to the base to execute a double play, most of the time your back is to the runner coming in. I could feel

Remy Says: Watch This

The Usual Suspects

You might think a team is always trying to pick off the fast runners, but most of the guys who get picked off are slow runners. Slower runners often try to get a bigger lead and become more vulnerable.

him. I could hear him. But I couldn't see him. So my chances of getting cleaned out on a double play were pretty good.

If you watch a second baseman during infield practice, you'll see him execute the double play and then make a little jump. When the game is on and a runner is getting ready to nail him, his jump becomes higher.

There's a picture of me when I was with the Red Sox kind of levitating above second base as I make the pivot to throw to first base on a double play. I see pictures like that and I say, "How the hell did I get in that spot?" I didn't know how high I would jump. I guess it depended on how high I had to get. The idea is to get out of the way of the guy trying to take you out.

As the second baseman, I knew who was on first base and his reputation. I knew if he could run. And I knew if the base runner was someone who loves taking out middle infielders or if he was a guy who was just going to slide in.

A successful second baseman can tell right off the bat how the ball is hit, whether the shortstop or third baseman is going to move for it, and whether he'll be able to turn a double play. He's done it so much that he knows, "I can turn this one" or "This one is going to be tough" or "I can't turn this one."

There are some times he's going to think: "With the way this ball is hit and the speed of the batter running to first base, we're not going to get him. So I had better eat it, or I may end up making a bad throw and giving up a run."

The third baseman can sometimes cause problems for the second baseman when he's throwing the ball to second base. Infielders prefer a low throw, but they've got to watch out for a sinker ball that can tail in toward the runner. If the ball comes in low, the second baseman can jump up and make the double play. That's better than reaching up for the ball, which makes him pretty vulnerable to the oncoming runner.

Dirty slides and revenge

In today's game there are many more rules than there used to be to protect the second baseman and shortstop. Years ago the runner could do just about anything: He could go get the fielder in the outfield grass if he wanted or throw a body block. Now the umpire can make an interference call if a runner runs or slides far away from the base.

That doesn't mean a runner won't still try to come at a second baseman on purpose. Let's say a runner is coming in on a second baseman or shortstop that he feels he can intimidate. It's the first game of a home stand, and the runner cleans him out. This might screw up that infielder for the whole series. On any play that's close, he may be a little anxious, and he may drop the ball or make a bad throw.

There are some situations when the second baseman expects a hard slide. For example, if there are runners on first and third with one out, the base runner is supposed to clean out the second baseman in hopes he makes a bad throw, letting the run score.

When I played I knew there were some guys coming to get me. It was their job not to allow the second baseman to turn the double play. I was very aware of them when they got on at first base, and I found myself hoping the batter would hit a nice grounder right at the shortstop, so that I could get that nice underhand flip. The goal was to turn the double play and get out of Dodge.

If a runner gets the second baseman cleanly, there's nothing the second baseman can do about it. If he gets him dirty, that's a whole different story. A dirty play involves the runner coming in spikes high, sliding late, sliding when he can't tag the bag, or laying a rolling block on the fielder. The second baseman's first instinct is, "I've got to make this double play." So he'll throw around the runner and that generally causes a bad throw.

A runner might make a mistake once in a while, but he won't make that mistake a second time because he knows the next time he comes

"I think Remy has the three things that are necessary to be . . . a great player: talent, aptitude, and he's coachable as hell. When he arrived in the majors, he just didn't know how to make the double play. Now nobody makes [the pivot] any better. Nobody."

CALIFORNIA ANGELS COACH
GROVER RESINGER, 1976

in, the second baseman may throw the ball right at his chest to make him slide. I'd tell the runner, "Make sure you get down next time." And then, if the game situation allowed, I had to hit him if he didn't get out of the way.

Another way to get back is through the pitcher, who can drill a batter when it doesn't mean anything in the game. Pitchers would call me over and ask, "Did he try to get you?" But you've got to pick the right spot in the game to retaliate. It could be the next game. It could be two games after that. Whenever it comes, the opposing player will know it's payback.

The Old Neighborhood Play

Some fans think infielders can be way off the bag and still get an out call from the umpire. It's usually not as drastic as many people think. If you slow things down on a replay, you'll often see that when the infielder caught the ball he was coming off the bag. You could call that a neighborhood play because he was not in contact with the bag, but it's not so far that it makes a difference in the play.

I can honestly say that I got away with a neighborhood play a few times. It's got to be pretty flagrant for the umpire to call the runner safe. The umpire may let an infielder get away with one, and say to him, "Give me a better effort next time."

Executing a pickoff play at second base

It's important to keep a runner on second base close to the bag, maybe even more so than at first base because at second base he is in scoring position.

The catcher is looking right out at second base, but the pitcher is facing toward home plate. Making a pickoff attempt at second base usually requires precise timing and coordination among the infielders.

Often, one of the infielders gives a sign to the pitcher, who is supposed to acknowledge with some kind of swipe or movement of the glove. It's a timing play after that. The pitcher goes into his stretch, and when he looks in a particular direction, the second baseman or the shortstop breaks for the bag and the pitcher throws the ball to him.

The catcher can also initiate the play; the catcher would make as if he was calling the pitch and put down five fingers, let's say, to call a pickoff play. And then he would show two fingers to indicate second base. The pitcher goes into his stretch, and when the catcher sees the second baseman break toward the bag, he drops his glove—that's when the pitcher turns and throws.

And then there is the straight daylight play. The second baseman or the shortstop comes in behind the runner and makes a break to second base; if the pitcher sees daylight between the fielder and the runner, he will turn and throw. If not, he has to step off the rubber and not make the pitch because now there's nobody in position at second base or shortstop.

The game situation is sometimes affected by the stadium. In Boston, for example, left field is very shallow with the Green Monster out there; you'll see many runners on visiting teams trying to get a bigger lead at second base in hopes of scoring on a base hit. If there's a slow lug on base, there's a pretty good chance of picking him off.

"Deking" out the runner

One fun thing for an infielder to try to do is to "deke" a runner into unnecessarily sliding, stopping short, or getting caught by a double-play throw to the base behind him. This can happen when a player is running on a pitch and the batter hits the ball in the air. Often when a guy is running, he doesn't know where the ball is going. So if the ball is in the air,

"Buy a steak for a player on another club after the game, but don't even speak to him on the field. Get out there and beat them to death."

LEO "THE LIP" DUROCHER, HALL OF FAME MANAGER OF THE BROOKLYN DODGERS, NEW YORK GIANTS, CHICAGO CUBS, AND HOUSTON ASTROS

the second baseman and shortstop try to act like a ground ball is coming to them and they're going to make a double play. (The runner, of course, is supposed to look to the third-base coach for help, but sometimes they don't have time to do that.)

One fielder will act as if he's going to go down to get a ground ball and make a feed, and the other guy goes to the bag. What he's trying to do is to get the runner to slide to slow him down and perhaps keep him from going to third base. And if an outfielder makes the catch, he may be able to double up the runner at first base.

It works sometimes. When it does happen, it's a lot of fun.

Making the throw on a double play as Richie Zisk of the Texas Rangers slides into the bag.

Photo courtesy Boston Red Sox

CHAPTER FOURTEEN

The Shortstop

A Demanding Position

After the catcher, the shortstop has the most demanding position because he is involved in so much of the game. The shortstop typically has the most total chances in the infield—other than the first baseman—and the greatest number of assists. And then there are throws from the catcher, relays from the outfield, slow rollers in the infield, off-balance plays, and so much more.

Shortstops need a strong arm or a quick release or both. And they need a lot of range.

I've already noted how Cal Ripken didn't have great quickness, but he knew how to get in the proper position, knew his pitchers, and knew the hitters. That increased his range tremendously. If you understood the inside game of baseball, you could watch him from the stands and pretty much call every pitch.

The amazing thing about Ripken was that he played 2,632 games in a row, most of them at shortstop. That position is so demanding, and there is a lot of contact on double plays. How did he manage not to get cut or hurt with ordinary injuries that would keep him out of the lineup for a few days?

But shortstop lends itself to great athletes and awe-inspiring plays: Think of Derek Jeter diving head-first into the leftfield seats in July 2004, saving the game for the Yankees and leading to a painful twelfth-inning Red Sox defeat. (But 2004 worked out all right in the end . . .)

Captain of the infield

The shortstop is in some ways the captain of the infield. To begin with he has to coordinate with the second baseman on coverage. The shortstop also gets involved in relay plays, most of the time as the lead man because he should have the better arm.

Like the second baseman, the shortstop can usually see the catcher flash his signs to the pitcher and learn what the next pitch will be. Many third basemen want to know what the pitcher is going to throw, so the shortstop signals if it's a fastball, a breaking ball, or whatever.

The signal to third base could be just a whistle, or it could be calling his name. If it is going to be a fastball, he might not say anything. Of course, he's got to mix it up so the third base coach or the hitter doesn't pick up on the signal.

Choosing between power and defense

A manager may have to decide between a power-hitting shortstop who is an adequate fielder and a superb fielder who is batting .220. A team can't put an inadequate fielder at shortstop because it would hurt too much; the manager would probably try to find another position for him like first base or the outfield.

Look at the shortstops playing today; these guys are remarkable. When I played second base, shortstops were usually the smallest guys on the field. They were quick, and they weren't expected to hit for power.

Remy Says: Watch This

Watching Infielders Adjust

If there's a right-handed hitter at the plate and you see the shortstop take a step left toward second base as the pitcher goes into his delivery, you can expect to see a fastball or something hard and away—a pitch that a right-handed batter would tend to hit to the opposite field or at least more to the right than he usually does.

In that same situation, if he moved to his right toward third base, you could guess it was going to be an off-speed pitch.

With a left-hander at the plate, if he moved to his left, it would probably be something off-speed like a curveball, slider, split-fingered fastball, or a changeup. If the shortstop stays where he is, it's probably going to be a fastball.

"Remy is genuine; there's no phoniness about the way he presents himself. Of all the people I know in broadcasting, he is the biggest creature of habit in the way he prepares for a game; that's the way the best players are, too."

SEAN MCDONOUGH, FORMER RED SOX PLAY-BY-PLAY BROADCASTER

Ripken was the first big shortstop I remember; he was 6'4". Derek Jeter, one of the more athletic shortstops in the game, is 6'3".

They remind me of linebackers in football. They're huge, but they're also fast and agile.

The Shortstop's Most Difficult Play

When it comes to the double play, the shortstop has the advantage over the second baseman; the play is in front of him and he can see where the runner is. Because of this, the shortstop knows exactly how much time he has and is in a better position to field the ball or take a throw, then get out of the way of the guy sliding into second base.

The most difficult play for a shortstop is going deep in the hole toward third base to make a backhand catch, then throwing a strike to first base. As a fan you look for a guy with arm strength and range. Can he get to the ball? And once he gets to it, what can he do with it?

I saw Garciaparra make that backhand play a thousand times; he'd grab the ball on the run, continue on toward third base, make an off-balance throw without planting his feet, and still reach first base with the throw.

Nomar's style excited the crowd more than the conventional play. When he let the ball go, everybody followed the ball to first base; if you looked back at him, you'd see him over near the stands at third base. No Little League coach would ever had advised someone to play like Garciaparra.

On deck in Anaheim.

Photo courtesy Los Angeles Angels of Anaheim Baseball Club

CHAPTER FIFTEEN

The Third Baseman

The Reaction Corner

In baseball a third baseman is probably the closest thing to a hockey goalie; the job calls for that kind of reaction time. Third base is the position that most requires first-step quickness.

Something like 90 percent of the ground balls to a third baseman are within three or four steps of where he is positioned before the pitch. And then consider that once the third baseman sets up, he might be 80 feet from the hitter. On any ball that has something on it, he doesn't have time to take three or four steps—it is usually a crossover step and a dive.

Brooks Robinson was one of the best I ever saw. He didn't have great speed, but he had first-step quickness, the ability to make diving plays, and he could make strong throws. On today's Red Sox, Mike Lowell is as smooth as silk.

I don't know if there's one personality that works best for a third baseman. I've seen guys like George Brett, who was very intense, but then there was Robinson, who seemed so laid-back. Graig Nettles looked as casual as could be. He'd grab the ball and flip it over to first sidearm and seem to get the runner by half a step every time.

The Third Baseman's Toughest Play

The most difficult play for a third baseman is handling a slow roller. First of all he's got to decide: Do I use the glove or do I barehand the ball? Then, once he gets the ball, he's usually at a difficult angle to first base. He's got to open up and throw across his body to first base, and he's got to throw a strike.

Remy Says: Watch This

Looking Down the Gun Barrel

One of the third baseman's nightmares is to charge in toward home plate expecting a bunt, only to find that the batter has pulled the bat back to take a swing at the ball. You don't see that very often. And you don't want to see it very often if you're a third baseman, that's for sure.

If the guy swings away, the third baseman is either going to get it in the throat or it's going to go by him; it's not likely he's going to catch it. He probably hopes it goes by.

The throw from this kind of play is usually made off-balance, and if the third baseman throws sidearm, he's got to know that the ball usually tails back in, so he's got to adjust for that in his throw to first base.

And then there are diving plays. The tough part is not the dive or the catch, it's the third baseman getting back to his feet, getting lined up, and making an accurate throw to first base. Another tough play is going to the right down the line and then making a long throw across the diamond to first base. On bunt plays, as with the slow roller, he needs to be able to charge the ball properly and make off-balance throws to first base.

Throwing plays

When it comes to making a play at the plate from third base, the challenge the fielder faces depends on where the ball is hit. If it is hit straight down the line, that becomes a difficult play because the runner heading for the plate may be blocking the throw. A third baseman grabbing a ball hit down the line looks up and says to himself, "Uh-oh. I can't see the catcher."

It's very dangerous to throw the ball over the head of the runner: It can sail over the catcher or make him stand up and allow the runner to slide in safely under the tag. The proper play is for the catcher to act like a first baseman and stretch out so the third baseman can see him.

The third baseman also has to make some split-second decisions about where to throw the ball. Let's say bases are loaded and there's a grounder to third. Depending on how the ball is hit and the speed of the batter, the third baseman has to decide whether to throw home or go for a double play. It's not automatic to throw to home plate unless it is essential to stop that run from scoring. Usually, if the third baseman's momentum is toward second base and the batter is not that fast, he will go for the double play at second and first.

These are instinctive things that come out of years and years of playing. Every fielder has to be thinking before every pitch, "What am I going to do if this ball is hit to me?" There's usually a plan A and plan B.

The third baseman's view of the plate

Third basemen are at a disadvantage in the infield because they can't see the catcher's signs to the pitcher. They sometimes can get help from the shortstop; for example, if the pitch is going to be a breaking ball, the shortstop might whistle at him, call his name, or open his mouth.

The third baseman usually wants to know if an off-speed pitch is coming. He doesn't need to know if it's a fastball because he's already set up for that. If he knows an off-speed pitch is coming, he might take another step toward the line if a right-hander is at the plate or a step away from the line if a lefty is at bat. The assumption, of course, is that a batter will swing early at an off-speed pitch and pull it.

Remy's Top Dawgs

Mike Lowell was the smoothest infielder on Boston's 2007 team; nobody else even came close.

Every position is different, but Lowell showed he knew the hitters and could be in position, knowing when to play in or play back, and knew how to play the bad hop. Third base requires first step quickness, jumping in on the ball.

Lowell just does it naturally, where other guys have to work harder at it. He's better than A-Rod, who is just average at third.

Around the league, I still think **Derek Jeter** is among the best at shortstop. **Placido Polanco** is unbelievable at second base for the Tigers. At first base, of course, there's Boston's own Kevin **Youkilis.** The kid over at Minnesota, **Justin Morneau,** is pretty good.

Four all-time-great Red Sox favorites (from left, Tommy Harper, Carl Yastrzemski, Dwight Evans, Luis Tiant—each of them an All-Star) attend Opening Day 2005 at Fenway.

Photo courtesy AP

Pickoffs and Rundowns at Third

There are pickoff plays designed for a snap throw by the catcher to the third baseman. Everyone has to be really careful because the runner is just 90 feet away from home plate. It's not like making an error at first or second; if a pickoff gets screwed up at third base, that runner is going to score.

Rundowns are also tough around third base because if the ball gets away, the run scores. The team on the field has to make sure the runner is going back toward third base. In a rundown the runner should never be chased toward home. If there's a bobble while the runner is headed to the plate, he's almost certain to score; if he's headed back to third base, that could limit the damage.

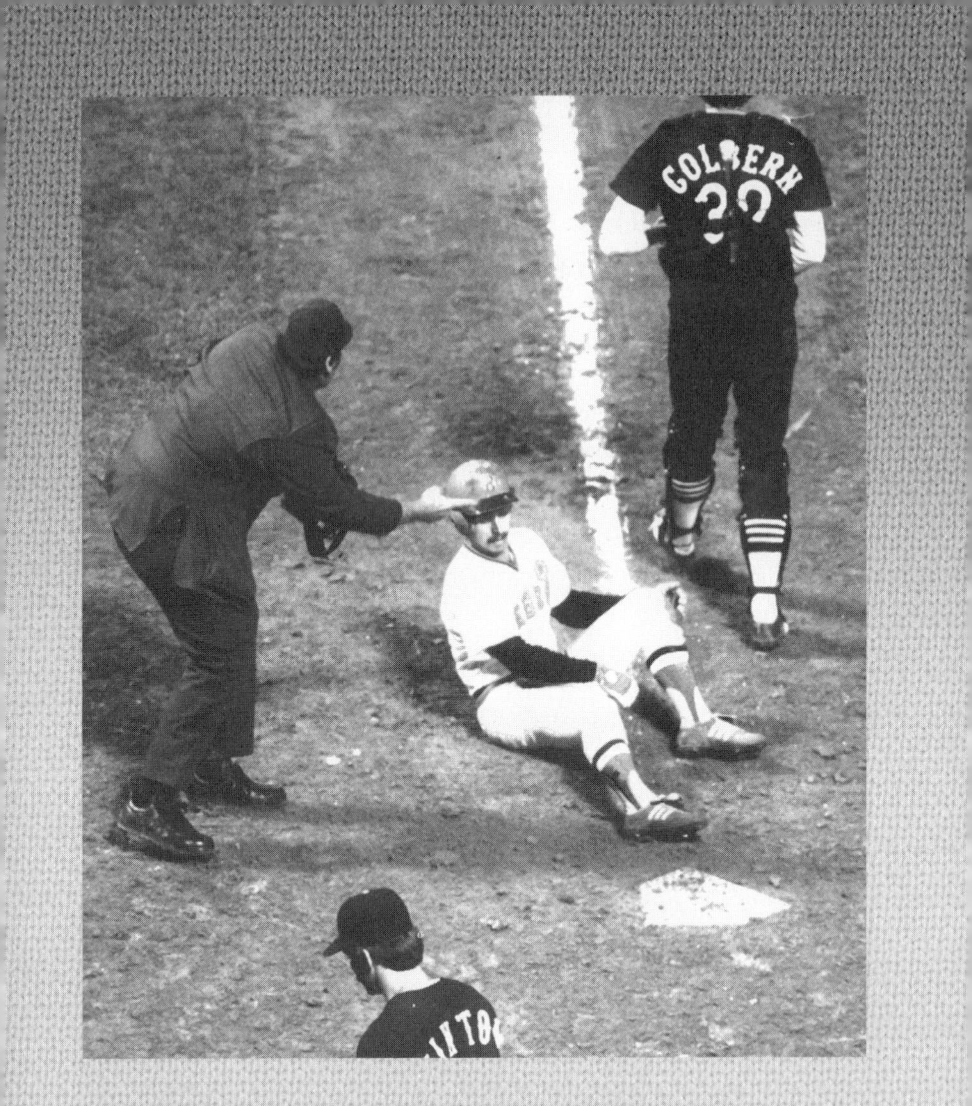

I'm tagged out short of the plate by Mike Colbern of the White Sox.

Photo courtesy Boston Red Sox

CHAPTER SIXTEEN

Pitchers as Infielders

Playing the Position

The pitcher shouldn't be a front-row spectator on plays in the infield. A Gold Glove pitcher gets into good fielding position after he delivers to the plate and can snare a ball hit back up the middle, pick up a bunt near the mound, and make a good throw to a base. A pitcher's ability to make a play on a grounder or a bunt and get that lead runner can make the difference in a close game.

That said, most pitchers are not good fielders; they put all of their effort into their windup and follow-through, which usually does not set them up to catch a rocket back at the mound. That's why it's so impressive to watch strong fielders like Mike Mussina, Tim Wakefield, or Greg Maddux.

I've been impressed with Daisuke Matsuzaka's infield skills, as well. In Game 3 of the 2007 World Series, he gave up a leadoff single to former Seibu Lions teammate Kazuo Matsui. Matsui made it to second on a fielding error by J. D. Drew in right field. But Matsuzaka erased him from the base paths when he snagged a hard ground ball back to the mound and ran directly at Matsui, setting up a rundown play that traded the runner on second for a slower man on first (and an out).

Some pitchers have difficulty throwing to first base; over the years that has been a small flaw in the skill set of Roger Clemens. Other pitchers won't even make a pickoff attempt because they can't make the throw well. Once teams get a sniff of that, they just send the runner as soon as the pitcher moves.

There is no question that a lack of fielding skills can hurt, but how much time does a team put into trying to make a pitcher a better fielder? The answer is not a heck of a lot; the number one job is pitching, and everything else is secondary. A pitching coach is not going to change a pitcher's follow-through for the purposes of improving his fielding. That's the last thing he'd want to do.

How to Watch a Pitcher in the Field

When you're watching a game, don't always shift your attention from the pitcher to the batter when the ball is in the air. Instead, take a look at the pitcher's follow-through: Does he finish squared up with home plate in a good fielding position that gives him a chance to make a play? Pitchers who fall off to one side are not going to have a chance at a ball back up the middle.

As it is at third base, most of the plays for the pitcher are like hockey goaltending: all reaction. But I think the real key is the ability to make plays on bunts. Does this pitcher have the ability to come off the mound, pick up the ball, make the right decision on the play, and get off a good, accurate throw? That's what separates an average fielder from a good fielding pitcher.

Remy Says: Watch This

"I Got It"

When there's a pop-up to the mound, most teams tell the pitcher to let one of the other infielders get the ball if he can. This has been a bugaboo of mine for years.

There are four infielders running up the mound and dancing around, everybody yelling, "I got it, I got it."

Many pitchers are good at pop-ups; during batting practice they're out shagging fly balls. If the pitcher is standing on the mound and there is a routine little pop-up, I say, let him catch it.

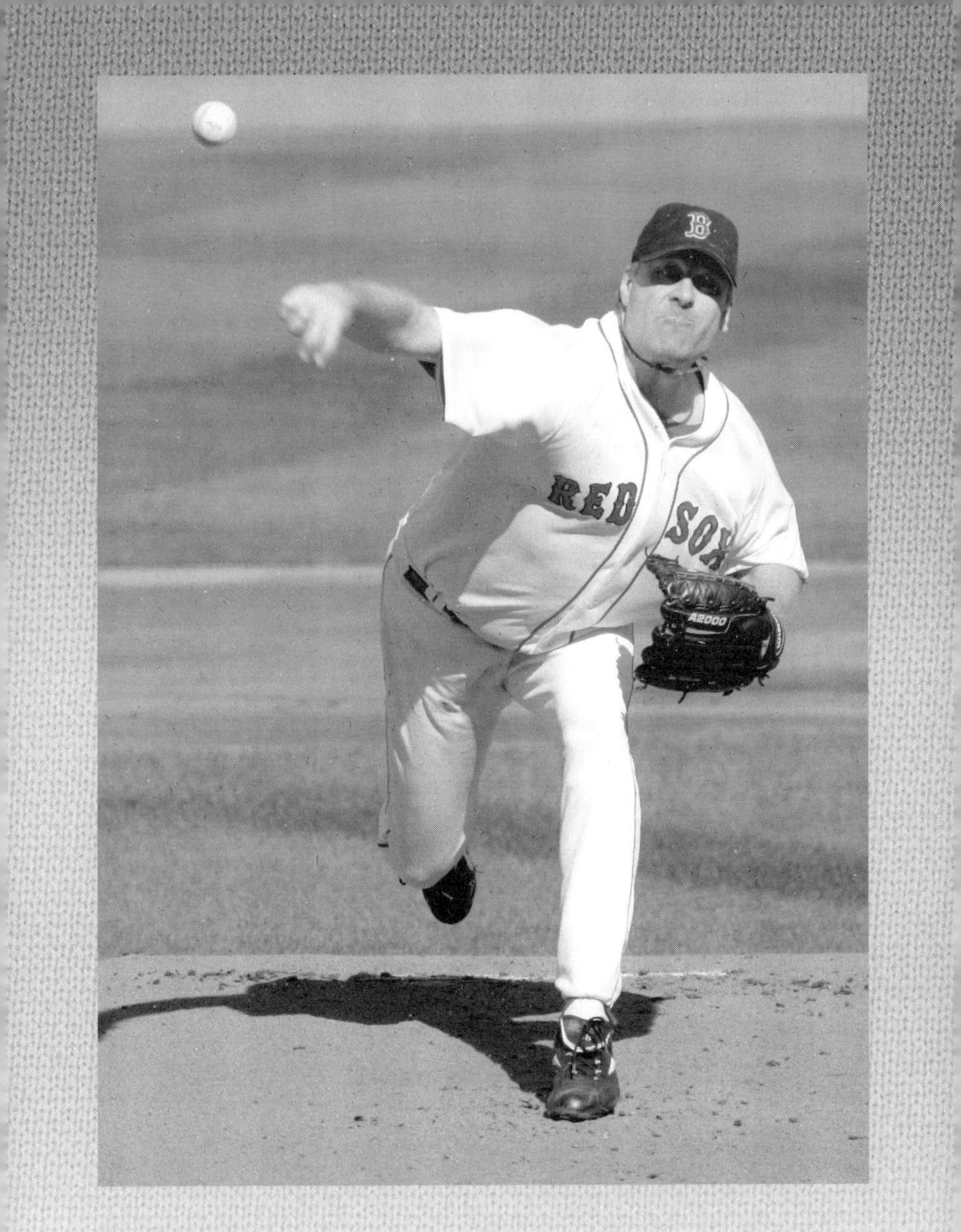

Curt Schilling pitched with power, finesse, and heart from the moment he arrived in 2004, and it is no coincidence that two new World Series trophies reside at Fenway.

Photo courtesy AP

The Pitcher's Toughest Plays

Keep in mind that when a pitcher finishes his delivery, he may be just 52 feet away from the plate. I've seen some ugly scenes when a guy gets hit with a line drive back up the middle. It's got to be a blur to a pitcher. All of a sudden, boom, he's smoked.

One of the ugliest of all time was September 8, 2000, when Red Sox pitcher Bryce Florie was hit in the face by a line drive in the ninth inning of a game against the Yankees at Fenway Park. He suffered a terrible injury, but he had the guts to try a comeback in 2001. In the first game he pitched, somebody hit a line shot right back at him again. That's got to make your legs shake.

When a pitcher or a batter gets hit in the head, he may tell the press, "No, no, I don't think about it." That's baloney.

Another heart-stopper: a pitcher reaching for a line drive with his bare pitching hand. It's just instinct. It's a good thing most of the time he doesn't touch the ball.

And sometimes you see some really wacky plays like the time El Duque—Orlando Hernandez, then of the Yankees—snagged a grounder back to the mound and couldn't get the ball out of the glove. So he threw the glove to first base to get the out.

And Julian Tavárez, a Red Sox pitcher who seems to exist in a world of his own, made at least two throws to first base in the 2007 season that were bowled along the infield grass. I called it "Candlepins for Dollars." Nothing personal; he got the outs.

Pickoff plays

On a routine pickoff play, it used to be that the pitcher was in charge and could throw over to first any time he felt like doing so. Nowadays, though, many pitchers take instructions from the dugout.

The pitcher might be instructed to take a step off the rubber, hold the ball, make a throw to first, or pitch out. The idea is to do anything possible to throw off the timing of the base runner. Some pitchers throw over to first just to buy time when they're not yet ready to pitch to the batter.

Bluffing to third, throwing to first

With a runner on first and third, every once in a while you see the pitcher bluffing a throw to third and then spinning around to make a throw to first. I don't think many pitchers use it at the right time. A good time to try it is with a 3–2 count and one out. The runner on first is probably going to be stealing.

The play very seldom succeeds, but when it does, fans or coaches might say, "How could that ever work?" It is such an ugly looking play and it is so obvious. But it occasionally works. I am living proof of that.

My very first game in the major leagues was April 7, 1975, at Anaheim. Before the game we had a meeting and we discussed the Kansas City pitcher, Steve Busby. One of the coaches said, "If there are runners on first and third, look out, because he fakes to third and throws to first, and he's good at it."

In my first time up to bat, I got a hit: a single to left field. I drove in Joe Lahoud for my first RBI and moved Dave Chalk over to third. Sure enough, I took my lead off first base and Busby faked to third, then spun and picked me off first base.

Dick Williams was the manager, and he told me to come sit right next to him in the dugout. He said, "Welcome to the Big Leagues. If I see that again, you're going back to Salt Lake."

The next time I was on first base with a runner on third, I took a lead of about 6 inches.

It was a thrill for me to play against the Red Sox. Here I am sliding in on the first-base side of the plate to avoid catcher Carlton Fisk, who was coming in from foul territory. Fisk later became a good friend of mine when I came over to Boston. The slide is not textbook—my hand is dragging, for one thing—but that happens when you're keeping away from a tag.

Photo courtesy Los Angeles Angels of Anaheim Baseball Club

CHAPTER SEVENTEEN

Catchers

The Tough Job behind the Plate

Catching is the most physically and mentally demanding job on the team.

Baseball players are pretty set in their ways. Most of them get to the park the same time every day, get themselves ready for the game, take batting practice, and do their infield or outfield practice. Catchers do the same—and they have to go to school every day.

As part of his job, the catcher has to sit down with the pitcher and the pitching coach and perhaps the manager and go over the other team's lineup, plus the players they've got on the bench as pinch hitters and pinch runners.

A good scouting report tells who is hitting the ball where. A team wants to learn as much as possible about its opponent's usual strategies. When do they hit-and-run? What are the changes since the last game between the two teams? To this an experienced catcher adds the knowledge he has of the other team and its pitcher.

Alas, today's game places more emphasis on offense than defense. Many defensive stars don't get proper recognition. They may get it from their own managers, pitchers, and their teammates but not from the fans. Look at the catchers you see in the All-Star Game; they are all players known for their offensive abilities.

There used to be a stereotype about catchers being a bit dim, wearing the "tools of ignorance." That is simply not true. Actually, most catchers are very intelligent and are much more involved with strategy and execution than any of the other players on the field.

Taking a beating

Catchers can have all kinds of temperaments and personalities. Some are really intense and others soft-spoken and calm. But the one thing they have in common is that they are tough.

Catchers are constantly getting beat up. They take pitches off the fingers, chest, shoulders, knees, feet, or shins. Runners come barreling toward them at full speed, and they've got to stick a leg out to try to block the plate.

I know more than a little bit about bad knees with my own history. I can't imagine being up and down on your knees like a catcher for an entire game. But there are guys who have played an entire career with bad knees and knee injuries. Carlton Fisk, the great catcher for the Red Sox and later the White Sox, had a career-threatening injury early in his career and went on to play for twenty-four seasons, until he was forty-five years old.

A perfect union

The pitcher and catcher would be in perfect sync if they agreed on every pitch before it was thrown. The less often you see the pitcher shaking off a sign and the fewer trips the catcher makes to the mound, the better the relationship. When the pitcher and the catcher are thinking along the same lines, they have probably done their homework together. They also know which pitches are working within this particular game and which are not.

Some proven veteran pitchers want to be in full charge. Nolan Ryan used to call his own game. But many younger pitchers won't shake off a catcher, because the catcher is calling the game or because the pitch calls are coming from the bench. Coaches are not going to tell a rookie never to shake off the catcher, but if they start to see balls flying all over the place, the catcher is going to be put in charge very quickly. Coaches will tell the rookie: "We know better than you how to get this guy out."

Midway through the 2003 season, I observed something I had never seen in uncounted thousands of baseball games: Red Sox reliever Todd Jones, recently arrived from Colorado, was on the mound in the eighth inning of a one-run game against the Blue Jays. Jones stepped off the rubber, walked behind the mound, and pulled out a little piece of paper.

"The wind always seems to blow against catchers when they are running."

YOGI BERRA

At first I worried it was sandpaper, but no pitcher would be that obvious. It turned out that it was notes from the scouting report. It must have worked because Jones pitched very effectively, and the Red Sox went on to tie the game in the ninth and win in the tenth. I wonder if it's just a matter of time before players start carrying little computers with them to consult the game plan.

And Curt Schilling may go into retirement as one of the great pitchers in the game's history, but he'll probably always remember June 7, 2007, when he shook off Jason Varitek's pitch call with two outs in the ninth inning . . . and a no-hitter an out away. Varitek called for a slider, but Schilling didn't agree and instead threw a fastball to Shannon Stewart who singled into right field. "We get two outs, and I was sure, and I had a plan, and I shook Tek off," Schilling told reporters after the game. "And I get a big 'What if?' for the rest of my life."

It was the third one-hitter of Schilling's career; as of the end of the 2007 season he had never thrown a no-no.

Throwing Out a Runner

Throwing out a runner requires much more than just a strong arm. Catchers have to have good footwork, allowing them to get into a good position to throw.

Think about what the catcher has to do to make a throw: He has to catch the ball, line himself up with second base, transfer the ball from the catcher's glove to his throwing hand, and then make the throw. You'll see catchers working on their footwork all the time.

And then think about the guys who are able to throw from their knees and still get something on the throw to reach second. Try it yourself some time; that's pretty difficult to do.

The key to success is not so much arm strength as it is quick feet, a quick transfer from the glove to the throwing arm, and accuracy. A catcher who has quick feet is generally going to have a quick release.

Picking a pitch to throw on

It used to be that catchers would call for a particular pitch when they expected the runner to try to steal. The old saying was that if you were hitting behind a guy who could steal, you were going. We don't see as much of that anymore. It seems as if many managers today don't particularly care about the running game. Their theory is: "Let's just get the guy at the plate."

Another reason this has changed is that the first two guys in the lineup used to be Punch-and-Judy guys who couldn't launch a home run. Today the guys hitting first and second, and throughout the lineup, have good power. So a pitcher is not going to make it obvious that the next pitch is going to be a fastball; if he does, all of a sudden his team is losing baseballs over the wall.

Here is another place where the emphasis on offense and bigger and stronger players has changed pitching patterns in baseball. It used to be automatic: on a 3–1 count a hitter would see a fastball. That is not the case anymore. Today, there are situations where a batter has to think backwards: on a 3–1 count he may well see an off-speed pitch.

Framing the Strike Zone

A good catcher always makes a tough pitch look good. Some guys are so smooth; the glove almost never moves. They will get the glove in the spot where they want the pitch to land—that's framing the pitch—and they leave it there. We used to call Carlton Fisk "Magic" because he was so good with his hands.

Other guys jab at the ball. If the catcher snares the pitch with his glove moving out of the strike zone—even if the ball is over the plate—the umpire may call it a ball.

If you see a catcher set up outside, you—and the umpire—expect an outside pitch. If the ball ends up going inside, the catcher will reach across to backhand it. The ball may still be on the corner of the plate but the pitcher won't get that call.

Catching a knuckleball

There's no certain way to catch the knuckler. I think Bob Uecker had it right when he said the best way to catch a knuckleball is to wait until it stops rolling and pick it up.

If you watch a good knuckleball pitcher like Tim Wakefield, you can't tell from one pitch to the other where the ball is going. The pitcher doesn't know, either. And so, how can the catcher prepare to catch something when he has no idea if it is going to dip, go inside, go outside, or rise?

Catchers try not to reach for a knuckleball. They keep the glove back and hope the ball finds the glove. Some catchers use an oversized glove when they're working with a knuckleballer. But then you see some catchers who can't get the ball out of that big glove to make a throw to second base.

Anytime a knuckleball pitcher is throwing, players who can run—and even those who can't run very well—want to steal a base. They figure it is fifty-fifty whether the catcher is going to catch the ball.

On defense, when a knuckleball pitcher is on the mound most fielders play everybody to pull because it is a very slow pitch and most batters are going to swing early. With a righty at bat, fielders will take a step or two to their right; against a lefty, they'll move to the left. You almost never see fielders expecting the batter to go the other way. It's just not going to happen.

Mouths in the Mask

Some catchers maintain a constant stream of chatter. There are guys who jabber all the time, and there are guys who don't say a word. Thurman Munson of the Yankees was always trying to distract hitters at the plate.

I remember once when Carl Yastrzemski stepped out of the box to tell a catcher to shut up.

The relationship between a catcher and an umpire is interesting; the catcher is always trying to get more for his pitcher. If he is not getting strikes on the outside of the plate, he is going to ask the ump why, and try to talk him into those pitches as the game goes on.

There are a lot of arguments that the fans don't see; there's an unwritten rule that the catcher doesn't take off his mask and turn around to argue with the umpire.

There are ways to communicate with umpires without embarrassing them; that's what most catchers try to do unless they are completely ticked off. That's not to say that there aren't days when the umpire might miss two or three calls in a row and the dugout starts giving it to him and the catcher gets involved.

The tough part comes when a catcher comes up to hit. If the catcher doesn't like a strike call, he might just bite his tongue. Or he will say, "Give my guy that pitch, too."

Reading the Signs

Although the catcher and starting pitcher usually have a plan for each batter before the game begins, in most situations the catcher calls each pitch by signaling from his position behind the plate. The basic set of signs is: one finger for a fastball, two for a curve, three for a slider, and four fingers or a wiggle for a changeup.

The catcher will change the signs when there is a runner on second base who might be able to see them and send a signal back to the batter.

He may use an indicator. For example, the indicator may be two fingers, and thus the pitch call will be the next sign after the catcher flashes two. He might send three, one, two, one, three; the sign after the indicator is one, which means fastball.

Television is a factor here, too. Players can go in the clubhouse and watch the game and they will be able to see if the catcher is using the same sequence all the time. There are some ballparks where the guy running the first-base camera will be in the dugout or nearby. There were managers who used to watch the little monitor on the camera; it was up to the umpire to see that, and if he did, he would get the monitor out of there.

Stealing the signs

Everywhere players go, there are rumors about one team or another stealing signs over television, with binoculars, or a telephoto lens. I don't know whether they are true or not.

I can tell you this, though: when a good pitcher is getting lit up, the coaches are going to try and find some reason. They might say he is tipping his pitches—doing something to give away the type of pitch he is about to throw. Or they might say the other side is stealing signs.

Years ago there was a rumor going around about a little box out near the bull pen in Yankee Stadium where the coaches could watch the game. It was just off-center from home plate, and the rumor started that these guys were stealing signs. Who knows?

When I played, we would go into Milwaukee and they would pound the heck out of us, and we were totally convinced somebody was stealing signs from the outfield.

Peekers

There are some batters who try to peek back at the catcher when they are up at the plate. I got caught doing it against Texas. Jim Sundberg was the catcher, and I had some pretty good success for a while just kind of glancing back. I wasn't really looking for the sign; what I was trying to see was how he set up. You can pretty much tell the location of the pitch from that. So I did it, and Sundberg saw me, and he said, "Peekaboo."

I got the message right away and that put an end to it. The message was: "If you keep doing it, you are going to get drilled."

In some parks at certain times of the day the hitter can see the shadow of the catcher out in front of home plate and he can see that shadow move outside or inside. In any case, that's why you'll see a lot of catchers switch location late, just before the pitch. They might start by setting up outside and then move inside. The catcher will also do this when there is a runner on second base, because many try to steal signs or location. The later he moves, the tougher it is to figure the location.

Collisions at the Plate

The rules say the catcher is not supposed to block home plate unless he has the ball in his glove. But that's almost never enforced; you'll regularly see the catcher with a foot out in front of the plate as he is reaching to get the ball.

What a catcher tries to do is get his foot on the third base line in front of home plate so that his knee is squared up with the incoming runner. He doesn't want to be caught opened up, or with his leg out to the side where a collision is going to blow out his knee.

Jason Varitek of the Red Sox is one of the best at blocking home plate. He is fearless. He will put anything out there: his knee, his foot. Of course it all starts way before the play; Varitek is as well prepared as any catcher in the game and tough as nails. If I wanted to show a young player how to go about his business, he's the one I'd point to.

In today's game we see more guys knocking catchers down than we did in the past. There seems to be less sliding at home plate and more collisions than I can ever remember.

Why? Because catchers are blocking the plate better. They are standing in front of home plate and the runner sometimes has no choice but to try to knock them over and kick the ball out of their glove or just knock them off the plate.

Headfirst into home

One of the most awful things to see is a headfirst slide into home plate. It's just a no-no.

Look at all the equipment the catcher is wearing: on his shins, his chest, his glove, and his head. He's like a knight in armor. In a collision he may fall on the runner or reach for a throw and come back and dive on him. Fingers and hands don't hold up well in those situations; just ask Manny Ramírez.

Then again, if a runner is coming in and sees the catcher reaching up the first base line for the ball and the plate is open . . . aw, forget it. My rule of thumb, if you'll pardon the pun, is: You generally don't come out well in a headfirst slide into home.

Watching a dustup at home

When you're watching from the stands and a play is developing at the plate, try to sneak a peek at the on-deck batter. His job is to get into a position that allows the runner coming from third base to see him. The on-deck batter is supposed to look for the throw, and tell the runner whether to slide or come in standing up.

If he wants the runner to slide, he'll be waving his arms down. If he puts his arms up, the runner can relax a bit and come in standing up because it is not going to be a close play.

The slide should be automatic unless the on-deck batter signals to stand up. Sometimes it gets messed up, and the on-deck batter doesn't get in position. The runner doesn't see the signal and ends up standing up at home plate when he shouldn't be.

The on-deck batter may also signal on which side to slide, but that's something the runner should be able to pick up by looking at the position of the catcher as he is coming in.

My fateful slide

I guess I know as much as anybody about sliding into home plate. I learned it on Sunday, July 1, 1979, the Red Sox against New York at Yankee Stadium, in front of 51,246 fans.

It was the first inning and I led off the game with a triple to centerfield. Rick Burleson was up next and he hit a pop-up down the first-base line. I can't tell you today if the third-base coach said to stay or go, but I made my own mind up to go. I thought first baseman Chris Chambliss was going to make the catch over his shoulder. Instead second baseman Willie Randolph made the catch coming in.

There were no outs, and I shouldn't have been going anyway, because with nobody out you've got to be 100 percent sure you can score. I think being in Yankee Stadium, I was a little juiced up in the first inning.

I was out by 10 feet. I went into this little hook slide and caught a spike. Jim Rice carried me off the field. That was the start of my knee problems.

RED SOX

PART FIVE

Against the Wall

Inside the high-tech television control room in a truck parked behind the rightfield bleachers.

Photo by Corey Sandler

CHAPTER EIGHTEEN

The Outfield

The Outfielder's Job

The outfield is where a manager wants home-run hitters and RBI guys. But a winning team also really needs a good defensive center fielder.

It is a beautiful thing to watch a good center fielder play defense: someone who can cover a lot of ground, make plays at the wall, and charge balls that are just over the infield.

Here are my benchmarks for outfielders:

- The **right fielder** should have the strongest outfield arm to help keep runners from going from first to third on an outfield hit.
- The **center fielder** should have the most range and the most speed; he needs to be able to go back or come in on the ball. He doesn't necessarily have to have the best throwing arm.
- The **left fielder** needs to be pretty sure-handed, able to keep balls he doesn't catch in front of him.

On an ordinary base hit to right field, the batter doesn't often stretch the hit into a double. One reason: because the right fielder could throw behind him and pick him off, the runner doesn't take a big turn around first base. If the ball is hit to left field, though, the runner will usually round first base toward second and then decide whether to take a chance on stretching a single into a double.

How to Catch a Fly Ball

Think about all the things that go into a full-speed chase after a little baseball. First of all, the fielder has to be able to read the ball off the bat.

How deep it is going to be? Is it going to sink fast? Will it slice one way or the other?

Then the outfielder has to make the proper cut to get himself into position. He has to keep his eye on the baseball, all the while running at full speed toward a wall that's not going to move. Finally, at just the right split second, he has to make the perfect leap to get the ball and hold on to it if he crashes into the wall.

I don't care if you make that play in Yankee Stadium or a Little League field, when you know you've taken away an extra base hit, it's a great feeling.

Catching a ball in the throwing position

When there are runners on base, an outfielder tries to catch the ball in a good throwing position. If he's a right-handed thrower, he'd want to catch the ball facing toward left field, so that his right arm is squared up to throw toward home plate or one of the bases. It's even better to make the catch coming in on the ball so that the fielder has a bit of momentum going in the direction in which he's going to throw.

It's also good to catch the ball with two hands so that transfer from the glove to the throwing hand is easy. And the outfielder wants to be on the balls of his feet, not back on his heels or drifting backward.

You can see how difficult it is for a right-handed thrower to end up in a good throwing position if he is running to his left to catch up with a ball. The same goes for a lefty running toward his right.

The right of way in the outfield

The center fielder is supposed to be in charge in the outfield, but that doesn't mean that he always catches the ball when he can. In certain situations, when there has to be a throw to home plate, for example, it might be better for one of the other outfielders to make the play if that fielder has a better throwing arm or is in a better position to make the throw.

But when the center fielder calls for the ball, the other two fielders are supposed to back off.

There are times, though, when communication doesn't work. It happens more in the outfield than it does in the infield because the outfielders are farther apart and the crowd noise can be overwhelming. When I played second base and ran out into right-center after a pop-up, I'd

"It was his solemn duty to catch a ball that wasn't in the stands."

MONTE IRVIN, HALL OF FAME OUTFIELDER FOR THE NEW YORK GIANTS, SPEAKING ABOUT FELLOW OUTFIELDER AND HALL OF FAMER WILLIE MAYS

sometimes hear both the center fielder and the right fielder calling for the ball.

The same rule applies when an infielder is chasing a pop fly into the outfield. The infielder goes as hard as he can until he hears an outfielder call him off.

A mistake some outfielders make is to call for the ball too soon and then not be able to get to it. This is a tough play because the outfielder is not looking at the other guy going after the ball, and the other player's not looking at the outfielder; they're both concentrating on the ball.

We saw a frightening example of this sort of situation in the final game of the 2003 divisional playoffs between Boston and Oakland. Former Red Sox center fielder Johnny Damon collided with second baseman Damian Jackson as they converged on a pop fly in shallow center. Damon was knocked unconscious and suffered a concussion that kept him out of the first two games of the American League Championship Series against New York.

There's got to be some kind of communication or there's going to be a collision. A fielder yells, "I got it. I got it. I got it." It's not brain surgery. If he doesn't hear someone call him off, he keeps going.

Working as a team

People sometimes talk about an outfield "team." I think more in terms of two outfielders at a time working on certain plays. You see that a lot in Boston when the left fielder goes for the ball up against the Green Monster; if it caroms off the wall, the center fielder is there to back up the play.

Outfielders talk to each other all the time, although not quite as much as the players do in the infield. They signal to each other to move

Rem Dawg Remembers

Hung Up in Fenway

Late in the 2003 season, Chicago White Sox left fielder Carlos Lee made a spectacular catch in front of the out-of-town scoreboard on the Green Monster in Boston, and when he came down, he ended up with his jersey hooked on the wall. That is something you don't see very often. It would have been even more interesting if it hadn't been the third out in the inning.

their position, sometimes changing position on counts, or to remind each other to back up in a particular situation. Let's say the center fielder is going to his left or right after a ball; he should get help from one of the corner outfielders or an infielder on where to throw the ball.

Every once in a while, you'll see an outfielder make a catch and then throw a lateral pass to another fielder for the throw back to the infield. Here's an example: The center fielder is charging hard toward the wall to make a catch, it's going to be very difficult for him to stop and turn around to throw. If the right fielder is coming over to help him, the center fielder can flip it to him because the right fielder is in a better position to throw.

The Outfielder's Most Difficult Play

The most difficult play for an outfielder is anything over his head going toward the wall. He's running full speed, he feels the warning track, and from that point he's got to know how far it is to the wall. A guy like Trot Nixon, for example, has no regard for a wall. He's just going to keep running until something knocks him down.

And then there are outfielders who defy gravity and climb the wall. Think of Torii Hunter taking away Barry Bonds's home run in the 2002 All-Star Game. For Hunter it must have been a dream come true. He's playing in his first All-Star Game. The most prolific home-run hitter in the game is at the plate and hits a long drive that is heading over the fence.

Hunter makes a great play and shows the world why he is a Gold Glove center fielder.

You might look at a catch like that and think it was a fluke. But many outfielders work on that play in spring training and during batting practice. It does, though, take a lot of athletic ability. If you'd asked me as a second baseman, "Why are you so good on plays diving to your right?" I couldn't give you an answer. I just did it. The same goes for outfield plays.

Defensive Positioning

One way to spot the difference between a veteran and a rookie in the outfield is to look for changes in positioning based on knowledge of the hitter and the intricacies of the game. When you see outfielders moving as the count changes, you know these guys are thinking out there.

Let's consider a straightaway hitter at the plate. If the count goes to 0–2, you are probably going to see that center fielder play the batter a little bit to the opposite field because with two strikes against him, he is not going to have the same swing. He is going to become defensive, likely to shoot the ball the other way.

In 3–0 or 3–1 counts, you're likely to see the center fielder move the other direction because the batter is probably going to swing more aggressively and pull the ball. The same goes for the right fielder and the left fielder, although the change in their position may be a bit smaller because they have less territory to cover.

Again it depends on the hitter. There are certain hitters who don't change their swing on an 0–2 count. They are still going for downtown. A home-run hitter like Sammy Sosa is not going to change his swing. He will be the same on 0–2 as he was on 0–0.

Directing the defense

The catcher is the only player who faces out at the defense. He will sometimes direct the outfielders; on most teams, though, players on the field are positioned by a coach in the dugout.

The coach who has this responsibility will have the scouting reports and the computer analyses of where hitters on the other team tend to put the ball. Although many veteran fielders are capable of making adjustments on their own, if the coach sees a guy out of position, it's his job to move him. That's why you'll sometimes see coaches on the top step of the dugout trying to get the attention of a fielder.

Playing shallow or deep

Some outfielders play deep and race in to try to catch balls hit just over the infield, while others play shallow and are ready to turn around and chase after balls hit toward the fence.

It comes down to preference and ability. For an outfielder the easier thing to do is to put his back against the outfield wall and charge everything. You and I could do that, but a lot of balls are going to fall in front of us or go to the wall to our right or left. The harder way to play the outfield is to play shallow and go back on a ball. To do that you've got to have great speed and be able to get a great jump.

The advantage of playing shallow is that you can take away some singles; the danger lies in giving up the extra base hit on balls that get past. But again, it depends on the situation in the game.

If his team has a one-run lead in the ninth inning, the center fielder is probably not going to play very shallow. Instead he is going to be protecting against the double; he doesn't want to allow a runner in scoring position to tie the game. This is the outfield equivalent of playing the lines in the infield.

Charge or lay back?

When a ball is heading to earth in front of an outfielder, he has to make a split-second decision whether to charge in and try to make a shoestring or diving catch or lay back and let the ball fall in for a hit. It's the same sort of thing an infielder goes through when he has to decide whether to stay back on a ground ball or try to get it on the first hop.

If his team is tied or one run ahead, the outfielder will want to keep the ball in front of him. He doesn't want to dive and have the ball get by and let the batter get into scoring position. It's difficult to do so, though, because a fielder's natural instinct is to try to catch everything hit toward him. That's why before the play happens, a player has to go over the situation. Where are the runners, and who are they? What is the score? Do I try to make a tough play, or should I play it safely and catch the ball on a hop?

Hitting the Cutoff

Cutoff and relay plays are essential parts of baseball but something that many fans may miss because they are concentrating on the runners or watching to see the play at the plate.

What I'm talking about here is a play involving a player getting the ball deep in the outfield and then throwing it to the infield. He may be aiming at the catcher at home plate, but an infielder is supposed to be in position to cut off the throw, redirecting the ball to another base or relaying it to home plate. The idea is to keep base runners from advancing an extra base unnecessarily.

On the infield, depending where the ball has been hit, one player is supposed to be the cutoff man. In general, it goes like this:

- If the ball is down the rightfield line or in the rightfield gap, the second baseman becomes the lead cutoff man.
- If the ball is down the leftfield line or in the leftfield gap, the shortstop is the cutoff man.

Now this is not set in cement. Let's say the ball goes into the rightfield gap, and the shortstop has a much better throwing arm than the second baseman. If the shortstop can get over to the right side of the infield, some managers have the shortstop become the cutoff man and the second baseman a trailer on the play.

On the other side, though, you'll never see a second baseman become cutoff man on a ball to left field. It's always the shortstop.

Remy Says: Watch This

How High Is Up?

The cutoff man should not have to jump to catch the ball because by the time he comes back down, his relay throw would be useless. So if the ball comes in too high, the cutoff man lets it go and the trailer makes the play on it.

Remy Says: Watch This

Outfield Assists

Some parks make it easier for outfielders to get assists on plays in the infield. Fenway is like that in left field, and Yankee Stadium in right field; outfielders can play shallow.

Tris Speaker, the Hall of Fame center fielder for the Red Sox in the early twentieth century, holds the major league record for total assists and is tied for the single-season record with thirty-five in 1909 and again in 1912.

Manny Ramírez, despite his sometimes casual approach on defense, is very quick in getting rid of the ball. He recorded eight assists from left field in 2007. In 2005 he had seventeen from the back corner.

The cutoff man has to decide how far out of the infield to go. If the outfielder has a strong arm, he should make a long throw to the infield and let the cutoff man make the shorter throw to the plate or a base.

The cutoff man takes up his position with his back to the plate. He yells at the outfielder and waves his arms so that as soon as the fielder turns he knows where the cutoff man is. The cutoff man concentrates on taking the throw from the outfield with two hands and getting himself into a throwing position. For that reason the cutoff man needs help from the trailer on where to throw the ball.

The trailer yells, "Third, third, third" or "Home, home, home" or directs the throw wherever the play is going to be. Or, if he wants the cutoff man to hold on to the ball, "Run it in, run it in."

Air mail

Outfielders are constantly told, "Hit the cutoff man," yet they don't always do it. An outfielder might fall in love with his throwing arm and want to show it off. Or he might just make a bad throw.

On a base hit to right field with a man on first, the fielder might try to throw out a runner going first to third. If the outfielder air mails one over the shortstop, the batter can see how high the throw is, and he'll keep going on to second base.

There are some situations in which an outfielder is expected to throw through to the plate. For example, if he is coming in on the play, moving toward the plate, and the ball is not hit that deep, a fielder with a strong arm should try to go all the way to the plate. If there's a man on third and no one else on base, the outfielder will probably try to reach the plate.

If there's a runner on first, though, the ball should be thrown on a trajectory toward the head of the cutoff man; if the trailer decides he's not going to get the man at the plate, the trailer tells the cutoff man to throw to another base, not home, to keep another runner from advancing.

Outfield throws to the bases

Not every throw from the outfield goes to home plate or to a cutoff man.

For example, let's say that a team has a two-run lead late in the game and the opposing team has a runner on second. On a deep hit to the outfield, there shouldn't be a play at the plate—instead the throw should go directly to second base to try to keep the batter from advancing to scoring position.

Before each pitch, every fielder is supposed to review in his mind where he will throw the ball if he makes a play. Outfielders also get help from the dugout and from infielders who may point to second base to remind them to try to prevent an unnecessary advance by a base runner. The message here would be: "Forget the guy running home and throw the ball here."

But many times players get caught up in the action of the play and don't think. Their normal reaction is to come up throwing and fire home.

Remy Says: Watch This

Off the Wall

If you arrive early for a game at Fenway Park, pay attention during outfield practice to see how the visiting team's left fielder is working on his game. You'll often see a coach whacking a ball off the wall, helping the fielder learn how to play the different angles.

Adjusting to Unusual Ballparks

Outfielders need to be aware of the idiosyncrasies of the park they're playing in. Fenway Park, of course, is one of most unusual, having the Green Monster in left field, but there's also Yankee Stadium with its short right porch and awful oddities like the catwalks hung from the ceiling of Tropicana Field, home of the Tampa Bay Rays. It's not just rookies who have problems at Fenway, either. I have seen guys play there for years and still have problems with the park. The wall makes for a strange game. It doesn't take much to put a ball off the wall, but balls that are crushed can hit halfway up the wall and end up as 300-foot singles. The carom is pretty true off the current leftfield wall; in years past players didn't know how the ball was going to bounce, depending on which seam it hit.

The most difficult decision for a left fielder at Fenway is judging whether the ball is going to hit the wall or fall just in front of it. That's why a lot of visiting left fielders play very deep; they figure that if the ball is over their head, it is going to be on the wall and they can come in to play the rebound.

But the better left fielders play shallow at Fenway because they can take away a lot of base hits. They've got the experience to recognize whether a ball hit over their head is going to make the wall or not.

At Fenway it's hard to score from second base on a ball hit to left field if the left fielder is playing shallow. Carl Yastrzemski didn't have a great throwing arm, but he played shallow and he charged the ball real well.

There's also the triangle in deep center field at Fenway, where the ball goes forever, 420 feet from home plate. And the foul pole in right field—the Pesky Pole—is just 302 feet away. You'll see a ball wrap around it for a home run. In another park that's a foul ball.

Down the third-base line, the wall juts out just past the infield cutout, and a ground ball that would be a double in another park can carom off the wall to the shortstop and end up as a single. The pole in left field—now officially called the Fisk Pole—is just 310 feet away.

Deking out the runner

In certain circumstances an outfielder can try to deke out a runner. We see that a lot in Boston because of the Green Monster. If a fly ball is hit high in the air, the left fielder may stand in front of the wall and act like he is going to catch it; what he is trying to do is deke a base runner into thinking he is going to make the catch even though the fielder knows the ball is going to hit the wall.

At the last minute the fielder will back off, turn around, and play it off the wall. He's hoping to freeze a runner at first or second base or maybe even throw out a runner who stayed at first base thinking the ball was going to be caught.

It very seldom works, but it looks good if it succeeds.

Falling Asleep in the Outfield

Sometimes you can look out to the outfield and see players practicing their swing. That doesn't happen much in the infield. There is a little bit less to do on every pitch, and some fielders have a tendency to stray a little bit. Rickey Henderson used to have a running conversation with the fans in the left field.

Sometimes I have pity on outfielders because some pitchers take forever to throw the ball. It's been a horrible inning; they've been out there for thirty-five minutes. This is not a snappy ball game where everyone is focusing on every pitch. But on the other hand, I will tell you it's hard to forget how many outs there are today. It's up there on the scoreboard and smaller boards at first base and third base. And the infielders are supposed to be reminding each other and the other position players about the number of outs already recorded in the inning.

But mental mistakes do happen and they can be as embarrassing as hell when they do.

In 2003 former Boston Dirt Dog Trot Nixon had a brain cramp in the ninth inning of a one-run game against Anaheim. With runners on first and second and one out, David Eckstein lifted a short pop-up to right field. Nixon caught the ball and tossed it into the stands and the runner on second came all the way around to score. It was ruled a two-base sacrifice fly.

PART SIX

On the Base Paths

I'm losing my balance reaching out for a bad throw and avoiding the runner, John Lowenstein of Cleveland, as he slides into second base in a 1975 game. I would have been set up straddling the bag, but the throw was into the runner and heading into short right field.

Photo courtesy Los Angeles Angels of Anaheim Baseball Club

CHAPTER NINETEEN

Running the Bases

The Running Game

Speed rules. A fast team can literally run themselves into a win with runners who take extra bases on hits, steal to move into scoring position, and score on sacrifices.

Or bad baserunning can take a team right out of the game.

Great speed can help someone become a great base runner even if his fundamentals are not that good because he can just outrun the baseball. But the art of being a good base runner requires much more than just speed.

There are a lot of things a runner has to be aware of when he gets on base. He's got to know the game situation: how many outs there are, the score, what kind of arm the catcher has, how good the pitcher's pickoff move is, the depth of the outfield, and who out there has a good arm.

Carlton Fisk was a great example of a player who was a terrific base runner despite a lack of blazing speed. He knew situations, the outfielder's strengths and weaknesses, and he cut the bases very well. Jason Varitek, another catcher, is a smart runner.

The rules of the road

There is a basic saying in baseball: Never make the first or third out at third base.

You don't want to kill an inning by getting thrown out at third base; if a runner stops at second base, he is already in scoring position if someone gets a hit, so there's little advantage to attempt going on to third. (A runner is more likely to gamble going from first to third with one out so he can score on a sacrifice fly.)

The score of the game makes a difference. You don't take chances if your team is three or four runs down. Nothing looks worse than a base-running blunder that takes a man out of scoring position when his team is trailing by just a few runs. It is just horrible.

When a ball is hit to left field, it is tougher to go from first to third because the fielder has a shorter throw to third base. But there might be some guy out there who has a weak throwing arm and the runner will challenge him.

The running game is also influenced by the ballpark. In a bigger stadium outfielders have to play deeper, so there's a better chance to advance an extra base. But in a small ballpark like Boston's, it is very difficult to go first to third on any ball hit to left field because a good outfielder plays shallow there.

A Runner's Style

There are beautiful runners who look like sprinters on the base paths, with perfect form. And then there are some guys whose arms and hands are flopping all over the place, but they still have good speed.

One of the most important skills a good base runner has to learn is how to cut the bases properly. I have known players who have gone to track coaches to try to pick up a step or so. But baseball is different because runners are not going in a straight line when they circle the bases. Runners don't need great speed to be able to cut bases the right

Rem Dawg Remembers

Running Smart

When I was running, anytime I saw the ball hit into the gap so that the fielder had to play it running to his glove side, I knew he would have to spin all the way around to make the throw. That extra second or two would make the difference on whether I would try to pick up an extra base or come around to score.

way. If a runner doesn't make the turn properly at first base, he can lose three or four steps, and that can end up costing a chance for an extra base hit.

Runners also have to learn how to touch the bag without injuring themselves. You'll see injuries at first base more than anywhere else because if the play is going to be close, many runners jump at the bag. The bag is between 3 and 5 inches off the ground; if they hit it off to the side, they can easily turn an ankle.

Rounding the bases

The way a runner rounds the bases can depend on where the ball is hit.

On a routine base hit to left field, a good base runner will probably take a large turn around first base; if there's a bobble in the outfield, he can advance to second. On a ball hit to right field, he can't automatically take that big wide turn at first base because a right fielder with a good arm could throw behind him and get him out.

The Art of Stealing a Base

Base stealers study pitchers in great detail. They know who has a good move and who does not. They know what counts to run on. They know how big a lead to take. And they are generally very explosive in their first two steps.

Rickey Henderson was so powerful in his lower body that after his crossover step he was at full speed. But it was more than that: He knew how to read pitchers.

Deciding whether to be a running club is a managerial decision. When Jimy Williams managed the Red Sox, he didn't put a lot of stock in stolen bases. In 2003 under Grady Little, we saw more horses turned loose, with Boston stealing eighty-eight bases, about double the average during Williams's years.

Terry Francona has not been afraid to use speed when he has it available. Red Sox fans will always remember Dave Roberts's swipe of second base in the ninth inning of Game 4 of the 2004 ALCS, which opened the door for Boston to tie the game against Yankee closer Mariano Rivera. Three innings later David Ortiz homered, and the Red Sox had the first win of their amazing comeback that led to the World Series. I'll return to Roberts in a moment. In 2007 the Red Sox had at least three players with real speed: Julio Lugo, Coco Crisp, and Jacoby Ellsbury. The team recorded 98 swipes in the season. Ellsbury, who may have the stuff to be a star, stole 9 bases in limited play; we'll also remember a great moment when he scored from second base on a wild pitch, one of the better bursts of speed I have seen in a long time.

Some managers think that players shouldn't steal at Fenway because it is a hitter's park. I have never bought into that; I have seen plenty of 2–0 games there. But the theory is that Fenway is a home-run hitter's park, where they don't play what they call National League baseball, which emphasizes running and stealing. In any case it depends on the team's personnel. If you don't have base stealers, you can't steal bases.

Red light, green light

When a runner gets the green light, it means he is free to steal any time he thinks he can, if it makes sense in the game. He may have the green light when he is on first base, but he may not have it going second to third. The manager might want to control that end of it.

Sometimes the manager will have the third-base coach flash the "don't run" sign. But if some dope tries to steal when his team is seven runs down and gets thrown out, he will probably never have the green light for the rest of his life.

The psychological part of the game comes into play here, too. When Ellis Burks was with the Red Sox, he was a guy who had shown great speed in the minor leagues and had a chance to be a very good base stealer. But he got thrown out a few times and lost confidence; he was the only guy on the team who was a threat to run, and he felt like he was letting everybody down. Then again, on a team where almost everybody runs, it doesn't seem to matter as much if a runner gets thrown out. That's the manager's style. In my rookie year of 1975, the Angels set a record with 220 stolen bases for the season. We had Mickey Rivers who stole 70 that year. I swiped 34, and we also had Tommy Harper, Dave Collins, and Morris Nettles each with more than 20 steals. We had good pitching with Frank Tanana and Nolan Ryan. What we didn't have were RBI or home-run guys. The only way we had a chance to score runs was to be aggressive

Rem Dawg Remembers

Turning Off the Green Light

Some managers like to control the whole game, while others will say to four or five guys: "You are on your own, but you have got to make good decisions. If you make two or three bad decisions in a row, you are no longer free to run."

That happened to me in Anaheim when I was a rookie. I tried to steal third base in a bad spot and got thrown out. Dick Williams took away my green light for two weeks. He never said a word to me; then one day he patted me on the shoulder and said, "You are back on your own." He wanted me to think for a while about the right and wrong times to run.

and steal bases. We lost a lot of 2–1 games and ended up seventeen games under .500 for the season.

The most stolen bases I had was 41 in 1977 for the Angels. I was traded to the Red Sox the next year and stole 30 in my first year there. When I came to Boston, they wanted me to run while we were on the road but be cautious at home because of the ballpark and the lineup behind me. We had guys who could pound the ball, so a stolen base wasn't a major thing at Fenway. I used to say that when I was on the road, I had a green light, but when I was playing at Fenway, it was a yellow light: run with caution.

I found it very difficult to turn it on and off like that. If you are a base stealer, you've got to steal all the time. To me that was like being a hitter and having a coach say, "When you are at home, we don't want you to pull the ball, we want you to go the other way."

Figuring out the pitcher

If I had the green light and I was thinking steal, I would pick the pitch I want to run on and then look for the trigger—either the shoulder or the knee.

A good base runner studies the pitcher to try to figure out whether he plans to throw home or to first base. Every pitcher is different, and there are different things to look for on a left-hander and a right-hander. But just like poker players say, nearly everybody has a "tell" that can tip someone off to his intentions.

Some pitchers will tip off by the movement of their head; for example, if they are going to throw to first base, they may hold their head a little lower.

The front shoulder is generally a good indicator; that was something I usually had good luck with. When that shoulder starts to tuck in back toward the throwing arm, a runner can take off because the pitcher can't go in and then back. If he does, that's a balk.

The other thing to watch is the foot that touches the pitching rubber. Once the pitcher starts moving, if the foot remains in contact, he has to throw home. In order to go to first base, that heel will come up and the pitcher will have to step off the rubber to make the pivot to go to first base.

In most cases a left-handed pitcher is better at holding runners on first base because he is facing the base as he prepares to throw the ball. But there are still things to look for. The rules say if the pitcher brings his foot behind the rubber, he is supposed to go home. So, if a left-hander brings his right foot behind the rubber, the runner can take off because the pitcher cannot go back without committing a balk.

The runner can also watch the pitcher's front knee. When he comes to the set position, if the knee bends, that means he is going to first base, because he is bending it to get into position to spin. If it just kicks back up, that means he is going home.

Now, many pitchers try to get away with a little quick bend that makes the runner think they are going to first, which freezes the runner, and then they throw home.

I always found that one of the toughest situations as a base runner was figuring out a right-hander who reacted quickly with his first move. Whatever he did, whether he was going home or to first, if it was quick, it could freeze me at first base.

There were other guys who were so easy to pick up that I couldn't wait to get on base, because I knew I had their trigger. Their delivery was slow and I had a great chance to steal a base.

Getting a good lead

One key to stealing a base is make the break with some momentum instead of starting to run from a dead stop. Another important element is to get a good lead. But there is no such thing as one perfect lead for every player. It depends, first of all, on the abilities of the runner. And there is the matter of how good a pickoff move the pitcher has.

A 5'10" guy is probably not going to be able to get as big a lead as a guy who is 6'2". Runners are supposed to be able to take one crossover step and a dive to get back to the bag. If I were to do that from the same place as a guy with much longer legs, I'd come up short of the base.

When a runner makes that dive, he's supposed to aim for the back part of the bag—toward the outfield—because that makes the tag a bit farther away for the first baseman.

The size of a lead depends on the runner's comfort level. You'll see some players who take big leads but don't get big jumps because they are thinking about getting back to first instead of moving on to second. Coaches talk about *one-way leads* and *two-way leads.*

With a one-way lead, a runner may be way off the bag but not planning to steal; he is prepared to dive back to first base. If he's got a two-way lead, he's prepared to go either way.

One time to use a one-way lead is to try to trick a pitcher. Let's say I was facing a left-handed pitcher who had a great move that I couldn't quite figure out. I might take a pretty big one-way lead, always leaning back toward first base, and hope to draw a few throws.

Then after a couple of throws, I might shake my head and reduce my lead. I want him to think that I've given up on stealing the base, but then as soon as he moves his foot, I'd be gone.

This is just one of those little games within the game. A runner might be able to get away with it a few times, until the opponent catches on to what he is doing.

Stealing third

A runner on second base has an advantage because there is nobody holding him on—the shortstop and the second baseman are in their fielding positions when the pitch is thrown.

The runner is told to keep an eye on the second baseman; he can see him out of the corner of his eye to his left. He has to rely on the third-base coach to watch the shortstop, hidden behind him when he takes a lead.

Just as he would if he were on first, the runner studies the pitcher. If the pitcher follows the same pattern—look at the runner once, get the sign from the catcher, take a glance over his shoulder at the runner again, and then throw the pitch—he's making it easy to steal third. If the pitcher mixes up his patterns, that throws off the runner's timing, and it becomes more difficult to run on him.

We know that left-handers generally are better at holding runners on first because they are looking right at the base. By the same token, it is usually easier to steal third base against a lefty. For a left-hander to make a throw to third base, he has to spin on the mound. And for some reason lefties also usually have a much slower delivery to home plate than right-handers, which makes it easier to steal on them.

But in any case a runner has to be careful. Standing on second base, he is already in scoring position. He had better be sure he can make it to third before he takes off.

Get Back!

The first-base coach is supposed to help runners keep an eye on the pitcher and catcher when they take a lead. But the truth is, by the time he yells "Get back," a base runner had better already be on his way back.

More important, coaches have the opportunity to watch the pitcher through the entire game from just behind first base, and they can study and time his move. The coach can help the runner decide how large a lead he can safely take.

When a runner is on second, the third-base coach can yell across the infield if the shortstop is coming in behind to take a pickoff throw from the pitcher or the catcher. The shortstop and second baseman are supposed to continually bluff moves in behind a runner on second to try to keep him close, especially with a right-handed hitter at the plate. If the infielder takes a couple of jab steps before the pitch, he may be able to get the runner moving back toward the bag as the pitcher delivers to the plate.

The third-base coach has to know the speed of runners and the way they run the bases. Coaches also have to know the strength of the outfielders' arms. Then coaches hope that their guy runs hard around the bases, as if they are going to score on every hit.

Running ugly

In the third game of the 2004 World Series, pitcher Jeff Suppan of the Cardinals put on one of the worst baserunning exhibitions I have ever seen, right up there with El Tiante's adventures in the 1975 World Series.

Suppan (a former Red Sox) was the starting pitcher for the Cardinals, and he was throwing well; he had given up just one run on two hits in the first three innings and the score was 1–0 Boston. Since this game was being played in a National League park, Suppan came up to bat in the bottom of the third and darned if he didn't beat out an infield hit.

Next up was Edgar Rentería (then with St. Louis), who hit a double off Pedro Martínez. With no outs the Cardinals had runners on second and third. The Red Sox infield played back, willing to concede a run to get an out.

Larry Walker followed with a sharp ground ball to second base. Suppan broke off third and started to come home, where he would have scored the tying run. Red Sox second baseman Mark Bellhorn threw the ball to David Ortiz, who was playing first base (because there was no DH).

For some reason Suppan stopped between third and home; he just

Remy Says: Watch This

Running for Home

When it comes time for a coach to decide whether to wave a guy home, my rule of thumb is this: With nobody out you've got to be 100 percent sure he can be safe. With one out that drops to 75 percent, and with two outs it's a 50-50 call.

If a coach is afraid of making mistakes and becomes tentative, he can't coach third base. He's got to stay aggressive.

froze. Rentería, who was already approaching third base to take his place, had to stop and run back to second. Ortiz ran a few steps toward third, pumped a couple of times, and then threw behind Suppan, and Bill Mueller tagged him out. It was your not-so-ordinary 4–3–5 double play.

As a base runner, that's one of the most basic plays you have at third. When the infield is back, you go on a ground ball. The third-base coach would have reminded him before every pitch.

In that situation the only ball you don't run on is one hit right back to the pitcher. That's it. On everything else you go.

It was just horrible. I have always been a fan of the DH; this was just another example why.

The pinch runner

If a pinch runner is on base with a pitcher who has a very slow move and a weak-throwing catcher behind the plate, you can expect the possibility of a steal. But when the manager inserts a pinch runner, it is not always to steal a base. More often than not, a pinch runner is inserted because he can go from first to third on a single or score on a double better than the man he is replacing.

A fast runner may be able to put some pressure on an infielder on a ball in the hole, removing the chance for a double play or forcing the infielder to move out of position or make a hurried throw because of the runner's speed. A fast pinch runner may also distract the pitcher and catcher from their plan. Coaches are always telling pitchers to concentrate on the hitter, but a runner dancing around at first base can still be a distraction.

I can recall the glory days of the Oakland A's in 1974 and 1975 when they had a pinch runner named Herb Washington. He'd be put in the game just to steal a base or to score from second on a base hit. He couldn't play a lick. He appeared in 104 games without ever getting an at bat or playing a position in the field. But in today's game there are pitchers, including many closers, who could not care less about the guy at first base. They don't have good moves. Their thing is striking out this guy at home plate. Their intentions are: "Let him steal. I don't care. I will get this guy out at the plate."

That said, one of the most important moments in recent Red Sox history came in the 2004 ALCS against the Yankees: Dave Roberts's pinch-run steal against Mariano Rivera in the fourth game of the ALCS. It was the bottom of the ninth and Boston was three outs away from losing to the Yankees.

If he had been thrown out, the playoff would probably have been over. This was pressure time. Roberts had to make it.

Most closers can be run against and that includes Rivera; that's no secret. But you just hope that when you decide to go everything goes right: you don't slip, you don't make a bad slide, and they don't pitch out.

All those things go through your mind. A lot of guys would say: "To heck with it, I am not going. I am not going to be the guy thrown out at second base and we go home."

The Red Sox needed the perfect stolen base and that's exactly what they got. Jorge Posada made a good throw, but Roberts stole the base off Rivera. The timing made it more impressive than the act itself.

"When Kevin Millar walked, Terry just looked down at me and kind of winked and said, 'You know what to do,' " Roberts said.

"Maury Wills once told me that there will come a point in my career when everyone in the ballpark will know that I have to steal a base," Roberts said. "When I got out there, I knew that was what Maury Wills was talking about."

Roberts moved on, but he'll probably never have to buy another drink for himself in Boston.

B
ED SOX

PART SEVEN

The Fields of Dreams

Fenway by night, with Johnny Damon at the plate and runners on the corners. With two outs the Marlin infielders have dropped back from double-play depth to their normal positions.

Photo by Corey Sandler

CHAPTER TWENTY

Looking around the Park

The Shape of Things

Many casual fans may not realize how much one ballpark differs from another. And even at one park, conditions can vary greatly from game to game.

Baseball's official rules lay out only the most general guidelines for the design of a field: The bases have to be 90 feet apart, the pitcher's rubber 60 feet 6 inches away from home plate, and the foul lines have to radiate out from the plate to first and third bases and beyond to the fences.

The distance from home plate to the nearest fence in fair territory has to be at least 250 feet, although a distance of 320 feet or more along the foul lines and 400 feet or more to center field is "preferable."

That's the heart of the description of the ballplayer's workplace, and within those broad definitions, we end up with places of perfect symmetry like Kaufman Stadium in Kansas City (leftfield line 330 feet from home, left-center 375 feet, center field 400 feet, right-center 375 feet, and right field 330 feet).

And then we have celebrated oddities like Fenway Park in Boston (left-field line 310 feet from home, left-center 379 feet, center field 420 feet, deep right field 380 feet, and rightfield line 302 feet, plus the 37-foot-high Green Monster in left field, a 17-foot-high wall in center field, a bull pen field 5 feet tall, a fence in short right field as low as 3 feet off the ground, and various ladders, garage doors, jut-outs, and triangles).

Fenway's leftfield wall changes everything. That's what makes it different from any other ballpark. There are balls hit off that wall that would be home runs in other parks but end up as singles at Fenway. There are balls that scrape the wall that would be outs at other ballparks.

New York's Yankee Stadium is also misshapen: 318 feet down the left-field line, 379 feet to straightaway left field, 408 feet to deep center, 353 feet to straightway right field, and 314 feet down the right-field line. The Yankees are building a new stadium, due to open for the 2009 season, and the layout is supposed to be more or less the same as the original.

And then there are the oddities like Tampa Bay's Tropicana Field. What makes Tropicana Field such a joke are the catwalks that hang from the ceiling; it can become a pinball game when the ball hits one. Most of the catwalks are in fair territory and in play. Other than that it's a pretty decent domed ballpark; I prefer it to Minnesota's.

The Metrodome in Minnesota is a strange place. It is tough to see the ball against the white ceiling, and there are speakers and other things hanging down from the roof. Also many of the seats are angled for football. I won't miss it when it closes; a new Twins ballpark is under construction and due to open for the 2010 season.

Looking at the field

Once they've figured out the layout of the fences and the stands, ballplayers have to think about the conditions of the field itself. Is it grass or artificial turf? Some infield grasses are thicker than others; some fields play quick, some fields slow.

If there's a speedy runner at the plate and a slow infield and thick grass, the defense has to play a little shallower. At a park with artificial turf, like Minnesota's indoor oddity, an outfielder has to be careful not to charge too aggressively on a short fly because if it hits the hard surface, it can easily bounce over his head.

The worst condition for an infielder is a wet infield; he gets no traction in the dirt part of the infield.

Before the game, especially at the start of a series, you may see players checking how the infield is playing. They may have a coach rolling ground balls so they can work on their mechanics and footwork.

Doctoring the field

Then there are the tricks the grounds crew can play with the baselines to help balls stay fair or roll foul.

"The Green Monster at Fenway changes the complexion of the game more than anything in any other ballpark in baseball."

JERRY REMY

When I was with the California Angels, one year we had a lot of speed but not a lot of power. And so the grounds crew monkeyed around with the slope of the field. Foul territory near the foul lines tilted in toward the playing field so that it was almost impossible to bunt a ball foul. Bunts would roll outside the foul line and then come back into fair territory.

I have been in other ballparks where the field was tilted the other way; if someone put a roller down the line, it would go foul. You'll see some ballparks where the infield turf runs right to the foul line. For a bunter that's great because there's more thick grass for him to drop a bunt on.

When Jimy Williams ran the Red Sox, he wanted the infield grass high and thick because the team didn't have a lot of range in the infield.

Teams have always doctored their fields to match their talents. Sometimes you can see it change from day to day. If the home team is starting a sinker-ball pitcher, the dirt in front of the plate may be mud and the next day, if they've got a power pitcher going, it is hard as a rock.

When Sparky Anderson was in Detroit, he had a bunch of sinker-ball pitchers on his staff, and they used to throw split-fingered fastballs, which generally result in ground balls. His infield didn't have a lot of range, so depending on who was pitching, they used to make it like quicksand in front of home plate. It was so frustrating to guys like me who hit ground balls. Even in batting practice, someone would hit a ground ball and *pfft* it would get stuck there. It wouldn't even make it through the infield.

And one more thing about the old Tiger Stadium in Detroit: Home plate was turned slightly toward right field. They had a short porch out in right field and a lot of left-handed power hitters throughout the years. That enabled those hitters to get on top of the plate and open up a little bit, which helped them pull the ball.

We went many years without even noticing it. But then somebody mentioned it and we saw the tilt—not enough to see on television or from the stands, but if you looked closely, you could see the difference.

At Angels Stadium, when we had a lot of guys who would steal bases, including me, it seems that our second-base bag was about 6 inches closer to first base than it was supposed to be. You would have had to use a surveyor's transit to see the difference, but that made a big difference at second base. On a bang-bang play, you'd be safe by 6 inches.

We knew nothing about it at the time. The secret came out later, from a groundskeeper who had apparently done the dirty job.

Swirling Winds and Jet Blasts

Wind is lousy to play in. Some of us would rather play in the drizzle than the wind. It's just brutal for fielders on fly balls and pop-ups. Depending on which way the wind is blowing, it can be lousy for hitters, too. Power hitters obviously pay more attention to wind than other guys. It didn't matter to me on my bunt which way the wind was blowing.

Before they installed the luxury boxes high above home plate at Fenway Park, there was a jet stream to center field. I remember playing second base on a hot and windy summer day with a southeast wind blowing straight out. You could see the ball go by, pick up speed, and just fly out of there like a space shuttle taking off.

Even today Fenway can play real big or real small. Early in the season, when the east wind is blowing in, it is a big ballpark; someone can crush a ball and it goes nowhere.

Watch the flags around the stadium. For hitters the ideal condition at Fenway is when the wind is blowing straight out. If the wind is blowing straight in from center field, it's a pitcher's day.

When the wind comes in, blowing from left to right, that's good for left-handed hitters; balls are going to carry out to the bull pen. They need all the help they can get because it's pretty deep out there. You almost never see wind from right to left at Fenway. And there is a swirling wind,

> **"Ninety feet between bases is perhaps as close as man has ever come to perfection."**
>
> PULITZER PRIZE–WINNING BASEBALL COLUMNIST RED SMITH

which is hard to describe. In some places the wind bounces off certain parts of the ballpark and actually carries the ball better in the direction opposite that of the wind.

Watching the Dugout

If you look carefully, you can sometimes see some pretty unusual goings-on in the dugout: from rally caps to a player being tied to a post with trainer's tape.

Many times silliness is a sign of boredom. In addition to the nine players in the lineup, sitting on the bench are backup players and perhaps some starting pitchers who are not due to be working for another three or four days. As a result there are all kinds of different mind-sets down there. There are guys who are totally into the game because they are playing in it, and there are backup players who are trying to stay involved as much as they can in case they are called on to come in.

And then there are the starting pitchers who know they are not going to be in the game. They are the ones you'll see carrying on conversations with the fans, fooling around with supplies from the trainer's kit, and otherwise doing whatever they can get away with. Pedro Martínez, as an example, can't keep still. He's the kind of guy who would like to be out there every day. The four days between starts drive him crazy. When we put the cameras on him in the dugout, he always seemed to be doing something.

By the way, when teammates taped Pedro to a post in 1999, that didn't sit well with the manager at the time, Jimy Williams. But what was he going to do? Cut Pedro and Nomar loose?

Rally caps are something else—it's just a bunch of guys trying to get involved, hoping to change momentum in the game by flipping their hats inside out or something like that.

The point is that every dugout is different; it depends on the personalities of the players. If you look in dugouts in some places, there's nobody there. They are up in the clubhouse eating or watching the game on TV. Most managers hate that, and some have rules against it.

If you watch the dugout carefully, you can tell a little bit about the team by the players' body language. If you saw Pedro getting taped up, there's a pretty good chance the Red Sox were winning that game. When a team is having a bad day, you will see guys sitting there stunned. And you can sometimes read on their faces which players are having a good day and which are not. If you see a jovial dugout, they are winning because not too many managers are going to put up with happy faces if the team is getting its collective ass kicked.

Going to the videotape

After they get back to the dugout, some players run into the clubhouse to watch their at bat on videotape. They might be looking at what the pitches were, what the sequence was, or the mechanics of their swing. They also can punch up an at bat from the last time they faced this particular pitcher, a week ago, or a year ago. And players—and coaches—could be studying the pitcher trying to pick something up. Is he tipping off his intention to throw a breaking ball? Is there something he does that lets you know if he's going to throw to first base instead of home?

Remy Says: Watch This

Playing in the Rain

In rainy conditions the advantage is always to the hitter. Even though you see the batter at the plate with water streaming down from his helmet, if he puts the bat on the ball, anything could happen. The ball skips through the infield quicker. And if a fielder picks up the ball, it's wet, which makes it difficult to throw with accuracy.

Rem Dawg Remembers

All Eyes on the Field

I remember manager Dick Williams used to walk up and down the Angels dugout during the game, and sometimes he would look at a player on the bench and ask, "How many outs are there?" Or, "What's the count?" And the player had better know; Williams wanted him involved.

Most designated hitters will go into the clubhouse instead of sitting on the bench through the whole game. They might watch a videotape of their last at bat. They might ride a stationary bike to stay loose. Or they might have someone in the clubhouse throw tape balls so they can swing and stay loose.

PART EIGHT

They're Only Human

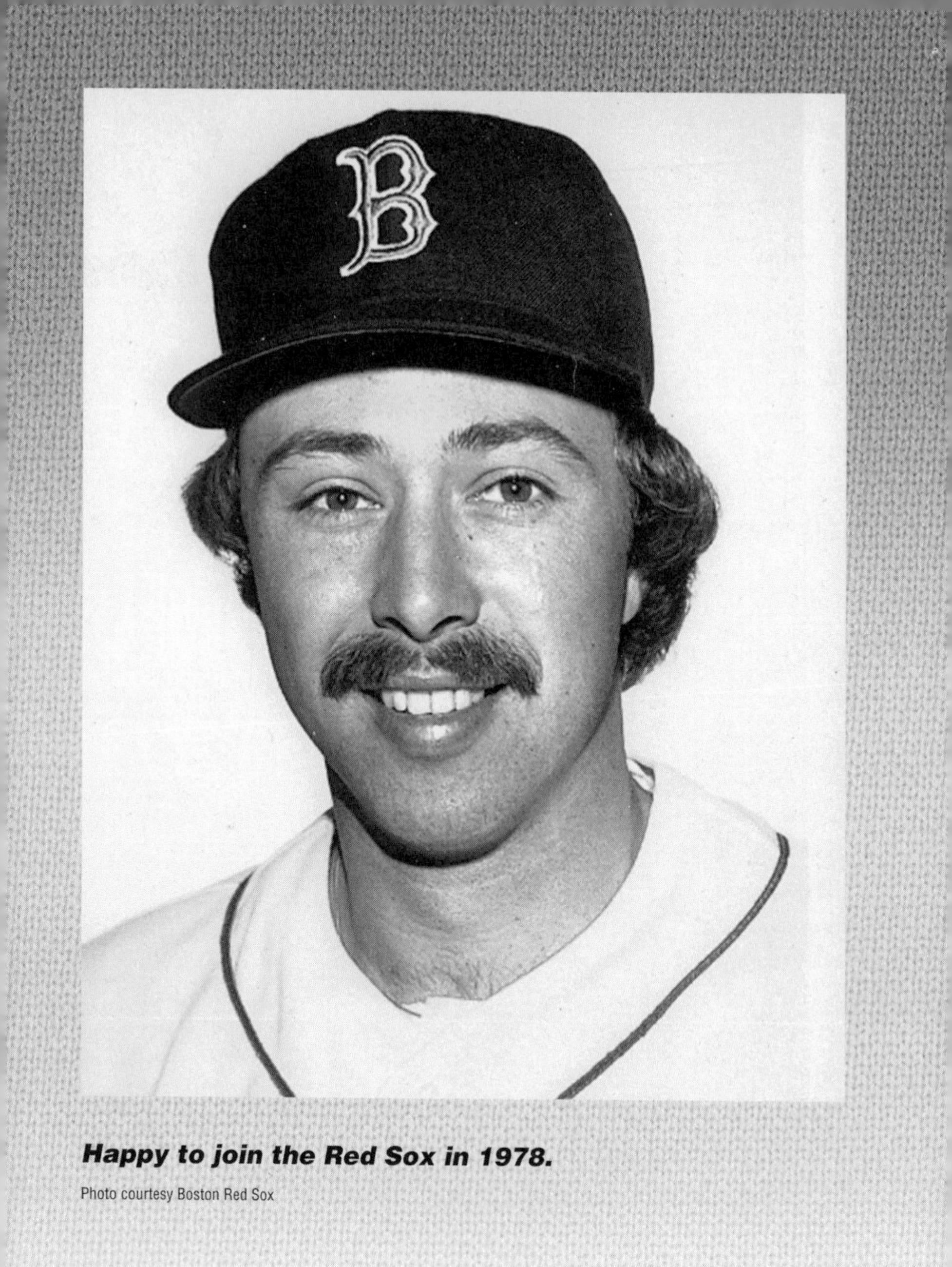

Happy to join the Red Sox in 1978.

Photo courtesy Boston Red Sox

CHAPTER TWENTY-ONE

The Mental Side of the Game

Watching Planes Overhead

We've all gone to a Little League game and seen the center fielder watching an airplane fly overhead or a third baseman with his fielder's mitt on his head instead of his hand. That doesn't happen in the major leagues, of course, but even pro ballplayers are not perfect. Every player's mind wanders sometimes. It's a mentally draining game.

In the major leagues teams play 162 games a year. There are times when a player is just not into it, and that's generally when he gets smoked. A lot depends on how the team is playing, how his own game is going, how fatigued he is, and whether he is sick or hurt.

We look at the players on the field as if they are robots. What you don't see from the stands is that one player has a tight hamstring. Another has a tender elbow. And another has something bad going on at home.

When fatigue sets in, the concentration level goes down. Players may have a Sunday afternoon game in Kansas City or Texas in ninety-degree heat and 90 percent humidity or thirty-five degrees and a cold drizzle in Boston in April. When you're focused on how poorly you feel, you don't play as well.

Losing focus on the game

In June 2002 Casey Fossum was pitching in relief for the Red Sox against the Yankees. It was the bottom of the ninth, and the Sox held a lead right there in the home of the enemy. The Yankees had runners on first and second with just one out. Fossum was pitching to pinch hitter Shane Spencer, and he hit a comebacker to the mound. Fossum caught the ground ball and threw to the plate. Unfortunately there was no runner

Rem Dawg Remembers

The Internal Dialog of a Hitter

The mental part of hitting can drive someone crazy; watching from the stands you have no idea what these guys are going through.

The internal dialog is constant with every pitch. We may talk about it during the broadcast, or the scoreboard may tell you that this guy hasn't had a hit in his last twenty at bats; trust me, he knows all about it.

Every time a slumping batter goes to the plate, it feels like he hasn't had a hit in three weeks, even though it has only been a couple of days. Ballplayers also talk to themselves throughout the game. "I'm 0 for 2 now, I've got to have a hit here to go 1 for 3, and then if I can get another one, I'll be 2 for 4, which is a great night."

Believe me: Hitters have many, many sleepless nights.

coming home. But catcher Doug Mirabelli had the presence of mind to throw from the plate to first base, and they caught Spencer anyway.

Fossum was an example of a guy losing touch with the situation at that moment. For some reason he thought there was a man on third. The thing that amazed me was that Mirabelli was paying attention; it was a good thing he was watching, or he would have gotten the ball right between the eyes.

Mental meltdowns

One of the more famous meltdowns in recent years was that of Rick Ankiel, a left-handed pitcher for the St. Louis Cardinals, who was a phenomenon in his first year in the majors in 2000. He had an 11–7 record during the season and then in the playoffs against Atlanta, he suddenly couldn't find the plate with a map. His pitches were out of the strike zone by yards, sometimes going right over the batter, the catcher, and the umpire.

That was so sad to watch. Here was a kid with a great arm, and then you're watching the nightly sports highlights and they're showing him banging pitches off the backstop.

I'm sure a lot of the problem was psychological. Once something bad happens, if you get it in your mind that it's going to continue to happen again, it's going to happen. After returning to the minors for a season, Ankiel made an unsuccessful comeback at the end of the 2004 season before leaving the pitcher's mound and trying to recast himself as an outfielder. He returned to the major leagues in August of 2007 and posted a .285 batting average with 11 home runs in the last third of the season.

Remy Says: Watch This

Keep Your Eye on A-Rod

It's not fair to lay the Yankee's troubles in the 2007 postseason on Alex Rodriguez. He may be the greatest player in the game, but unfortunately the postseason has yet to work out for him in New York.

During the season A-Rod seemed so fluid and smooth when things were going well. And then in the playoffs you could see him pressing with a very mechanical swing. When you press, I don't care how great you are, you are not going to be as good.

To many of the fans in New York, the only way he can earn his Yankee pinstripes would be to not only win a world championship but to be a major part of it. (This is a guy who is probably going to break Barry Bonds's home run record if he can stay healthy.)

After the 2007 season, it looked like he was going to be leaving New York, and if he had, he would have been remembered as a great player who never won a championship. Now A-Rod and the Yankee ownership have kissed and made up, and so we'll see how he performs in years to come.

I thought his agent's activities, coming out with the news about A-Rod's contract plans in the middle of Game 4 of the World Series, were disgusting. It was pathetic to see him try to make one of his clients bigger than the game at a time when all the focus should have been on the Colorado Rockies and the Boston Red Sox.

Sometimes these guys get so powerful that they think that they just control everything. It was poor timing and bad taste. Had he been my agent, I would have been pissed off at him because his actions made his client look stupid.

Rain Delays

Rain delays are the worst baseball "events" possible. I have already said how important it is for ballplayers to get into a comfortable routine. Anything that interrupts the routine throws the whole day out of whack.

If the delay comes at the beginning of the game, the players have done all their work to get ready to play and all of a sudden they are put on hold. It's especially bad to have the starting pitcher loosen up and then not be able to start the game.

A rain delay in the middle of the game is another kind of disaster. You are in the flow of the game and all of a sudden it is stopped and you have no idea how long the delay will be. Let's say one of the team's best pitchers started the game. After a delay of an hour and a half, does it make sense for this pitcher to go back out there again? He runs the risk of injury or a bad performance—at best, it's a wasted start.

Some managers have chosen not to start their best pitcher in a game when there is a good chance the game will be interrupted by rain. They might start a relief pitcher, and once the rain delay is done, bring in a starting pitcher.

When the rain comes, players head up to the clubhouse; some play cards or watch TV. It is hard to keep a mental edge. When the grounds crew takes the tarp off the field, they've got to get themselves back in gear.

I have come to the conclusion that every ballpark should be built like Safeco Field, with a retractable roof. There are no rain delays there, even though it rains a lot in Seattle. You know when you start the game, you are going to be playing at least nine. Even when the roof is closed, it is a beautiful place; the roof covers the field, but you can still see a piece of sky.

Nobody likes a rain delay except the hot dog and beer vendors.

Extra Innings

I hate extra innings. I never liked them as a player, and I like them less as an announcer.

Baseball strategy is built around the nine-inning game, and it can really mess up your plans to go deep into extra innings. Strange things

Remy Says: Watch This

If I Were Commissioner . . .

If they made me commissioner of baseball, I would want to find ways to speed up the game. There is no clock in baseball, which is a great thing, but some games go on and on. It's ridiculous.

Get pitchers to stay on the mound and throw the ball. Don't let hitters leave the batter's box.

Why should a pitching coach be allowed to go out to the mound? Would the hitting coach come out in the middle of an at bat and talk to the batter? No. Would an infield coach go over to chat? No.

I watch the 1978 Red Sox–Yankees playoff game when they show it every once in a while. Ron Guidry gets the ball and he's on the rubber ready to go. Batters never left the box.

TV has something to do with it, with commercial breaks. But if I were commissioner, I would get them out there to make them pitch and make them hit.

I think the idea of instant replay is a good one. In some parks it is tough to make some calls. The umpires are making calls about whether a ball is fair or foul or home runs looking up from the field. That's tough. When we look at the replays, we're looking down from above, and we can slow things down and look at them in detail.

They should have an umpire somewhere with a monitor. When it is necessary, he makes the call. I think it is only fair.

The more I see interleague play the less I like it. It is boring to me. But fans apparently like it, so it is not going to go away.

The other thing that bothers me is having two sets of rules. In the World Series, Colorado came to Boston with their team set up with a bunch of versatile bench players but no regular designated hitter.

They put up a guy as DH and he batted ninth, striking out four times in the game. And then when Boston went to Colorado, they had to sit down one of their better hitters and fielders, Kevin Youkilis, so that they could put David Ortiz into the lineup. So it is not fair for either team.

And again I don't find anything interesting about watching the pitcher hit, even when Daisuke Matsuzaka got an RBI hit in the third game of the World Series.

Good for him. I still don't like it.

happen in extra innings; it seems like everybody is trying to end it with one swing, and it doesn't usually work out that way.

It is mentally and physically draining to play all those innings. On the bench everyone is wondering when the heck somebody will win this thing. It is almost like they are caught by surprise when they do win.

The manager has already played out his plans for a nine-inning game. Extra-inning games can tear down the pitching staff. The manager may have to use a pitcher he wanted to rest, or he might end up using a pitcher for two or three innings when that pitcher is not used to going that long. As a result the team may lose that pitcher for two or three days.

If you look at the bench, it is not always full because a lot of guys are out of the game and have already made their way into the clubhouse. Teams have different rules; some managers let them go in and some don't.

Extra innings also means it becomes a one-run game. If a power hitter is up, everyone is hoping for a home run. If a team gets a man on first, they are probably going to try to bunt him to second. I have seen guys bunt with one out to get a man into scoring position, something you wouldn't ordinarily do.

If the game is at home, it becomes a sudden death situation: one run

Remy Says: Watch This

The Day After the Night Before

As a fan, when you leave the ballpark or turn off the TV at 11:00 p.m., you go home and to bed. But a ballplayer may have physical therapy or other things he needs to do after a game, and it may be midnight or later before he heads home, and then he's still wired. Some guys eat; some stay up watching TV. They may go to bed at 2:00 a.m. and sleep until 10:00 or 11:00 the next morning.

Some managers call off batting practice on a day game, or hitting might be optional. You may not see all of the star players in the lineup because a day game after a night game is the perfect time to give guys a day off. Often the catcher who worked the night before gets to rest.

But when it's crunch time in a tight pennant race, you can expect that all the regulars are on deck.

and it's over. Teams even get that feeling on the road: "If we can score one run, we've got a shot." But when a team gets the lead on the road, there's another problem. In most cases the best pitchers have already been in the game, so the manager may have to try to protect a one-run lead with a guy who wouldn't normally be used in that situation.

The Effect of the Schedule

Players and managers sometimes look with dismay at the upcoming schedule, especially when it includes cross-country trips. There are some road trips that are sure to be tough, with a lot of travel and crazy hours.

In recent years I've seen horrors like this: a night game in Anaheim followed by a flight to Texas for a game the next day. The team loses two hours on the clock as it heads east, getting to the hotel as the sun comes up. *USA Today* is outside the door when the players check into their hotel rooms. After a few hours of fitful sleep, it's off to the ballpark.

Most teams will send the next day's starting pitcher on ahead so that he will get a good night's rest. If they are going to get in at four in the morning, the pitcher is not going to be with them. That way they'll have at least one rested person on the diamond.

One time while I was with the Angels, sending the pitcher ahead didn't help. We were coming from California to New York, and when we got to the hotel, the pitcher who had been sent on ahead was coming in from a night on the town. That didn't go over very well.

The Roar of the Crowd

How can players communicate with each other when there's a wave of noise coming from the stands? The truth is, they don't really hear it. It's crazy, but they are so focused on what they are trying to do that it becomes a buzz. Can it become a problem on a pop-up? Sure it can. One fielder calls for the ball and the other doesn't hear him. They've both got to concentrate. But as far as what they've got to do as fielders, and what their responsibilities are on plays, I don't think the crowd has any effect on that at all.

A good ballplayer can communicate pretty well in any situation. It's like taking signs from the third-base coach. The player should never miss them because he should always know what to look for in a particular situation. For example, if there is a man on first, the batter should be looking for the hit-and-run or the bunt. He's not looking for the squeeze. So he shouldn't miss the sign.

It's the same idea for players on defense. Do they have mental lapses? Sure. But a good player is thinking before the play: "Okay, we've got runners on first and second. The batter could bunt or he could swing away. Here's where I'm going to play and what I'm going to be prepared to do."

On some teams the fielder might look to the dugout, and a coach there would let him know where he should move or what play is on.

Watching the players on the bench

I like to watch players' reactions. That said, you can't always tell how a player is going to behave when he gets back to the dugout. There are certain guys who never change the way they act; they will be the same whether they got a hit or made an out. You will have other guys who just flip out, and you know they are going to be upset when they get back to the bench.

Instead of watching the next batter walk up to the plate, follow the last batter back to the dugout. If the guy is really pissed off, watch as he prances up and down the dugout. And if he does something really dumb, once he walks by, you'll see other guys laughing at him.

You may also learn something by watching where the players sit. Some always seek out a particular seat in the dugout. You might see one guy who always sits at the end of the bench; that's where he is most comfortable. Players not in the game that day are usually more relaxed and may sprawl on the steps.

When pitchers come off the mound, some will go to the far end of the dugout to be as far away as they can from the pitching coach or the manager, while other guys will go and sit right next to their coach and the catcher.

Catchers generally stay near the manager and coaches and are usually constantly discussing the game. Depending on what happened in the last half-inning, a coach might ask the catcher what pitch was thrown, why was it thrown to a particular location, or why the pitcher had shaken off a call.

Root, root, root for the home team

I'd rather hear 35,000 happy, buzzing fans than be in front of 5,000 people after a rain delay, drunk and screaming at me after I've struck out. You can hear every one of them.

There may be some leather lung in the stands, and every time you move or do something wrong, this guy is all over you. You saw him last week, and he was doing the same thing. It gets personal sometimes. Ballplayers are not always the most mature people, and sometimes you say something back and it becomes ugly.

There were some places we would go to as players where the crowd was really raucous, like Yankee Stadium. Actually, it was fun to go to New York and have those people get on us. You don't expect the people on the road to like you. You want them to get on you. At least you're recognized.

It's harder at home when people yell at you. This is your house; these are your fans. It takes a strong guy to ignore it. There are some guys who can't adjust to it. I've known guys who were so intimidated at Fenway Park that they had a hard time playing there.

Wives, family, and friends

I hated it when my parents were at the ballpark. I knew they were in the family section, but I didn't know who was five rows behind them. It could have been some jerk who just couldn't stand me, and he was just going to eat me up the whole game.

Remy Says: Watch This

Standing at the Plate

If you are a guy who hits forty or fifty home runs a year, you're allowed to stand at home plate and admire the flight of the ball. But some clown who hits four a year and flips the bat looks ridiculous. That's the kind of stuff that drives me crazy.

Like Jim Brown used to say about celebrations after touchdowns: Act like you've been there before.

Or if I made an error, the next time I came to the plate, I would get booed, and nobody wants his family to hear that. I think the players' wives become more immune to that because many of them are there all the time. They know it is part of the business.

And finally, there is nothing more embarrassing than making an error. Everybody is watching you, and you make a horrible play; it's not a good feeling. I guess my all-time most embarrassing moment was when I made two errors on two consecutive balls while playing for Anaheim. Some friends of mine from Somerset had come out to California on a visit, and they had great seats in the front row.

There were back-to-back balls hit right to me, and they both went right between my legs. Even our own fans were booing me; they were all over me. I didn't make another error for the rest of the day, but I knew I didn't want another ball hit to me for a while.

Putting on the Game Face

It used to be that when someone hit a home run, he came across home plate, took congratulations from the guy on deck, and went into the dugout. That was it. No tipping the cap; no curtain call. Ballplayers rarely showed any emotion on the field; you didn't see guys hit a home run and then pump their fist as they circled the bases.

One of the unwritten rules was to never show up the pitcher; players knew if they did, the next time they got up to the plate, they'd get drilled.

Players today show more emotion. It is not as splashy as basketball when a guy dunks, or the celebration in the end zone when a football player scores a touchdown. Traditionalists don't like it. But baseball is entertainment, and people seem to like it.

When David Ortiz or Manny Ramírez launch one, they don't show up the pitcher—but they do sometimes take a moment to admire their work. Lately, Manny has taken to holding up his arms like a football ref signaling a touchdown; it's just Manny being . . . Manny.

And then there are players who operate on a completely different plane. From the day Rickey Henderson came into baseball, people called him a hot dog. He did everything with style. I am sure he took a lot of abuse for that early in his career. But Henderson acted the same throughout his whole career. That's Rickey's game, and unless he unretires again (and that's not out of the realm of possibility), he will be eligible for election to the Hall of Fame in 2009 or 2010 and he's going to get in.

Reggie Jackson was another example of a guy who was entertaining to watch. People loved to watch him swing; even when he missed it was exciting.

Another kind of hotdogging are stunts that seems to come up every ten years or so: Some outfielder comes in to pitch an inning or some player wants to get into his team's record book by playing every position in a game or a season.

José Canseco, who was a bit flamboyant, almost ruined his career in 1993 when he was playing for the Texas Rangers against the Red Sox. Texas was getting creamed by Boston and they were out of relievers, so Canseco came in to pitch the ninth inning. He ended up tearing a ligament in his right elbow and a month later had to have surgery and was out for the rest of the season.

After the at bat

We know that even the best batters make an out somewhere between six and seven times out of every ten at bats. Some hitters just jog back to the dugout and take their seat; others may throw their helmet or commit assault and battery on the watercooler.

A batter gets upset when he strikes out by swinging at a bad pitch. The pitcher didn't do it, and the fielders didn't make a great play; he got himself out. It's especially galling if he had a chance to drive in a run.

Looking at some players, you couldn't tell whether they were 4 for 4 or 0 for 4 in a game with four strikeouts. That's just their makeup. Freddie Lynn was a great player who was laid-back and relaxed; it's the same thing with Manny Ramírez. On today's Red Sox, you can watch the face of Kevin Youkilis to see how he feels about his last at bat. It would be nice to think that everybody remembers the baseball season is 162 games long, that an everyday player is going to get at least 500 at bats, and that athletes can take failure in stride. But for most players, it's not that way; it's life and death with every at bat.

Managers have to be careful in handling their players. Just because one player shows his emotions, that doesn't mean he cares more than the

Remy Says: Watch This

The Warning Sign

These days, after a retaliation, you'll see the umpires warning both benches to put an end to this stuff. If the umpire feels a pitcher is purposely throwing at somebody after that, the player and his manager are tossed out of the game.

If you're watching from the stands and you see the umpire hold up the game and point to both dugouts, that means they have been warned. What he is trying to do is take control of the situation before anything else develops. If there was an incident the day before, sometimes the umpires will warn the managers before the start of the next game.

other guy. It doesn't take long for a manager to get to know his team. He sees them in battle every day and sees how they react to events.

As a manager or a teammate, it's not a great idea to go up to some players and say, "How the hell could you swing at that pitch?" You might end up getting knocked out. You let a teammate cool off and talk to him later. But other guys don't mind talking. Players on the bench might be in conversation with a teammate and talk in great detail about what the pitcher is throwing, and it will help them when they go up to bat themselves.

The same thing goes for hitting coaches. They're not likely to go up to a batter immediately after the batter makes an out to remind him that he wasn't supposed to swing at a certain pitch. They know that the player is not intentionally going after bad pitches. A good hitting coach has to know when to approach somebody and when to leave him alone.

Brawls

Have you heard the line about a guy who goes to a boxing match and a hockey game breaks out? Brawls are pretty rare in baseball, but a few times each season something happens that pushes a team over the line.

When a pitcher starts head-hunting, you know something is going to happen. It often is a carryover from the night before. Let's say a hitter had a great night the night before, going 4 for 4, with a couple of home runs. On his first time up the next game, the pitcher knocks him on his butt. That is probably going to draw a retaliation; his team's pitcher will choose someone to knock down himself.

There also may be a personal thing between a hitter and a pitcher that could go back three years, and now it is the right time for the pitcher to drill him. Well, the hitter hasn't forgotten, either, and that may cause a brawl.

And sometimes there are bad feelings that develop between teams, like the unpleasantness between the Red Sox and Tampa Bay a few years ago. Almost anything could set it off. A player may go into second base with cleats high, and other teammates will try to protect their second baseman or shortstop.

If a brawl happens, although it may look like mayhem on the field, there are usually only a few players fighting. There are always some clowns who come charging across the field from the bull pen because they think that is what is expected of them.

Sometimes in the middle of a brawl, other players go in to try to settle an old score with someone not involved in the original fight. They just take advantage of the craziness to get in a shove or a punch.

But most of the guys out there are just trying to keep other people from fighting. And if the star pitcher is involved, he may end up surrounded by teammates who are there to protect him. They are not going to let anybody get to him; he's their bread and butter, and whether they think he is right or wrong, they are going to make it hard for the other team to get to him.

Baseball Superstitions

Like I said before, baseball is a game of habit. Players have the same routine every day: go to the park, take batting practice, take infield practice, and play the game. Somewhere along the way, habits can often become superstitions and compulsions.

Some players will take the same number of swings in batting practice and the same number of ground balls in infield practice. Some guys will run the bases; other guys won't.

Then there's the way they dress. Some players will always put on their right sock first, then their left, or the other way around. Or they will have a favorite uniform for batting practice and another for the game. They'll have a special glove they use. Or they'll insist on wearing a tattered old undershirt all season, or use a batting helmet cruddy with five seasons' accumulation of pine tar.

Then again, if things go badly, they'll switch anything and everything.

When I was going out to the field between innings, I used to have to touch second base. I don't know why I did it, but it had to happen every time, and if somehow I forgot whether I had touched the base, I would run over and touch it again.

There are many players who don't want to step on the line when they take the field and always jump over it. Other guys have to touch the line. Wade Boggs used to go out and run his sprints at 7:17 before a 7:30 game. Not earlier and not later. He would eat chicken for lunch every day.

I have long worried that when some players get out of the game, they're going to have to get treatment for obsessive-compulsive disorders, because without baseball they'll have to find something in the house they've got to do every day.

Breaking up a no-hitter

In May 1976, I was on the other side of a pitching gem. I broke up a no-hitter by Ken Brett of the Chicago White Sox in the ninth inning with two outs. I checked my swing and ended up hitting a slow roller down the third-base line. Jorge Orta put his glove down, but the ball went underneath.

I was stunned when I got to first base and saw that the official scorer had given me a hit. Usually, at that point in a no-hit game, whether it is the visitors or the home team, the scorer is going to give the pitcher the benefit of the doubt.

The score was 0–0 going into the tenth, and Brett came out to pitch that inning, too. I doubt that you'd see that today. He ended up winning the game in the eleventh inning with a two-hitter.

That said, when a player comes up to bat in the ninth inning and the other pitcher is throwing a no-hitter, the batter sure wants to break it up. He has been battling this guy all day, and he is 0 for 3. But you want a solid hit. I would never bunt in that situation to break it up. That would be bad form. But I also didn't go to the official scorer and ask that my hit be scored as an error.

I kidded Brett about that game for years; sadly, he passed away in 2003 after losing a battle with brain cancer.

Rem Dawg Remembers

On the Bench and Field in a No-Hitter

One of the best-known superstitions in baseball comes when a pitcher has a no-hitter going. The players are supposed to leave him alone, or at least never mention the line score of the game.

As announcers, do we tell listeners? I think we have to. People are flipping around the dial and you want to hold them. The announcer could say, "The Angels don't have a hit yet." I don't have a problem with just flat-out saying, "Clay Buchholz has a no-hitter through seven innings." But in the dugout, when it gets to that point, you don't mention it. The pitcher knows he has one going, but teammates don't want to jinx him.

A no-hitter is one of the most difficult things to do in sports. Players want to make sure they handle everything cleanly; they don't want to allow an extra guy to come to the plate by making an error. I was on the field behind Nolan Ryan when he threw one of his no-hitters, this one against Baltimore. I can't say it was fun; it was a nerve-racking experience.

The unwritten rules

How much is too much? That was one of things that crossed more than a few minds on the night of June 27, 2003, when the Red Sox drubbed the Florida Marlins by a score of 25–8. In the first inning the Sox scored ten runs before the first out was recorded and fourteen before the third out was made on a close play at the plate.

Among the many great records of that day came when Johnny Damon got three hits in three at bats in that first inning.

But many in baseball were also unhappy later in the game when it seemed to them that the Red Sox were piling on extra runs. Here's another of the unwritten rules of baseball: If you're way out in front, you don't steal bases, you don't swing for the fences on 3–0 counts, and you don't send the runner from third to home on a close play. The way I see it, if you've got to slide at home plate in that sort of a game, you shouldn't be going.

Not everyone agrees with me, but for a century of baseball the unwritten rule was: Win the game, but don't go out of your way to embarrass the other guys. And don't you know it, but the next night the Marlins came back in the ninth inning to deliver a crushing loss to Boston.

I'm sliding on an attempted steal; the play is going to be very close.

Photo courtesy Boston Red Sox

CHAPTER TWENTY-TWO

Slumps, Streaks, and Errors

A Case of the Yips

Sooner or later, every ballplayer gets the *yips*. That's when nothing seems to go right.

A hitter can go to the plate fifteen times in a row and feel on top of the world. Every pitch looks hittable; nothing is too difficult for him to get to. Or he's in a series when he's not seeing great pitching. Every time he swings the bat, he's making good solid contact and getting hits.

All of a sudden, on that sixteenth time at bat, he's out in the Twilight Zone. Now he puts together four or five bad at bats. He may have three line drives in those at bats, but they're right at somebody.

Rem Dawg Remembers

Throwing It Away

Sometimes players get in the habit of making bad throws or develop a phobia about throwing, like what Chuck Knoblauch went through when he was with the Yankees. From the second baseman's normal position to first base is the easiest throw to make in the whole game; it's only about 40 feet. But sometimes that's worse, because the more you think about it, the more the chance you have to make a bad play.

I've seen catchers who couldn't throw the ball back to the pitcher; Mackey Sasser went through that with the Mets.

Who knows why that happens? A player might make one bad throw, it gets in his head, and after that he just anticipates something bad happening every time he throws the ball.

They tell players they're supposed to feel good about it anytime they hit the ball well. Baloney. I wanted hits. I didn't care what those hits looked like. I didn't care if they were bloops or bunts. I just wanted hits.

Hitters can go 4 for 5 without hitting the ball out of the infield and feel like they're on the greatest streak in the world. And they sleep well that night. Or they could hit five hard line drives right at somebody and be 0 for 5 and not sleep a wink.

Breaking the slump

When they try to get out of a slump, most players go back to the basics, working on their mechanics. And for many it finally gets to the point where they say, "Okay, what is my main trigger? What is the *one* thing that I think about to get me going when I'm swinging well?" It could be making sure his shoulder stays in, making sure his head is on the ball, making sure he's lining up back through the middle, or making sure his hands are high. Whatever it is, players usually get down to one basic thing and work on it and eventually come out of it.

But mentally it kills you.

One thing about baseball is that even when things go well, players don't get to enjoy it very long because they're out there every day. A player may have a great night and win the game for the team. But when he wakes up in the morning, he's focused on the next game.

And it is the same with slumps. The days roll one into another. Players get down on themselves and depressed and they get to thinking all kinds of things: "My season's going down the tube. I had a man on second and I couldn't drive him in, and we lost by a run." It just builds and builds and builds.

Through the course of a long season, the best players adjust to those things better than others. A lot of it has to do with personality.

Sports psychologists, hypnotists, and voodoo

One season the Angels were playing horrible baseball, and so management brought a hypnotist into the clubhouse. In those days that was the cutting edge. He was giving us this stuff about positive thinking and getting negative thoughts out of our minds. Almost all of the guys were rolling their eyes and poking each other in the ribs.

"I like radio better than television because if you make a mistake on radio, they don't know. You can make up anything on the radio."

FORMER YANKEE SHORTSTOP AND
BROADCASTER PHIL RIZZUTO

All of a sudden Frank Tanana is standing up and the hypnotist is telling him, "Walk here, walk there," and he was doing it. Tanana was a great pitcher, but he used to like to have fun. To this day, I don't know if Tanana was faking it or if he was for real.

Looking back, I guess we should feel bad for the poor guy who came in to help us. I imagine he was used to working with people who were serious and looking for help, and there he is with a bunch of people who are saying to themselves, "What are we doing here?"

I remember walking out of the place, and everybody was just shaking their heads.

We went out and got killed again that night.

What Causes Errors?

There are many reasons why good fielders make errors: bad mechanics, bad hops, and bad reads on a ground ball or fly ball, among them. Players sometimes go through stretches where mechanically they feel they are doing everything right, but it seems as if every hop they get is a bad one. Sometimes the things that go wrong are so minor that players don't even know the cause.

I know that some coaches say they want players who would like to have the ball hit to them on every play. Maybe there are those guys, but I think there are more guys who say, "I'll take it if it comes to me, but I'd prefer it to go somewhere else right now."

Defensive slumps

Ballplayers compete nearly every day. It's not like football where they play a game on Sunday and then they have five days to correct whatever problem they had in that one game.

When a hitter goes into a slump, he may go 0 for 20, which sounds bad, but that's really only four games. And the same sort of thing can happen defensively. There can be a stretch of a few games where the ball is just eating up a fielder; it seems as if he's always out of position to make the plays, and that when he is in the right place, he gets a bad bounce and it hits the heel of his glove.

Hitting Streaks

When a batter is hitting very well, players sometimes say he is "in the zone" or "in the groove." It could end with the next at bat, but for the moment everything seems to be working the proper way. He is staying back on the ball, he is soft on his feet, his eyes aren't jumping, his swing is perfect, and he is not getting any nasty pitches. It seems like every pitch is down the middle of the plate, and the ball looks the size of a basketball.

That is heaven, what hitters dream about. Players who bat .350, hit 40

Remy Says: Watch This

Hands-Down and Backs Up

One of the crazy things about baseball is that you can't play if your hands are messed up. Football players will laugh at you; they play with broken arms. But so much of baseball involves the hands that any kind of injury to the wrist, hand, or fingers is a devastating injury for a baseball player. He can't throw, catch, or swing a bat.

Players like Derek Jeter who tend to lean into the strike zone get plunked on the hands often; more and more guys, including Jeter, are wearing another piece of body armor on the backs of their hands.

Finally, there's nothing worse than trying to do anything with a bad back; just think about swinging a bat and playing a base in pain.

"Remy is very dedicated and reminds me a lot of Pete Rose in that he's hustling all the time. He loves to play. As a matter of fact, he's the first one at the park. He gets there before anyone else."

CALIFORNIA ANGELS COACH JIMMIE REESE, 1976

home runs, and drive in 100 runs have to feel that way a lot more than I ever did.

My big days

On May 12, 1979, I went 5 for 5 in a game at Fenway against the Oakland Athletics, four singles and a double. The starting pitcher was Rick Langford, and he was someone against whom I had a lot of luck. I remember one time I bunted on him for a base hit and he got really ticked off. And I guess he was still frustrated because he never managed to pitch very well to me.

There are certain guys whose pitches a hitter sees exceptionally well. There is nothing they throw that makes the hitter feel uncomfortable. The pitcher could be a future Hall of Famer or some guy they just called up from Triple A.

I had good luck against Luis Tiant when he was with the Red Sox and I was with the Angels. He had this big herky-jerky windup, he had chains that you could hear jangling, and he had his wallet and his keys in his pocket. And yet for some reason, his ball looked good to me. I also faced lousy pitchers, guys other batters were just pounding the stuffing out of, and I couldn't hit them.

One Boston and American League record I share is hitting six singles in one game. The game, at Fenway against Seattle, began on September 3, 1981, and went nineteen innings before it was suspended at 1:00 a.m. Then we came back the next night to resume the game. I got my sixth hit in the bottom of the twentieth inning, with a man on first, and I was left standing on second base with the game-winning run when the last out was made. Six hours of baseball, I go 6 for 10, and we lost 8–7.

In 2003 my record got company: Nomar Garciaparra had six singles in six at bats plus a walk in a disastrous thirteen-inning loss at Philadelphia.

Injuries Come to Us All

Once a player gets established in the major leagues, unless he gets injured, batting averages are usually pretty stable from year to year throughout the prime of his career.

If a player is a career .290 hitter, most years his batting average will be right in that range. The occasional off-season is usually due to injuries or personal problems. You almost never see a complete drop-off unless the guy is at the tail end of his career and he is just gone—he's slowed up and he can't physically do what he used to do.

Midseason rehab

One recent trend, and I think it's a good one, is sending major leaguers down to the minors for rehabilitation from injury. A player hurt in the middle of the season and out of the lineup for a month doesn't have the benefit of spring training when he returns. And his team may be fighting for a spot in the playoffs and not too happy about putting someone in the lineup who is not playing to the best of his ability.

If that player goes down to the minors, he can take at bats against live pitching and in game situations. It is not going to be the same quality of pitching he sees at the big league level, but it helps a lot. And when he plays in the minors, the games don't mean anything—to him—and the stats are not going to end up on his baseball card. That takes a lot of pressure off.

My bum knee

As I've already noted, I originally hurt my knee sliding into home plate in 1979 at Yankee Stadium when I tried to score from third on a short pop-up.

I never should have gone, and I ended up catching my spikes as I tried to slide into home plate. I only played in seven more games for the rest of

"Does Cal know?"

RYAN MINOR, BALTIMORE ORIOLES THIRD BASEMAN IN 1998, AFTER BEING TOLD HE WOULD START IN PLACE OF CAL RIPKEN JR., THE FIRST TIME RIPKEN HAD MISSED A GAME IN 2,632 CONSECUTIVE OUTINGS

the season. And though I had averaged thirty-five stolen bases in my first four seasons, the most I would get in the rest of my career was sixteen.

It was a major concern for me because I injured my left knee, the one that is always exposed to the runner coming in on a play at second base.

As my career went on—and with each operation I had on the knee—I was more concerned and probably not fundamentally as good as I should have been at making double plays. I became protective, getting that knee out of there. I would find myself throwing off one leg instead of nicely planting myself and making a good throw. For example, I might lean on my back leg, get my left leg out of the way, and make a sidearm throw. It's not something you plan on doing, but you know that one more blow to the knee puts you back in the operating room, having it worked on again.

I've had ten operations on my knee and one on my back. I used to love to play tennis, but I can't do that anymore. Even golf bothers me. I can still jog straight and slow; the side-to-side stuff I can't do. I'm not going to get anywhere very quickly. Now my goal is to have an injury-free off-season.

Way back when, as a member of the Twin Falls Cowboys in Idaho, part of the Rookie League.

Photo courtesy Boston Red Sox

CHAPTER TWENTY-THREE

Coming Up to the Bigs

A Rookie's First At Bat

Pay attention the next time you see a rookie taking his first at bat in the major leagues. This is it: He is in the Show.

If he is anything like I was, his knees are shaking. He might be facing a pitcher he has watched on TV for the last four years, and all of a sudden there he is, 60 feet 6 inches away.

Getting a major league uniform and putting it on for the first time is a pretty awesome experience. The rookie is the story of the day for the sportswriters, and they're all going to ask him the same question: How does it feel to be here?

The Role of the Minor Leagues

From the point of view of major league organizations, the purpose of the minor leagues is player development. The teams down there try to win games, of course, but if the major league team needs help because of injuries or problems, it can promote the best players in Triple A to the big club overnight.

Players do not always make their way through the minors in a step-by-step fashion, from high school or college to a rookie league and then A, Double A, and Triple A leagues. A guy out of college, a high draft choice, may start in Double A baseball. A kid out of high school may begin in a rookie league.

At the rookie league level, the kids have to be taught everything. A lot of the players are from other countries, and in addition to baseball, they have to be taught how to live here and learn the language.

I think a player who can make it to Double A ball has a legitimate shot at getting to the major leagues, sometimes without spending time at Triple A. The scouts and coaches at minor league levels can pretty quickly recognize the proper level for a young player.

At the Triple A level, you see veteran players who have spent time in the big leagues and hope for another shot, and solid but unspectacular utility players stockpiled by major league teams as insurance in case one of their regulars goes down with an injury.

Players the organization thinks are two or three years away from being major contributors at the major league level are often at Double A.

Moving through the minors

Teams generally expect their high draft choices to speed through the minors. And in today's game pitchers who have any ability at all are likely to rise even faster.

Years ago almost every player spent four or five years in the minor leagues to ensure that when he got to the big leagues, he was prepared to play. But today the huge sums of money clubs give to their best prospects pushes them through much more quickly. If the organization gave a prospect a ton of money, it wants to move him up to the major leagues fast.

Rem Dawg Remembers

A Career Begins

I love to see guys get a hit their first time up because I know how much pressure that takes off their shoulders. One of the coaches will usually ask an umpire for the ball, and it will be kept in the dugout. The kid will write on the ball that it was his first major league hit, and it will be something he will have his whole life.

I still have the baseball from my first hit in 1975. I wrote the date and the pitcher; I left off the fact that I got picked off base. I put that on my shoes.

"I think about baseball when I wake up in the morning. I think about it all day and I dream about it at night. The only time I don't think about it is when I'm playing it."

RED SOX GREAT CARL YASTRZEMSKI

The chances of making it to the major leagues are also improved if the player is coming to a weak team. A good club may try to filter in one or two new guys each year. Teams that aren't very good rush their players more.

When it comes to pitching, nearly every major league team is always looking to improve. Every year we go to spring training and look at the press guides and see young pitchers who have been in the minor leagues for just one or two years. That's practically nothing when it comes to baseball experience, and here they are getting a crack at the major league team.

Predicting success

Teams are always looking for players with the "five tools": hit for average, hit for power, blazing speed, exceptional fielding, and strong throwing ability. If a player has all five at the Triple A level, he is probably going to be a pretty good big league player.

A player's stats in the minor leagues give some idea of his likely numbers in the big leagues, but there is no certainty. There have been many players who come up from a great career in the minors and end up as total disasters in the big leagues. And there are players who make it to the majors and turn out to be much better hitters than their minor league record indicated.

In 2007 Dustin Pedroia was given the chance to be the Red Sox starting second baseman on the basis of his success in the minor leagues and his history as a star at Arizona State. Playing college ball in 2003, he batted .404 across sixty-eight games. Once he signed with Boston, he moved rapidly through the minor leagues, batting .308 for his minor league career.

As a starter for the Red Sox, he struggled for the first few months of the season, but you've got to give Red Sox management and coaches credit for sticking with him; he went on to post a very solid rookie year, batting .317 with 57 RBIs and 8 home runs.

Jacoby Ellsbury put up similar numbers as a minor leaguer and performed very well as a late season call-up and then in the postseason in 2007. He shows great promise as a speedy outfielder who can hit for average.

Teams depend a great deal on the expert advice given by their scouts and coaches. A good scout can look at a young man and project a year or two ahead to his likely capability.

Let's say there's a hitter at Double A who is leading the league in batting average and has hit twenty home runs. Good scouts and coaches know if this guy is a good hitter or not. He may be facing weak competition in the minor leagues, but he may have a beautiful swing. Or his batting skills will not match up well against a major league curveball.

That's what makes a good organization: scouting, smart draft choices, and the development of the players they have under contract. When all of the scouts for all of the teams decide a player is not major league material, it's probably not a mistake.

And when young players get to the big league level, there are many other factors that help—or hurt—them. The lighting is better for night games, which may help them as hitters. On the other hand, the pitchers are much better, and so is the defense. A ball that would have fallen for a triple in the minor leagues is going to be caught by a major leaguer.

Life in the Minors

Each time a player moves up a level in the minors, his lifestyle improves—a little. There's a major improvement in the jump from Double A to Triple A because making that move is pretty much the end of six-hour bus trips from city to city.

Triple A is pretty good nowadays. Under the latest collective bargaining agreement, a player who signs a contract with a major league team

Remy Says: Watch This

Watered Down

An unfortunate side effect of quickly promoting the better pitchers to the majors is that minor league hitters end up facing less-substantial pitching than they'll see in the big leagues.

received a minimum of $30,000 in his first year in the minors, with his salary doubling if he signs a second contract or if he plays at least one game in the major leagues.

Some of the low minors, though, are not part of a major league organization and there the money may be very thin. But coming to the big leagues is a whole different story. You play in the best stadiums, on perfect fields, and under great lighting. Someone picks up your luggage and delivers it to your room when you're on the road. The team bus drives right onto the tarmac at the airport to get you to the chartered plane. And you get enough meal money to eat very well.

The minimum salary for a major league player in 2008 is $390,000, plus first-class airline travel and hotels and an $85 per day meal and tip allowance. That's why they call it the big leagues.

Stuck in the minors

Sometimes you have to wonder which is worse, having the lowest batting average in the majors or being the batting champion of Triple A. Actually neither is bad because you will get attention from one major league club or another. What's worse is being a lousy hitter in the minors.

Then there are players who set batting records in the top minors and stay there; they're sometimes called Four A players because they find themselves somewhere between Triple A and the major leagues. They get stuck in the upper minors because they may have home-run power but can't do anything else. They might not be able to run or are weak fielders. They don't quite have the skills to get up to the majors or to stay there.

That's got to be frustrating. They know they are not going to be great players in the big leagues. They're making a decent living at the minor

Remy's Top Dawgs

Wade Boggs was a guy who had been in the minor leagues for a long time, and when he came up to the Red Sox, we thought other teams would find a way to get him out. They never did, and he had a fantastic career as a batter.

What impressed me most about Boggs was that he became a good defensive third baseman; he was not one when he came to the majors. He spent as much time and effort on making himself a better third baseman as he did on hitting. I give him a lot of credit for that because most guys just want to hit. He took it personally when people didn't think he was a good third baseman, and he got to the point where he won a Gold Glove.

league level, but they really have to love to play to be down there for years.

Spring training

There's an awful lot going on at spring training besides major leaguers getting into shape for the coming season. Teams bring to camp their best prospects from Triple A, Double A, and sometimes lower.

The major league manager and front office may be seeing a young player for the first time. This kid may not be ready for the big leagues, but early in the spring, he may get more playing time than the regular players. Veterans may take two at bats and then head to the clubhouse or the batting cages; the minor leaguers play the rest of the game. It's hard to judge their skills because they're probably batting against the other team's minor league pitching. Even so, some kid may catch the eye of the manager. He may not be a top prospect in the organization, but the brass may like what it sees.

Still most minor league players know they have no chance for an immediate promotion. They are there for the first couple of weeks, and then they are going to start filtering down to the level where they belong. Every spring there are maybe three or four or five players who are on the bubble—guys who could be called up to the majors or sent down to the minors, depending on the team's needs and a judgment by the managers.

My Road to the Show

I began my minor league career with the Twin Falls (Magic Valley) Cowboys, hitting .308 for the 1971 season. Next stop was Stockton in the California League, batting .265. Then Quad Cities in the Midwest League, batting .335 in 1973.

I made the jump from the minors directly to the opening-day lineup of the Anaheim Angels in 1975. I had a good year at Double A El Paso of the Texas League in 1974, hitting .338 with 34 doubles, and they called me up to Triple A at Salt Lake City in the Pacific Coast League toward the end of the season, where I batted .292 in forty-eight games.

At Salt Lake City I met a guy named Grover Resinger. He told me, "If you come to spring training and play like you have this year, you've got a good chance of making the team." I thought, "Yeah, right."

In the off-season I went down to Mexico to play winter ball. I hated playing down there, but it gave me some good experience.

I was shocked when I got to spring training with the big club in 1975 and saw Resinger in uniform as a coach for Dick Williams, the manager. He had sent word to the brass, and Williams focused on me the whole spring. He liked what he saw, and they were looking to remake the team with some younger players, and that's how I got my crack.

As I look back, I realize I could have gone to spring training and messed up and not have made the team and maybe never gotten another chance. But I got off to a good start, hitting .313. It wasn't until late in the spring that I was told that I was going to make the team and that I

Remy's Top Dawgs

Carl Yastrzemski was one of the players I looked up to as I was coming to the majors, and then I had a chance to play with him at the end of his career. The thing that will always stick out in my mind about Yaz was how passionate he was about hitting. To the day he retired at age forty-four, he could still hit a fastball. He constantly made adjustments to be able to handle that pitch late in his career.

was going to be the starting second baseman on opening day. I couldn't believe it.

I remember I was interviewed by a reporter for the *Los Angeles Herald-Examiner.* I told him: "It's the thrill of my life. In the minor leagues you are so far down you can't even see the big leagues. You wonder if you can make it to Triple A ball. Then you are in the lineup opening day."

The Angels had Denny Doyle at second base, and because I was doing well, that gave them the chance to trade him to Boston, where they really needed a veteran, and he helped the Red Sox win a pennant that year. Ironically, when I was traded to Boston, I ended up replacing Doyle again. He couldn't have been a nicer guy, though.

That's Captain Remy to You

In my third year in the major leagues, at age twenty-four, I was named captain of the Angels by manager Norm Sherry. According to the sportswriters, I was the youngest captain in recent years and maybe the greenest ever. I was honored but not all that comfortable; there were a lot of older and more experienced players in the clubhouse. The opening day roster on that club included Don Baylor, Bobby Bonds, Joe Rudi, and Frank Tanana. Nolan Ryan was in his eleventh year in the majors and already on his way to the Hall of Fame.

But if the manager asks you to be captain, what are you going to do, say no? I looked at the newspaper clippings. "I've been thinking about it for a while," Sherry told the *Herald-Examiner.* "Jerry isn't the star type. He's a tough kid. He plays hard every inning. He's a peppery little guy."

I boldly made a prediction: "It's a real honor," I told the press, "to be captain of a team that probably will be the best in our division in October." As it turned out, we had a lot of injuries that year, and I ended up as the captain of a sinking ship. We finished 74–88, far back in the pack.

I appreciated what Sherry was trying to do, though. I felt like I played hard all the time, ran out every ball, worked hard at batting practice, and was a dirt-dog player. I think I was named by Norm as an example of the way you are supposed to play the game—not because I had the best ability.

The previous captain had been Frank Robinson, who had the job for just a month in 1974 before he was traded. Anyhow, there's probably no need for a captain on a major league team. I think there are guys who lead by example. You could name the best player on your team as captain, but he may not be the guy other players will talk to or who will quietly go to other players and give them a prod.

Maybe it would have been better if it happened later in my career. Fortunately, Anaheim was not a huge media market like Boston, where the captain might have thirty reporters hanging around his locker after a game asking him to speak.

There are no official duties in baseball for the captain. I got to bring the lineup out to home plate every once in a while and do some ceremonial things. Today many teams do not have a captain. The player rep deals with grievances and union matters, and he is chosen by the players and not the manager.

My swan song

My next-to-last game, on May 15, 1984, was Roger Clemens's major league debut. The Red Sox were in Cleveland and Clemens got knocked around, giving up eleven hits in five innings before a crowd of 4,004 people in huge old Cleveland Stadium, where they could fit something like 78,000 fans. I drew a walk, and Glenn Hoffman came in to pinch run for me. My knee was real bad and I couldn't run; Hoffman had some kind of injury, too.

My last game was a few days later at Minnesota, where I came in as a pinch hitter in the seventh inning and flied out to left. We lost the game. I didn't know it was my last game at the time, but I knew I was getting close.

Unfortunately most guys don't know when it is their last at bat. They either leave because of injury or when nobody wants them any more. When Cal Ripken played his last game, it was against the Red Sox, and he ended up left on-deck when the final out was made. The Red Sox got a lot of abuse about that, but the manager wanted to win the game.

On the road with the Red Sox at Safeco Field in Seattle.

Photo by Corey Sandler

CHAPTER TWENTY-FOUR

Lineups, Substitutions, and the Bench

Setting the Lineup

Over more than a century of organized baseball, the basic strategy for constructing a lineup has not changed all that much, except for the addition of the designated hitter in the American League.

There are a number of elements that go into making up the lineup, including the ability to get on base, speed, and power. And many managers like to do things like alternating left-handed and right-handed batters if they have good ones available; that makes it tougher for the opposing manager to make pitching changes late in the game.

Reading the stats

The most basic statistics to watch for a hitter are batting average, home runs, and runs batted in. But they rarely tell the whole story. In today's game many general managers and some coaches are very much into all kinds of other stats, including on-base percentage. Among the latest stats is OPS, which is a combination of on-base percentage and slugging percentage.

Let's define some of the more common statistics:

Batting average (AVG). This is the simplest to measure, calculated by dividing total hits by the number of at bats. A player is not charged with an at bat if he walks or makes a sacrifice hit. So the formula for batting average is AVG = H ÷ AB.

On-base percentage (OBP). OBP is a measure of how often a batter reaches base. It is calculated by totaling hits, walks (BB), and times hit by a pitch (HBP), then dividing by total plate appearances, including at bats, walks, sacrifice flies, and times hit by a pitch. The formula is OBP = (H + BB + HBP) ÷ (AB + BB + SF + HBP).

Slugging percentage (SLG). Slugging percentage is a measure of total offensive production, emphasizing the relative value of extra-base hits over singles. It begins with a calculation of total bases with this formula: TB = 1B + (2 x 2B) + (3 x 3B) + (4 x HR). In this formula 1B means singles; 2B, doubles; and 3B, triples. Then total bases are divided by at bats. Thus, the formula for slugging percentage is SLG = TB ÷ AB.

OPS. OPS is a relatively new way of looking at offensive production; this is a total of on-base percentage and slugging percentage. The formula is OPS = OBP + SLG.

OPS seems to hold up pretty well. The all-time career leader for OPS is a guy by the name of Babe Ruth, with a 1.1636 rating. The single-season record for OPS was set in 2002 by Barry Bonds with a 1.3807 rating, a few ten-thousandths of a percentage above Ruth's one-season best. In 2003 Bonds slipped just a bit to an OPS for the season of 1.278.

Reading the Players

Throughout its history baseball has been a game of statistics, but they are not the whole story. Managers also have to know the individual accomplishments of the players. A player who may deliver a few more home runs, RBIs, and a better on-base percentage may not be as good for the team as a guy with lesser numbers who has the heart of a lion. A manager may rather go to war with that guy than with the big slugger.

Anytime you talk about a great player, you've got to look past his numbers on paper and ask some questions. When do those numbers come? Are they coming at key times in a game? Are they coming in blowouts? Are they coming against lousy teams?

"Jerry was an igniter, which is what you want from a leadoff guy. He knew how to get things going. And he used every ounce in his body to help the team get a win. When he rolled, we rolled."

FORMER RE SOX STAR
OUTFIELDER JIM RICE

Who gets that big hit late in the game when the team is down by a couple of runs? Who is the guy who has great stats but has to take a day or two off each week?

What about the guy whose stats might not be as good but who is going to go out and give everything he has every time he's in the game?

Some players are criticized for having a relatively low on-base percentage, but getting on base might not be their primary role.

The key is to see how to fit a good player into the right spot in the lineup.

The leadoff hitter

The ideal leadoff hitter has good speed and a high on-base percentage. That usually means a player who can hit well, bunt, earn a walk, take lots of pitches, and run once he's on base.

Teams love a leadoff hitter with a high on-base percentage because he is likely to come up to bat five times in the game; managers want their best hitters at the top of the lineup, so those hitters get up as many times in a game as they can.

Second batter

If a manager has a leadoff hitter who regularly gets on base and can run, he wants a number two hitter who is a contact hitter, can bunt, and can work the hit-and-run. A good contact hitter can move the ball the other way, so if there's a runner on second, he can move him over.

Ideal is a guy who is comfortable going to two strikes so that he can give the leadoff hitter a chance to steal.

Third batter

Teams may bat their best overall hitter third; on the Red Sox in recent years that spot has belonged to David Ortiz. Like the first two batters, he should be expected to get on base in front of the power guys behind him. But he also should be able to drive in some runs.

Sometimes it comes down to how a player is hitting at the moment. If a strong hitter is struggling for a while as the cleanup hitter, the manager may move him up to bat third. When he gets hot again, he may move back to fourth in the lineup.

Cleanup

The fourth man in the batting order, the cleanup hitter, is supposed to clean the bases. This is usually the place for the most reliable run producer, someone who drives in a lot of runs.

An RBI leader usually—but not always—has a pretty good batting average and good power. At his peak Manny Ramírez is among the best. In 2007 Manny battled some injuries; he managed to turn himself around and start banging the ball just when it counted—at the end of the season and into and through the World Series.

Fifth batter

The fifth man in the lineup is just a tad below the cleanup man as a hitter. He may not maintain as high a batting average, but he may hit with more power.

One of his most important roles is as protection for the number four hitter; having a strong hitter in the fifth slot may convince the other manager not to intentionally walk or pitch around the cleanup hitter. Mike Lowell filled this role with great skill in 2007, leading the team in RBIs.

Sixth through ninth batters

In general, production slips a little bit as you go down the batting order. But the sixth hitter should still be a guy who can do damage with one swing of the bat.

I don't want to degrade guys hitting seventh and eighth, but let's face it: If they were better hitters, they would be hitting at the top of the lineup.

Now here comes a difference between the leagues: In the National League the eighth batter is probably not a great hitter, but he might lead the team in intentional walks, because the other team will often walk him to get to the pitcher if it makes sense in the game situation.

In the National League, the ninth position is usually held by the pitcher, and he is generally considered an automatic out. Take a look at the batting averages: Many pitchers are down around .100, meaning they make an out roughly nine out of every ten times they come up to the plate.

When he came to the National League after a long career as an AL manager, Tony La Russa experimented with having the pitcher bat eighth and a better hitter come up ninth. I think what he was trying to do is make his ninth batter like a leadoff hitter, so by the time he got to his power guys—like Mark McGwire at the time—the bases could have a lot of runners on them.

In the American League, with the designated hitter, some managers like to do the same sort of thing, putting someone with a bit of punch and speed in the ninth spot in hopes of setting the table.

162 lineups for 162 games

From the player's point of view, there's a lot to be said for a lineup that remains the same through whole stretches of the season, except for the occasional injury or scheduled day off. That used to be the case with many managers, including Ralph Houk and Don Zimmer; players could walk in and not even have to look at the lineup card.

There is more changing of the lineup now from day to day because there is more data available to managers. They will adjust their lineup based on who is pitching and the success individual players have had against him.

Another reason is the increased use of platooning: sharing one position between two players, usually with one batting against right-handed pitchers and the other against lefties. I've seen situations in which you may have two players for right field, and if you combine their numbers, they are as good or better than an everyday player.

Platooning works when a pair of players has different but complementary strengths or weaknesses against certain types of pitchers. And ideally, they are equally capable on defense. If you have one player who is a complete stiff defensively and he costs you games because of his defense, it is not a platoon situation.

That said, nobody wants to be a platoon player. Pro ballplayers want to be in the game every day.

The Designated Hitter Rule

I like the designated hitter. I always have.

Baseball purists will tell you that there's so much more strategy in the National League where pitchers hit. That's true, but I just don't find it exciting to watch a pitcher come to the plate; even when he gets a hit it doesn't excite me.

The sacrifice play also does not thrill me. You may be down five runs in a game and here is the pitcher up to bat, and all the manager can ask for is a sacrifice.

Pitchers are so valuable, especially in today's game where talent is a bit thin. If I was a manager, I would not want to take a chance with Josh Beckett, Curt Schilling, or Daisuke Matsuzaka being hit by a pitch and losing him for the season.

I think a pitcher is a pitcher. I am not saying that all of them lack the ability to hit, but I don't want to take the risk of having him go to the plate, and I hate the fact that most of them are an automatic out. (And yes, I know Matsuzaka got a key hit in Game 3 of the 2007 World Series. I still would have preferred to have seen David Ortiz as DH and Kevin Youkilis at first base.)

The effect of the DH on brushbacks

One of the arguments against the DH rule is that because the pitcher doesn't come up to bat there is no way to retaliate for a brushback or a beanball. That's a legitimate point.

If a pitcher doesn't have to go to the plate, he may feel free to drill somebody because he knows he won't have to pay the price personally. But on the other hand, one of his teammates may face retribution from the other team's pitcher or an infielder.

In the National League they police themselves a bit more because the pitchers do have to hit. Then again we don't have brawls in baseball every week.

Despite the difference in the rule, there was not that much difference between the two leagues in 2007. For the season Daisuke Matsuzaka led the Boston pitching staff with thirteen hit-batsmen; no one has accused him of being a headhunter—he does pitch inside and nibbles at the plate. The AL leader for the season was Justin Verlander with nineteen plunks. Over in the National League, the top of the list was held by Byung-Hyun Kim of the Florida Marlins, hitting sixteen batters.

The problem with interleague play

A related problem with the DH is the fact that the two leagues operate under different rules. I think that is dumb.

That's one reason I particularly don't like interleague play. Management builds the team to play in their league and division, and then they've got to play eighteen or twenty games against unfamiliar opponents. When an AL team is in an NL ballpark, they've got to take their designated hitter out of the lineup and slap the pitcher in there. If he's been in the American League all his career, he has little or no experience in hitting or bunting at the major league level.

It becomes a joke. You see American League pitchers laugh when they are up to bat, laugh when they strike out, and laugh when they get a hit. I think the American League is at a tremendous disadvantage when that happens.

The other reason I don't like interleague play is that I think it takes something away from the World Series and the All-Star Game. Years ago there was a pride in your league when you went to the All-Star Game. That doesn't mean that the games were always played with 100 percent intensity, but it was the National League against the American League. When I was an All-Star in 1978, I recall the president of the league giving us a speech about how important this was to win for the American League.

It is a little tougher to do that now that everybody is kind of mixed together during the season. But the fans like it. They have responded to it pretty well. They like seeing teams come in that they don't ordinarily see.

The Role of the Bench Player

The ideal utility player is a guy who can play three or more different positions; for example, an infielder who can fill in at shortstop, second, and third. They're not great players with extraordinary range and abilities, though. If they were stars they would be put in the lineup every day. What you are hoping for is a player who will not hurt you defensively; anything they can give you on offense is a plus.

The everyday player is going to remain in shape all season, but the utility player who doesn't play consistently has to work a little bit harder during the pregame to keep his body in shape. It's also hard for him because he doesn't get to see much live pitching. Batting practice is not the same as facing live pitching.

Perhaps the most difficult thing someone on the bench has to deal with is the fact that he's not an everyday player. Anybody worth his salt wants to be in the lineup. They've got to realize that for most of them, they are best off being utility players. It is going to keep them in the big leagues a lot longer than if they were trying to hold down a position every day.

A young kid who comes up from Triple A was probably a starter in the minors, and then in the majors only gets into a few innings per week. The young guy wants to make his mark, to get in the game, show them he can play, and make his money. Going from being an everyday player in the minors to sitting on the bench is hard.

It seems to me that the veteran near the end of his career becomes a better utility player once he accepts the fact that he can't play every day anymore. Alex Cora showed a lot of class as a bench player for Boston in 2007, playing very well at second base or shortstop when needed and contributing some key hits as well. And he never groused about it.

RED SOX

PART NINE

The Bosses

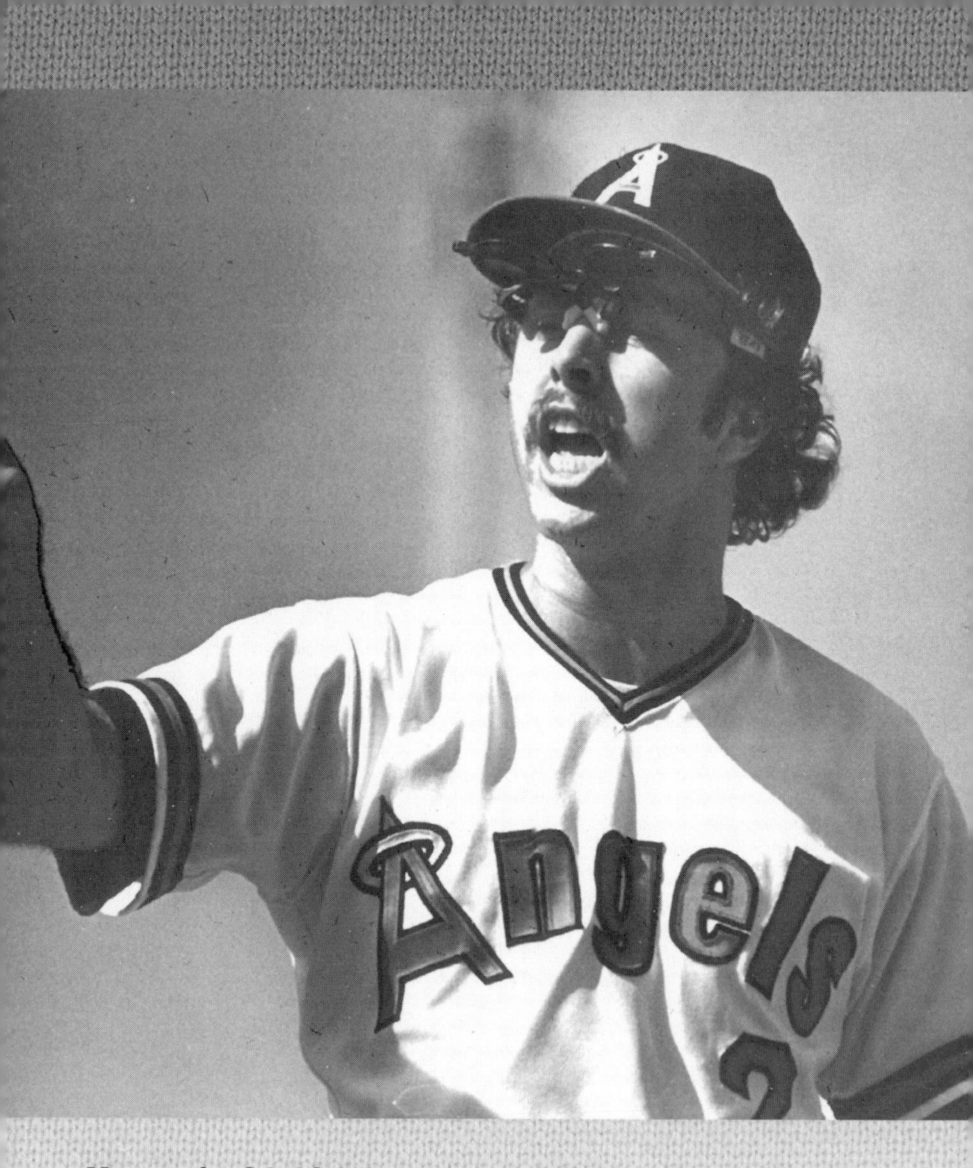

Me arguing? I think I must have been directing an infielder or an outfielder. Yeah, that's my story.

Photo courtesy Los Angeles Angels of Anaheim Baseball Club

CHAPTER TWENTY-FIVE

Managers

My Way or the Highway?

Years ago, managers had much more power. The old-school type of manager used to say, "It's my way or the highway."

Baseball is very different from football. For example, in pro football many contracts aren't guaranteed; if a football player doesn't perform, he's gone. But in baseball, when a player is being paid $20 million a year, the front office expects him to be in the lineup every day. A manager has to have the support of the front office before he can take a high-paid superstar out of the lineup.

Today managers have to learn how to cater to each different personality in the clubhouse: superstars, solid regulars, and bench players. The manager has to develop a relationship with each one of them to get the most out of their personalities and talent.

But the manager still has to maintain some rules that everybody has to live by. Then he hopes the veteran and star players are willing to abide by them, because if they are not, it can be chaos.

Judging the manager

When it comes down to it, the easiest part of the job is managing the game itself. The most difficult thing is dealing with the players and dealing with the media. Managers are constantly second-guessed on moves that they make, especially in major media markets like Boston, New York, Philadelphia, Chicago, and Los Angeles.

What loses managers the most games are poor pitching choices late in the game: staying with a pitcher too long or bringing in a guy who has pitched too much recently. Those decisions are more important than things like whether to position players on the lines in a particular situation or bunt or hit away on offense.

The money factor

Managers are now paid better than they used to be, with several earning a million dollars or more per year, which is a nice piece of change in any situation, but it's still an unusual situation because many of his employees are pulling down three, five, or fifteen times as much. The pay scale in baseball has been way out of whack for a long time. Among the highest-paid managers in baseball: Bobby Cox of the Atlanta Braves, Joe Torre of the Los Angeles Dodgers, Tony La Russa of the Saint Louis Cardinals, and Boston's own Terry Francona.

It's hard to deal with a superstar, but it can be done. The manager has to develop some kind of relationship and hope he can communicate in a way that makes the player respect the boss.

I'm not saying that players walk in and say, "I am making $10 million, and you are only paid half a million, and so I am going to walk all over you." But there is a certain sense of independence for a guy making $10 million a year.

In some ways the situation is similar to that in the world of entertainment, where a big star earns more than management. Baseball is entertainment. When folks buy tickets to a game, they are there to watch Josh Beckett or Daisuke Matsuzaka pitch or Kevin Youkilis play first or David Ortiz or Manny Ramírez come up to bat; they are not paying to see the manager make a pitching change.

But it is the manager who takes the heat when things go wrong. The manager is measured in wins and losses; it's pretty much as simple as that.

Types of Managers

A good manager has to keep a bit of distance. When I was playing, I had managers come into the bar and have a cocktail with me; that was fine. But if the manager gets too chummy with one guy, other players become resentful.

There are all kinds of personalities in a manager's uniform: screamers, player's managers, and disciplinarians.

"I never thought home runs were all that exciting. I still think the triple is the most exciting thing in baseball. To me a triple is like a guy taking the ball on his 1 yard line and running 99 yards for a touchdown."

HALL OF FAMER AND
HOME-RUN KING HANK AARON

I learned long ago that if you scream at your children all the time, they stop listening. The same goes for screamers as managers.

A player's manager really tries to get along with the team. They may have different sets of rules for different members of the team. They try to earn the respect of their players by standing up for them.

When a team with a player's manager doesn't perform well, the front office will often make a change to somebody who is supposed to bring some discipline. It's a never-ending cycle. Owners just hope they catch one personality type that works for a while.

Dick Williams, one of my managers when I was with the Angels, was one of the hardest men in the world to play for. He was a very good baseball guy, but he was very demanding and not afraid to get in your face. But I remember talking to him later in his career when he was with Seattle. He said, "I can't do this anymore, it is not the same. I can't handle myself the way I want and have the same success as I did in the past. It is a different game."

And I know what he meant by that. The change is mostly about money. Managers are not only dealing with the player, they are dealing with the player's agent. And if it is not the manager, then it is the general manager who hears from the agents, and then he gets on the phone.

In his tenure with the Red Sox, Grady Little certainly qualified as a player's manager. He was a quiet, one-on-one type of manager, a laid-back Southern guy. But that didn't mean he didn't burn inside when things went wrong.

Double Bubbles: Terry Francona

There's no arguing with results: two World Series rings in four seasons for Red Sox manager Terry Francona.

There is no question he is a player's manager. He treats them with respect and he has gotten their respect. There are no surprises for the players; they know what to expect. And he is very smart in surrounding himself with very good people like his bench coach Brad Mills and pitching coach John Farrell.

He is a much different guy than when he first got here. In the beginning he was always on edge with the media; success brings confidence.

In 2007 he did a good job adjusting to the type of players he had. He had some guys with speed, so he had them run more. He had a few guys who could hit-and-run, so he called for more of those plays. He called more sacrifices.

Is everybody happy?

Everybody wants to be liked, whether they are a hard-ass or a cream puff. That's very difficult in baseball. There are twenty-five players on the team during the season, and maybe another ten or fifteen move onto the squad for parts of the season because of injuries or trades. The manager can't keep all of them happy. There are only nine or ten starting in a game, and all of the others are not.

Can you imagine going to work each day knowing that some players are really ticked because they haven't been playing and knowing they're going to come in and argue?

And throughout baseball there are certain players who are cancers on a team. There's no point naming names—if you follow baseball, you know the guys I mean. They are never-ending problems in the clubhouse and on the field.

Remember that many players on a major league team are just kids, young adults in their early twenties. They have been playing ball their whole life. A lot of them don't have the skills to be out in the business world and know how to conduct themselves. And then some clown comes into the clubhouse and they are easily misled. It can destroy their career for a couple of years, until that cancer is gone.

A team is together from February 15 until October 1, and with luck a bit longer. That's a long time, and it's every single day with very few days off. They travel on airplanes for long coast-to-coast flights. They are in that same crowded clubhouse day-in and day-out.

There are all sorts of personalities from different parts of the world. There are guys who come from wealthy families and kids who didn't have shoes growing up. Somehow they all have to click together, and the bonding force is the game they play. The one thing they all know is baseball.

There have been clubs that have been successful even though they have had an unhappy clubhouse. The Oakland Athletics back in the 1970s and the Yankees in the 1980s had a lot of trouble between players. And there was a lot more going on that fans never heard about.

Can a team be successful with that kind of environment? Sure. But is it pleasant to be around? No.

Players have a tendency to shut up if the team is winning because they'd look like idiots if they said something was wrong. But once the

Remy Says: Watch This

The Firing Line

In the end a manager is judged by wins and losses. If a player signs a five-year deal, he is not likely to be fired if the team does poorly. But the manager takes wins and losses very seriously, sometimes more seriously than the players.

When things go badly, the firing order usually starts with the manager. The general manager gets a break for a while, but eventually, if the losing keeps up, it's his turn to go.

I thought the treatment of Joe Torre by the Yankees at the end of 2007 was disgusting. Had I been Joe Torre, I would have just left. But I think he wanted them to fire him. Torre was the perfect guy for that job. But perhaps Joe needed a change himself. How much can you take? The Yankees won all those championships and still they expected to win a championship every year. Well that's not going to happen.

How much abuse can you take before saying, "I don't need this."

I always thought that George Steinbrenner was a little bit jealous of Torre because Joe got a lot of credit when they won.

Joe knew the position he was in. He could call his own shots. And he did.

team starts sliding, that's when it all comes out, and then it just steamrolls out of control.

Motivating the team

As I have said this is not football, where the coach gets the whole team fired up before it goes out on the field. But it is important to have a manager who can motivate in all sorts of ways. There are some players who need their rear end kissed, and others who need a kick in the same place.

We always had these speeches at the beginning of spring training, and many of them were silly. The manager would stand up and say something like, "I feel we've got a real good club this year. We've got a chance to do something." As a player, you look around the room and you know if you have a good enough team to go to the World Series. But you get that same speech.

Over the years I've thought about what I would say if I was a manager. I would tell the team:

> I want to get to the World Series, and I want to win it. What I want you to do is go out and have the best possible year that you individually can have. If you do that, we are going to have a good team.
>
> I am the one who's got to worry about the wins and losses. Motivate yourself, be prepared to play every day, and you will reap the rewards through a world championship or a better contract.

Let's face it, baseball is an individual game. A manager can talk all he wants about the World Series, but a player's personal goal is to have his best year ever. And if a few players on the team do just that, together they've got a good chance to win.

Team meetings

There is no such thing as a time-out in baseball. During the game a manager is not going to call a team meeting. There aren't even all that many team meetings in the clubhouse. There may be a "go kick ass" meeting once or twice a year. "You know we are better than this," the manager or one of the coaches will say. "We are as good as the team that's in first place. Let's get our act together."

If a team loses five in a row, a manager might not be able to help himself. He may not be seeing the effort that he wants to see. Players are not running hard. Runners are not trying to take out the second baseman on a double play. He'll have a meeting for a pep talk, or a screaming match, or something in between.

But team meetings are rarely effective. You get more out of individual conversations with players.

What Makes a Good Manager?

It would be easy to sit here and say that catchers, second basemen, or shortstops are particularly well suited to be managers because they are always involved in the game. But I don't think that's true. Much more important is personality. As a manager, can he get along with people? Is he a leader? Can he discipline people the right way?

He's got to be able to communicate with the players and care about them as people. They have feelings. They have families and personal problems.

Can this person deal with newspaper, radio, and television? If he can't handle the media in serious baseball towns like Boston or New York, he'll get crushed no matter how good a manager he is.

A manager who has played in the major leagues commands some immediate respect because players know he has been to war. He understands the ins and outs of being a player and living the big league life. It's very difficult for a guy who never played at a major league level. Players believe that he doesn't understand them because he has never gone 0 for 20 at the plate.

Managing day to day

On a day-to-day basis, the manager's job is centered around making up the lineup. Working with his coaches, he goes over scouting reports and individual matchups of his players against certain pitchers. The manager usually scribbles the lineup on a piece of paper three or four hours before the game and hands it to the bench coach, who will transfer it to the official lineup card given to the umpires; a copy is posted on the wall of the clubhouse.

Many times, though, the manager has to wait and see if players are physically capable that day. A regular may have to go through physical

Remy Says: Watch This

The Right Man for the Job

I think another key to success as a manager is not asking a player to do something he can't do. You don't ask Manny Ramírez to try to sacrifice to move a couple of base runners along. He hasn't done it, and he is not going to do it. (For the record, in Manny's first fifteen years, he came to the plate more than 8,200 times, and he had exactly two sacrifice hits; they both came early in his career. I'm sure there's a story behind each of them.)

You win consistently by not putting players in positions where they are going to fail.

therapy before he knows whether he can play or not. And sometimes a player gets hurt in batting practice or comes to the clubhouse with the flu.

During the game, the most difficult decision is handling the pitching staff. The challenge is to use the right pitcher at the right time, and in the right matchups, especially late in the game.

Other decisions come down to the manager's style. Some guys like to put on the hit-and-run play; others don't. Some managers like to have their players steal. Some build their game around waiting for the three-run homer, while others try to manufacture runs one at a time with bunts, steals, and sacrifices.

From player to manager

Today, when a ballplayer who has been in the majors for a few years retires, he is pretty much set for life. How do you convince this guy to go back to Class A ball and ride buses and make forty grand a year managing rookies? At the minor league level, managers are not doing it for the money because there is little there. It comes down to motivation. How badly do you want to remain in the game? How much do you want to manage?

There are guys who walk away from the game when they retire, and you will never see them again. And then there are former players you'll see at the park every day. They can't get away from it.

In recent years we've had a few broadcasters come down from the booth and go into the dugout as manager. Bob Brenly had a couple of good teams at Arizona. If you've got Randy Johnson and Curt Schilling, that's not a bad place to start your career as a manager. Buck Martinez didn't have the same success in Toronto, but he didn't have the same talent to work with.

Some people in baseball felt it wasn't right for Brenly and Martinez to jump in at the major league level like they did, because they hadn't put in years working as a coach or manager in the minors. Brenly had just one season as a coach for the Giants. But observing the game for a number of years from the broadcast booth, you see a lot more than you would if you were just focusing as a hitting coach on your hitters. And Brenly and Martinez had played in the majors, both primarily as catchers.

And in 2008, Joe Girardi took over as manager of the Yankees. Girardi went from catcher to broadcaster to bench coach to manager (Marlins) to broadcaster and back to manager. He replaced Joe Torre who went from player to manager (Mets and Braves) to broadcaster and back to manager (St. Louis, Yankees, and Dodgers).

Manager Remy

When I finished playing, I worked for a season as a bench coach with the New Britain Red Sox in Connecticut. I went down there when the team was at home. At that time I felt that my future would be to start as a coach and eventually manage somewhere in the minor leagues and then the majors, but it hasn't worked out that way.

I am still doing what I love to do, being around baseball, but I certainly don't have anywhere near the pressure of a manager.

Is managing a goal of mine? Not at this stage of my life. You should never say never to anything, but I can't imagine it ever happening.

As a manager I couldn't go out there and play when the team needs help. I would just have to sit and watch, and I don't think I would do it very well. And knowing my personality, I am not sure I would be cut out for it right now.

Although I'm pretty much an old-fashioned guy when it comes to baseball, I think I could adjust to today's game and players and treat them individually. But I think the focus on wins and losses would just eat me up, because I know how I felt as a player when I was not playing well, and it wasn't pleasant.

Watching a Manager Lose His Job

The 2003 season was very exciting and almost brought the Red Sox into the World Series; there was that little problem in the seventh game of the American League Championship Series when those New York Yankees came back to tie the game against Pedro Martínez in the eighth and win it in extra innings on Aaron Boone's home run. It was also the last Boston game managed by Grady Little.

For most of the season, the Red Sox had been forced to make do without a strong closer. It took a long time for that bull pen to settle down. As a matter of fact, it took until the playoffs. I remember sitting with Little in his office and hearing him say, "Flip a coin. Who do we go to tonight?"

Little had been criticized during the season for not staying with the starters longer. Then finally, in the ALCS, he got into trouble for keeping Martínez in the game when the bull pen was pitching lights out.

Let's imagine the conversation when Little went out to the mound in that inning. Grady asks, "How're you feeling?" And Pedro says, "Fine." That's it.

If you ask a pitcher how he feels and he says, "I'm cooked," he's out. But when a pitcher with Pedro's stature says, "I'm okay," he stays.

What would have happened if Grady had pulled him out and the bull pen had coughed up the game? He would have been criticized for not staying with Pedro.

What would have happened if Pedro had told him he was cooked? Now Martínez is a quitter, right?

There are not many good scenarios here. Pedro was only up to about one hundred pitches when he began the inning, and as I watched that game, my gut feeling was that you could get another inning out of him.

I would have let Pedro come out for the eighth inning and let him try to get through another three outs, but I definitely would have taken him out after he gave up a hit. He was cooked.

Grady Little was not fired for that one incident. If things had worked out and they had won the game and gone to the World Series, he probably would have stayed; but because things didn't work out, Little's decision made it easy for the Red Sox to let him go.

Watching the Umpires

Umpires are trained to get themselves into the best position to make calls on every conceivable play. You probably couldn't find ten people in the stands—unless they're the umpire's family—who watch them that closely, but it's an interesting routine.

The umps have a rotation they go through for every game situation. Everything has got to be covered; if there is a fly ball to the outfield that is not clearly out of the park, or if there is the possibility of fan interference, the umpire has to get out there and see it up close. Umps have to make sure the outfielder catches a ball and doesn't trap it between his glove and the grass. And if one umpire goes out into the outfield to make the call, another ump has to cover for him in the infield.

As far as the quality of umpiring, I think all players will tell you the same thing: They want an honest and consistent effort from the umpires. If they get that, they can live with the occasional bad call. Players, managers, and attentive fans can see the difference between an umpire who is hustling and some hack who is just phoning it in.

You can tell if the home-plate umpire is having a good or bad day by the amount of conversation he has with the catcher and the hitter, and sometimes the pitcher. If you see a lot of long stares by the pitcher, you know he is not happy with the ump. If you see many batters stepping out of the box and questioning the umpire, you know they are not happy with his calls. Or, if you see catchers getting out of their crouch and having conversations with the umpire after a call, you can figure they're not talking about the weather.

Me arguing? Manager Ralph Houk steps between me and the umpire at home plate. First-base coach Tommy Harper has a foot in there, too, and Dwight Evans reaches in from behind.

Photo courtesy Boston Red Sox

CHAPTER TWENTY-SIX

Coaches and Trainers

The Supporting Cast

The manager is in charge of day-to-day operations on the field, but in modern baseball he is by no means alone. Today's Boston Red Sox, as an example, surround the manager with a bench coach, pitching coach, hitting coach, bull pen coach, plus first-base and third-base coaches on the field. Other support staff include a head trainer, assistant trainer, rehabilitation coordinator, and bull pen catcher. In the clubhouse are an equipment manager and staff.

The Bench Coach

Many managers like to have a bench coach beside them in the dugout as another set of eyes and ears, someone they can consult with to kick around some ideas. As slow as the game seems to some people, it speeds up when it comes time to make decisions.

Most bench coaches have had managerial experience at either the minor league or the major league level. Don Zimmer was with Joe Torre on the Yankees for many years and is a great baseball mind; there were times when Zim was responsible for running the offense.

On some teams bench coaches deflect a lot of the petty things that a manager doesn't really need to deal with; players can go to the bench coach with their complaints, and then he can pick the right time to go to the manager and tell him what the player is a little ticked off about. In some ways it's a bit of a good cop–bad cop deal. Even though the bench coach probably feels exactly the same way as the manager, he can tell the player, "Maybe you are right, let me talk to him about this."

Way Off Base

One of the most important moments in the 2007 World Series came late in the second game when bench coach Brad Mills flashed a sign to Jason Varitek; Tek passed along a message to Jonathan Papelbon who promptly picked Matt Halliday off base. Mills had learned something in his preparation for the game, and they executed it perfectly.

Mills knew from scouting reports that when Halliday tried to steal a base he often would do it on the first pitch; he was half way to second base with his lead and Papelbon eliminated the threat.

Mills is a hard worker and he gets along with the players. He is a manager waiting to happen.

The Pitching Coach

The pitching coach is the most important specialist on the team. As I've said before, the game starts with a guy throwing a ball. A good pitching coach not only knows the mechanics of pitching and how to teach, but he also can communicate with his players. When a starting pitcher gets pounded, the pitching coach has to build up his confidence and get him squared away mentally and mechanically before he goes to the mound again.

Pitching coaches are probably more focused on one task than any other coach. They generally don't deal with anything but their pitchers; they pay little or no attention to what hitters or fielders are doing.

Sometimes you'll see a pitcher who's struggling look into the dugout in the middle of the game to catch the eye of the pitching coach. The coach may give the pitcher a signal that says "keep your shoulder in" or "tuck your hands" or whatever they may be working on.

The pitching coach watches the starter on the mound, looking for problems; he will also let the manager know when he thinks it's time to get out the hook. He is the one who has to bring the news when one of the relievers in the bull pen isn't throwing well. He has to monitor how many pitches a reliever made in his last game and how many days in a row he has appeared. He will make the recommendation to the manager about who is available for that day's game and who needs a day off.

Remy Says: Watch This

On the Mound

When the manager or the pitching coach comes out to the mound to make a change, he sticks around until the reliever arrives from the bull pen. What he usually wants to do is remind the new pitcher of the game situation: "You've got guys on first and second, and the batter may be bunting." Or the pitcher may get the word that the manager expects a runner to try to steal a base.

Most managers listen very closely to their pitching coach. They would be foolish not to; the pitching coach knows the pitchers better than anyone. John Farrell is another hard worker, well prepared. You can see the respect the pitchers have for him.

Visits to the mound

One of the protocols of modern baseball is that the first visit to the mound is usually by the pitching coach, and the second is by the manager, coming out to change pitchers. The old baseball saying is: "I am the manager, I make the decisions, and you are out of the game."

There are, though, managers who don't even go out there to say good-bye. It might look like a lack of courage by the manager, but I disagree. The relationship the pitching coach has developed with the pitcher is much stronger than the one the manager has.

The first visit to the mound could have all sorts of purposes. It could be a motivational thing: "You're throwing well. I don't see any problems. They got a couple of cheap hits, so don't worry about it." Or there might be a young pitcher on the mound who has started the game by walking the first guy on four pitches and has thrown balls one and two to the next batter. Here comes the pitching coach just to change the pattern. "Calm down. Focus on throwing strikes, and let your fielders help you out."

The coach might have noticed something in the pitcher's delivery. Or he might visit to talk about a game situation, such as planning for a possible bunt or suicide squeeze.

Rem Dawg Remembers

A Coach Cares

A good coach is a guy who works with you, knows your personality, and knows when to approach you and when to stay away. The best coach I ever played for was Walt Hriniak, when I played for the Red Sox. If you didn't hit, he couldn't sleep. He cared very much.

There are also times when the coach goes out to the mound to delay, giving the reliever in the bull pen a chance to get loose. Many times the manager will signal the catcher or one of the infielders to go to the mound to kill some time. He will get back to his position, and then here comes the pitching coach to kill more time.

In any case pitchers are not fools. They can look behind them and see a reliever warming up in the bull pen.

The Hitting Coach

A hitting coach usually has a particular philosophy. But the problem is that players have a tendency to listen to anybody they think can help them. A player might have a good relationship with the first-base coach and seek his advice instead of that of the hitting coach. He will listen to his brother. His father will call him, and his wife is going to offer an opinion. The guy in the fifth row is going to tell him something, and the parking attendant has a great suggestion.

Even when the hitting coach and the player have a good rapport, it's a tough job. The coach has to deal with mechanics. He's got to know the hitter's strengths and weaknesses, what he does when he is swinging well, and what's wrong when his swing has gone bad. The coach has to know the opposing pitchers, and he's got to review videos with each batter.

And he has to deal with the individual psyches of the hitters, which is probably the most difficult thing to do. There may be one guy the coach can go to after every at bat and another player who had better be left alone until tomorrow.

Much of the work takes place in batting practice. Or a player may want to work one on one with the coach in the afternoon before a night game. The coach has to be there to do that for the player, and he's got to be available to listen to him cry about why he is not hitting.

Judging the hitting coach

You would think hitting coaches could be judged on some very specific bottom lines: the team batting average, on-base percentage, and a few other measures. I have seen hitting coaches fired when all the offensive numbers look good: top five in batting average, second in runs, fourth in on-base percentage. What's wrong with those numbers?

And even if the results are not that good, it is not easy to directly blame the hitting coach. He may be very good at his job, but it is out of his hands once he does the preparation work. He's not going up to the plate—the players are. He may not have much to work with.

But if the relationship between the key players and the hitting coach is not good, he is gone. To be blunt about it: If four or five of the best players complain to the manager about the hitting coach, he will probably lose his job.

Hitting coaches always are sent packing when the team doesn't hit, and they don't get enough credit when it does.

Remy Says: Watch This

Individual Stats in a Team Sport

When a hitter goes in to negotiate his contract or enter into arbitration, he doesn't take the team's wins and losses in there; he takes his batting average and how many runs he drove in. He is not being rewarded based on the team finishing first or finishing fifth. He is rewarded on what he did individually.

The Bull Pen Coach

Bull pen coach is another unusual specialty. He's a guy who is dealing with players who are not involved in the play by play or flow of the game. Most of the men in the bull pen have roles that bring them in late in the game or in particular situations. One of the coach's most important jobs is keeping those guys mentally prepared.

The bull pen coach will bring lineups and the scouting reports with him to the bull pen. Doing so allows him to go over with the setup man the batters he is likely to face when he goes into the game or prepare the closer for the batters due up in the ninth.

"The first guy you are going to see is Jim Thome. What's our plan against Thome? How have you gotten him out in the past?"

He helps warm up pitchers and keeps in constant touch with them. If the call comes to get Corey to loosen up and he throws three pitches and reports that his shoulder doesn't feel right, the coach has to let the manager know right away so they can make other plans. The coach has to be able to know when a pitcher is on and when he is not. He shouldn't be fooled if a pitcher has an injury and wants to pitch anyway.

Remy Says: Watch This

Weight Training

The idea of weight training started about twenty years ago, pretty much toward the end of my career. Today, every team has a conditioning coach and they travel on the road with the team. Everything they do is focused on baseball. Players are not going in lifting weights just to lift weights. There is a purpose for everything.

There are lots of things I wish I had when I played. There's the whole area of video libraries. Batters can go into the clubhouse between at bats and look at what they've got on the pitcher they are going to face. They can see every at bat they have had against him and how he tried to get them out.

The Trainer

The manager will meet with the trainer daily for the update on injuries major and minor. The trainer may see twenty guys a day for one thing or another, whether it is to put on a Band-Aid, tape an ankle, rub down a shoulder, or whatever. He handles immediate injuries. Beyond that, though, the trainer has an unusual relationship with the players. Players spend a lot of time in the trainer's room with whatever injuries they may have. They also go in there for their normal daily routines, which might include things like stretching, applying hot packs, or taking whirlpools. And there is a lot of gabbing that goes on there; a trainer pretty much knows everything that is going on with the club.

Players have to trust that the trainer is not going to go running down to the manager if they are complaining in the trainer's room.

Strength and conditioning coaches

In years past players used spring training to get in shape. There was no such thing as a strength and conditioning coach. All they had was a trainer in the clubhouse, and much of his regimen involved basic things like stretching and postgame whirlpools or ice packs.

Now teams are hiring college-educated physical specialists. They set up nutritional programs for the players. They design workouts and stretching plans. They are also responsible for rehabbing players with injuries and watching their progress very closely. And they set up off-season programs for many players.

From the front office's point of view, the strength and conditioning coaches are responsible for keeping the players healthy and on the field. The quickest way to be out of a job is to have a lot of guys get hurt. And that was just what happened to the specialist hired by the New York Yankees for the 2007 season; as the team stumbled (and players broke down) in the first few months of the season, there were calls for the firing of the manager and the general manager . . . but the fall guy became the strength and conditioning coach.

Rem Dawg Remembers

Intelligence Agents

After a trade, when a team plays against a former player, the third-base coach is going to have to change his signs, because the ex-teammate knows them. When a new player arrives, coaches may ask about the signs on his former team and ask about individual players. A team may hire a catcher and then ask for his ideas on how to pitch to his former teammates. Sometimes it works; sometimes it doesn't.

Drugs in the Dugout

At least now baseball is doing something about abuse of drugs by some players; they ignored it for years and years.

Players are always looking for a competitive edge. If that had come through a needle in my playing days, more guys would have used it. There is no question about that.

I have always said amphetamines were more widely used in baseball than steroids. I wouldn't say it is a bigger problem, but it was more widespread than steroids.

As a sport, baseball wanted to close its eyes because they wanted offense back in the game. Now they've got it and they are paying the price for it. It is sad that a spurt of incredible offense ruined some of the legitimate stats in baseball. But baseball should have done something about it because they knew about it.

I can't blame those who did it because they weren't violating any of the rules of baseball at the time.

Watching the Bench and Coaches

It's fun to keep an eye on the bench. Watch the manager flashing signs to the third-base coach. On some teams someone other than the manager may be relaying the signs; the manager may not be the best one to give the signs because he may be more predictable with his signs than one of the coaches. If the team is worried that someone on the other side is trying to steal the signs, I have seen situations where a coach or even one of the trainers may give the signs.

In any case there are many different ways to disguise the signs. One way is for the manager to give a sign—let's say the bunt—and then put a hold on it. From that point on the batter is not looking for the bunt sign, but instead he is waiting for the hold to be removed.

Out on the field the third-base coach gets the most attention because he is the one relaying the signs. The hitter, the base runner, and the opposition are all focused on him.

There is not much to learn from the first-base coach. When a runner gets on, his conversation is pretty basic. He will make sure the runner knows how many outs there are. He'll remind him about any player on base in front of him—if the guy on second is particularly slow, the coach will remind the runner not to overrun him. And he'll discuss the depth of the outfielders, which can affect baserunning on a hit.

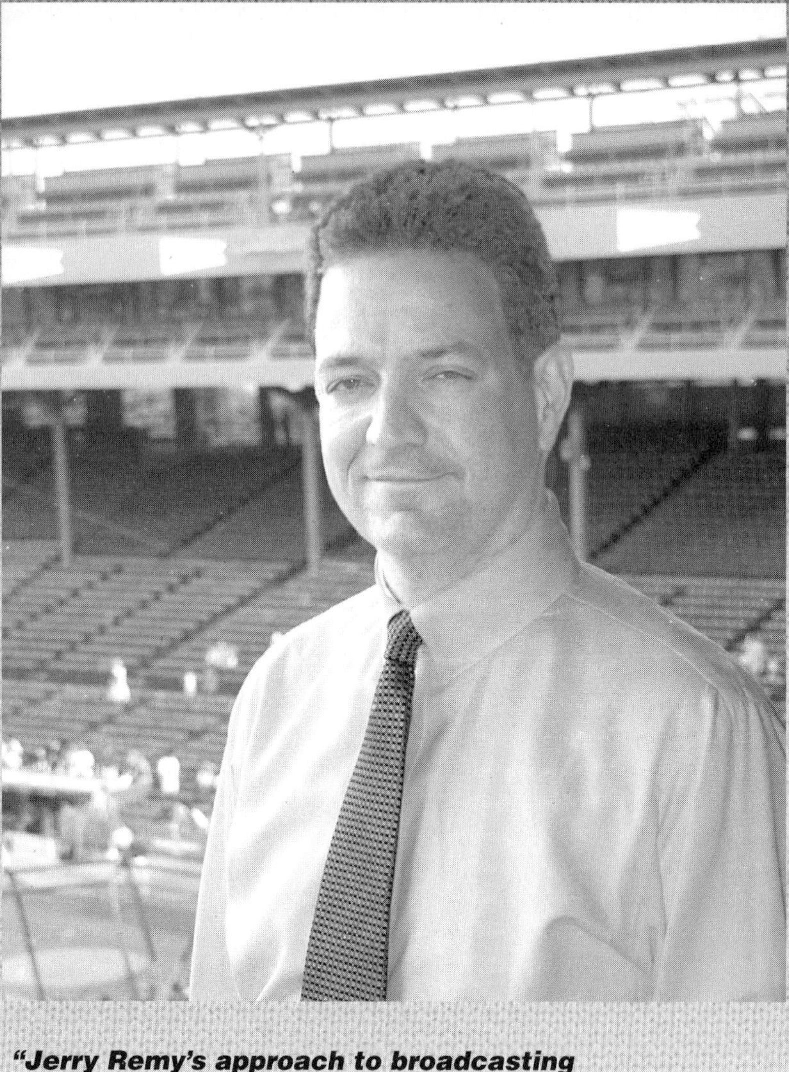

Photo by Corey Sandler

"Jerry Remy's approach to broadcasting is similar to the way he played the game—with great intensity. He's not afraid to be honest, and the players and the fans respect him for that."

SEAN MCGRAIL, PRESIDENT OF NESN

CHAPTER TWENTY-SEVEN

The Front Office

The General Manager

The basic job of the general manager is to put together a baseball team, working within the budget made available by ownership. A good GM has to be skilled at negotiating deals and contracts, including hiring and firing the field manager and coaches.

Today's general manager is more than ever likely to be a young college graduate; many of these GMs have never played the game at the professional level. They rely heavily on numbers and statistics—something I don't always agree with—and try to surround themselves with advisors who have played or been involved in player development, scouting, or coaching.

The field manager looks at his team all the time and thinks about how it can get better. At the end of the season, he might make some suggestions to the front office. And if the general manager and the owners agree, and if there is money available, they may try to follow up on his suggestions. Or they may go down a completely different path.

In the end it is the general manager who has to negotiate the deals and stay on budget.

Money makes the league go round

Of course the general manager's shopping list has to be realistic. A team in Florida might struggle under a budget of $20 million, while the free-spending New York Yankees might have $190 million or so in the kitty for 2007; the Red Sox payroll for the same year was north of $143 million. Thus one team may have difficulty holding on to its stars when it comes time for contract renewal, while another may be able to go out and hire the best available free agents.

If the GM is working with a virtually unlimited budget, his job assignment is to get the best players. He has to convince them that his town is where they should be playing. Actually it's a matter of convincing not only the player but also his family and his agent.

Then there's the GM who has to work with a tight budget. He is not going to get the big-name superstar player; a superstar's salary alone could eat up a quarter or a third of the team's entire budget. Instead this sort of team may rely very heavily on scouts to make good draft picks and on player development staff to teach kids how to play at the major league level.

In general, when you see an organization that has a solid minor league system, you will likely see a general manager who has done a good job; the organization has scouted well, drafted well, and developed its players well, and their homegrown players have had success at the big league level.

Unfortunately, when these good young players get to the big leagues, they're not likely to stay with a club that doesn't have a lot of money to spend on salaries once they have enough seniority to become free agents.

The importance of character

Baseball is a statistical game, but there is more to it than that. As far as I am concerned, it is just as important to know the player as a person. You need to know what this guy brings to the plate other than the numbers. Is he a good citizen? Is he a good presence in the clubhouse? Is he a guy you're going to have to worry about in the community?

Sometimes a second-tier guy may be able to help the team a lot more than a troublesome superstar. You might have a player who put up great numbers last season, but now he's going through a divorce. If he has off-the-field problems, how good is he going to be this year?

Billy Martin once told me that he learned more about his guys when they were struggling than when they were going good. That's when he knew the character of his players.

And there is something to be said about having a general manager who played the game. He knows what it feels like to be in a prolonged slump. He knows what it's like to blow a play with the game on the line. He knows what the clubhouse feels like after a team loses a tough game.

Making trades

Teams don't make trades just to make trades. The best reason to move a player is to do something to improve the club. That could mean plugging a hole in the lineup or the defense or sometimes getting rid of a bad influence in the clubhouse. And, increasingly, trades are made for economic reasons.

Sometimes a team makes a trade when a player is getting to a point in his career when he is going to command more money than the club is willing or able to pay. Or a team may have a good player under contract for another two years, but management is convinced that he will not stay with the organization when he next negotiates a deal. In that sort of a situation, a team may choose to trade him with a few seasons left on his contract in order to get something for him before he walks away. It is probably going to be an unpopular move, but one that makes sense from a business point of view.

Players understand that trades are part of the game, but it is an uncomfortable part. It can be very unsettling to have their names floated around as part of possible trades.

For many players in the prime of their career, life is pretty good. If they're lucky, they enjoy their situation. They love living in the community. Their wife is happy, and the kids are in school and have made friends. They get along with their teammates. They like their manager.

But hanging over it all is the uncertainty of knowing they could be traded. Unless they have a no-trade clause in their contract or a limit on the places to which they can be traded, players can be dealt anywhere at any time. It is not fun for them to pick up the paper and read that they may be involved in a deal.

When I got the call

In my career I was traded only once, from the Angels to the Red Sox in 1978. It was a good trade for me. But if it had never happened, I would have been happy to stay in California. That was the organization I had been with from day one as a professional. I was with guys I had played with in the minor leagues and the big leagues.

When I was traded to Boston, though, I was going to my home team, the club I grew up watching when I was a kid in Somerset, Massachusetts.

The idea of playing at Fenway Park with guys I admired made it a nice trade for me.

When I had traveled to Boston with the Angels for six games a year, the pressure to have a good game was tremendous. In those days not every game was on TV, so my friends and family weren't going to see me play very often; those six games were what they were going to remember.

My trade didn't come out of the blue. In 1977 the Angels had put together what looked to be a real good team but injuries killed us. We had Don Baylor, Joe Rudi, and Nolan Ryan. The team had signed Bobby Grich, an All-Star second baseman, but he was going to play shortstop while I stayed at second. Grich ended up hurting his back and couldn't play short; the Angels wanted to put him back in his natural position at second base. So I became expendable.

I had a pretty good sense something was in the works. I remember there was talk about San Diego, which didn't excite me. And then when it started to heat up with Boston, I was very anxious for it to happen. I had a good relationship with the Angels, and I think they accommodated me by sending me to Boston. The Red Sox were happy because I was a local kid, and I was young and had speed.

I was traded in the off-season, which gave me a couple of months to prepare. A midseason trade is much tougher. It's like living full-time on the road. The player is living out of a suitcase, staying in hotels away and at home. He is put into a situation where he is supposed to be an immediate help; that's why they made the trade. He is trying to impress his new manager, his new teammates, and his new fans.

Sometimes the guy a team traded away was very popular in the clubhouse. But players don't take it out on the new guy coming in; they know he had absolutely nothing to do with the trade. Some of the coaches, though, may ask him about the signs and strategies of his former team.

A New Winning Tradition in Boston

After winning the World Series twice in four years, some people are wondering if the Red Sox have replaced the Yankees as a dynasty in baseball. That's not close to being true, at least not yet. But the Red Sox have become a very, very solid organization. How many repeat winners are there in championships in any sport? Not many. The new owners, of course, deserve some credit for fostering a winning team. From the player's point of view, a good owner is a guy who signs a big check. It's also nice to have a guy who is interested in you as a person, and cares about your family

To the fans, a good owner is a guy who puts a winning team on the field. They wish for owners who have the resources to spend, and spend wisely.

It is hard to find anything negative to say about the new owners of the Red Sox. They came in as outsiders, which is never an easy thing to do in Boston or anywhere else, but they immediately understood the team's history and Fenway Park.

A couple of years ago, all we were talking about was getting a new stadium: Instead, they took a special place and made it better, adding the Green Monster seats and rightfield roof seats, and making lots of other improvements.

PART TEN

In My Humble Opinion

The Red Sox and the Marlins square off in a confrontation after a batter was hit by a pitch near the end of a crazy 25–8 Boston win in 2003. No punches were landed.

Photo by Corey Sandler

CHAPTER TWENTY-EIGHT

2004: The Curse Is Reversed

Duck Boats in the River Charles

At 11:40 p.m., on October 27, 2004, Keith Foulke snared a one-bounce comebacker to the mound. The hands of time seemed to drag as if they were slowed by eighty-six years of frustration. Foulke ran five or six steps to his left and then underhanded the ball—ever so carefully—to Doug Mientkiewicz at first base.

And the 2004 Boston Red Sox were World Series champions.

Three days later, I was on a Duck Boat with the team on an unbelievable parade through Boston. The noise was deafening. It never stopped from the moment we left Fenway all through the streets of Boston. I looked out into the crowd and I saw old ladies and grown men crying. People were yelling "thank you" to us all. I have never experienced anything like that in my life.

And along the way I also saw kids who knew only this team; they didn't know anything about the history since 1918, about the fact that it had taken eighty-six years—entire lives—between World Series wins in Boston. They didn't know about Babe Ruth, Bucky Dent, or Bill Buckner; they didn't know about Ted Williams, Carl Yastrzemski, or Carlton Fisk, either.

There are people here in Boston who thought a celebration like this would never happen. And although every one of the Red Sox players knew it was going to be something special, it was beyond anything they could have ever expected.

But it happened all right. In our lifetime.

The 2004 team will always be remembered. There will be a generation of people who will know every player on this team; they will always remember their names.

Were the Red Sox Cursed?

Bucky Dent in 1978. Bill Buckner in 1986. Grady Little in 2003.

Did it all start in 1920 when Babe Ruth was sold to the Yankees? Was there a curse of the Bambino on the Boston Red Sox?

I never believed in that stuff. In most cases we simply weren't good enough to win, and in other instances things have not gone right. Is that a curse? No.

That said, the way the seventh game of the 2003 American League championship between Boston and New York ended was the greatest heartbreak in the history of the Red Sox.

The Red Sox had that game won and they were going to the World Series.

Remember that in the 1986 World Series, when the Red Sox were one strike away from winning before a ball went between Bill Buckner's legs, it was Game 6. They could have won Game 7.

In 1978 Bucky Dent's home run came in a tiebreaker game to get to the playoffs. And that was a good game; nothing happened in that game that was bad.

From Cursed to First

So how did we get from the most disastrous loss in Red Sox history to Duck Boats in the River Charles in 2004?

After the disaster of Game 7 in 2003, Red Sox ownership decided it had to take the team to another level.

The greatest need was to add a closer and another starter. One month to the day after the end of the 2003 World Series, Red Sox general manager Theo Epstein took Keith Foulke to a basketball game (the New York Knicks against the Boston Celtics, as a matter of fact), trying to acquaint him with the sport culture of the city. Foulke got a huge ovation from the fans at the game, and he hadn't even agreed to pitch here yet.

And then there was Curt Schilling. He had a choice: Boston, New York, Philadelphia, and probably some other teams. I think what the Red

Sox told him was something like: You can go to New York where they have already won the series more than a few times, or you can come to Boston and do something that this place hasn't done in eighty-six years. Schilling accepted that challenge.

It Was the Way They Did It

With their victory in 2004, the Red Sox were freed from their biggest demon, the feeling that they could not get past the Yankees. They are absolutely past that, and mostly because of the way they did it.

Believe me, there were some very long faces around the Red Sox executive offices when they were down 0–3 in the ALCS. Everybody was in disbelief because nobody expected the series to go that way.

They were probably already thinking, "How are we going to handle this?" To be swept away by New York would have thrown a whole season's goodwill out the window. It would have been absolutely crushing because the team was put together to go to that next level. If they had lost in seven games, that might have been a different story, but to be swept would have been shattering.

Then they turned it around. They won the last four against the Yankees and then swept the St. Louis Cardinals in four games in the World Series. To win eight postseason games in a row against the best teams still standing is remarkable; it is hard enough to win eight in a row during the regular season.

But once the Yankee series was over, there was no stopping the Red Sox. Boston's pitching was far superior to that of the Cardinals. St. Louis had a very good offense, but the Red Sox were able to expose a lot of their hitters' weaknesses, which is a credit to the scouting department.

The Red Sox went from trying to figure out "What the heck are we going to do next?" to the greatest victory they ever had, the greatest comeback in the history of baseball.

The comeback erased a lot of things: It erased the Bambino. And we're not going to hear the chants of "1918" at Yankee Stadium. That is all gone.

The Pivot Point

The Red Sox started out strong in 2004 but went into an extended period of .500 ball in midseason, and at one point it looked like they might not even get the wild card playoff spot. What was the pivot point? Was it the fight between Alex Rodríguez and Jason Varitek on July 24, the trade of Nomar Garciaparra a week later, or something else?

The fight may have been a factor. It made a statement that Varitek and the Red Sox were not going to take a backseat to anybody.

The Garciaparra trade was obviously big because it—along with other deals made at the trading deadline—made the Red Sox a much, much deeper team.

One of the things that was killing Boston was that its defense was inconsistent, giving up so many unearned runs. So, they added Doug Mientkiewicz for defense at first base, picked up speed with outfielder Dave Roberts, and got a very steady shortstop in Orlando Cabrera. Then they got Bill Mueller back from knee surgery, and he began to hit.

The way I looked at it, they had played the middle three months of the season like they were running in quicksand. When things came together in a short period of time at the end of July, the team started to play with the confidence that we expected them to show from the beginning of the season.

I really can't say if this team would have been as good at the end of the season with Garciaparra as it was without him. I do know he was not healthy, and the front office was very, very concerned over the fact that the team was going to be in a pennant drive and he was not going to be able to play. So the Red Sox thought they had to make a move. And the fact that Nomar was at the end of his contract played a part. It didn't look like they were going to be able to sign him again.

To me it was like trading Yaz or Jim Rice. Nomar was the most popular Red Sox almost from the first day he came up from the minors. He was never booed. He always hustled and played hard. The people loved him. He was an All-Star player.

I'm sure they were holding their breath in the front office; they weren't quite sure how this was going to play out. But it turned out to be one of the most courageous, gutsy moves that any organization has made.

The team immediately started to play better, so it took pressure off Cabrera. Toward the end of the year, nobody was even talking about Nomar. In some ways it was kind of sad, because he was such a great player for so many years. On the other hand, it just goes to show that all people want is a championship. It doesn't matter how you get there, just get there and win.

Arroyo and A-Rod, Round Two

Bronson Arroyo, who stepped in and did a very solid job as the fifth starter for Boston in 2004, was involved in two of the most memorable moments of the championship season. He's a breaking ball pitcher who fooled a lot of guys with good stuff.

I've already mentioned the July 24 fight between Alex Rodríguez and Jason Varitek—and the rest of the Yankee and Red Sox teams. Arroyo threw the pitch that hit A-Rod. It was an accident, not a purpose pitch. A-Rod had some unpleasant words for Arroyo, and Jason Varitek stepped up to protect his pitcher, and there was yet again a Red Sox–Yankees push-and-shove.

That seemed like ancient history by the night of Game 6 of the ALCS, as the Red Sox were battling back from losing the first three games of the playoff. Arroyo came in to relieve Curt Schilling in the eighth inning with Boston holding on to a thin 4–1 lead. Arroyo gave up a double and a single, and suddenly the Yankees were only down by two runs with A-Rod at the plate.

Arroyo got Rodríguez to bounce a weak grounder to the right of the mound; the pitcher grabbed the ball and ran toward first base. At the last minute, he chose to tag A-Rod instead of stepping on the bag or throwing to an infielder. And A-Rod slapped the ball out of Arroyo's glove.

At first I didn't think there was anything wrong with what A-Rod did. I was trying to figure out the difference between that play up the first-base line and one involving a player trying to knock the ball out of the catcher's glove at home plate.

I searched the rule book to see where it says you can't slap at the ball, and it is not in there. But it is in the umpire's interpretation of the rules, and they ruled A-Rod out and brought Jeter back to first base. The Yankee's rally was over.

A-Rod should have run right through Arroyo and knocked him over. That's what most guys would have done.

The 2004 World Champion Roster

The Boston Red Sox won it all, which is proof enough that it was a fine team. Curt Schilling was every bit as good as advertised, Pedro Martínez had a solid year, and Keith Foulke shut the door almost without exception when games were on the line. And the lineup was one of the best, supported by a strong bench with some key strengths. Let's take a look at some of the key contributions by players who brought the trophy home to Boston.

Curt Schilling, SP

2004 Regular season: W–L 21–6, 3.26 ERA, 226.2 IP, 203 K, 35 BB, 1.06 WHIP

2004 Postseason: W–L 3–1, 3.57 ERA, 16.2 IP, 13 K, 4 BB, 1.08 WHIP

2004 World Series: W–L 1–0, 0.00 ERA, 6.0 IP, 4 K, 1 BB, 0.83 WHIP

Curt Schilling's performance in the season was great, but his pitching in the postseason is a story that will always be remembered in Boston. He had a nagging ankle injury through the second half of the regular season; it became much worse in the ALDS in Anaheim. And then he had a bad start in the opening of the ALCS against the Yankees, and there was some doubt whether he would even be able to pitch again in 2004.

By the sixth game of the ALCS, the guy probably didn't belong on the pitcher's mound, but somehow he was able to go out there and not only pitch, but also pitch well. That's probably the lead story of Boston's championship season, because without him the Red Sox would not have been able to do what they did. They would not have come back.

Schilling's story is going to be up there with guys like Larry Bird coming out of the trainer's room to score some points for the Celtics. Or Kirk Gibson of the Dodgers hobbling up to the plate to pinch-hit a game-winning home run against Oakland's Dennis Eckersley in the 1988 World Series.

Schilling's accomplishment was even greater because he had to pitch most of a game, and not just come up for one at bat. He had to pitch seven innings against the Yankees and then six more against the Cardinals with his ankle sutured together.

Pedro Martínez, SP

2004 Regular season: W–L 16–9, 3.90 ERA, 217.0 IP, 227 K, 61 BB, 1.17 WHIP

2004 Postseason: W–L 2–1, 4.00 ERA, IP, 26 K, 13 BB, 1.33 WHIP

2004 World Series: W–L 1–0, 0.00 ERA, 7.0 IP, 6 K, 2 BB, 0.71 WHIP

For a stretch of time, Pedro Martinez was the best pitcher I have ever seen. He could come out and throw 97 MPH on the first pitch of the game. By 2004 he couldn't do that any more, but he still showed that when he had to, he could get up there—94 or 95 MPH—when he needed it.

Pedro is a very proud man, and sometimes he makes that much too obvious. In September 2004, after a game in which the Yankees finally got to him in the eighth inning to defeat him, Martínez faced the press and let loose with the following: "What can I say? Just tip my hat and call the Yankees my daddy. I can't find a way to beat them at this point. . . . I wish they would disappear and not come back."

He had faced the Yankees so many times over the past few years, and things had not always gone well for him in those games. That was what came out of his mouth, and it became a lightning rod for Yankee fans. He had no secret plan.

But I also think the best game Pedro pitched in his life was against New York in Yankee Stadium. That came on September 10, 1999, when he pitched a one-hitter (giving up a Chili Davis home run) while striking out seventeen Yankees.

Keith Foulke, RP

2004 Regular season: W–L 5–3, 32 saves, 2.17 ERA, 83.0 IP, 79 K, 15 BB, 0.94 WHIP

2004 Postseason: W–L 1–0, 3 saves, 0.64 ERA, 14 IP, 19 K, 8 BB, 1.07 WHIP

2004 World Series: W–L 1–0, 1 save, 1.80 ERA, 5.0 IP, 8 K, 1 BB, 1.00 WHIP

To me Keith Foulke was the MVP of the 2004 postseason. In the Yankee series he pitched in five of the seven games, giving up one hit and zero runs over six innings. In the World Series he threw in all four games, giving up just four hits in five innings and a single run.

For the entire postseason he had an ERA of 0.64, winning one game, saving three, and making appearances in eleven of fourteen games. He gave up a total of seven hits in fourteen innings.

Over the full season he had a few ups and downs, but when it was on the line, he was unhittable. It gave the whole team a level of confidence to know that when the game was close, you could bring in a guy like Foulke and the team was going to win. And that just filters down through the whole team.

Johnny Damon, OF

2004 Regular season: 621 AB, .304 average, 35 doubles, 6 triples, 20 HR, 94 RBI, .380 OBP

2004 Postseason: 71 AB, .268 average, 3 doubles, 1 triple, 3 HR, 9 RBI, .297 OBP

2004 World Series: 21 AB, .286 average, 2 doubles, 1 triple, 1 HR, 2 RBI, .286 OBP

Johnny Damon was the catalyst for the team, and when he didn't hit well, they didn't play well. He had the best year of his career, driving in and scoring runs from start to finish; one of the ways you win pennants is when individual players put up career numbers.

Mark Bellhorn, 2B

2004 Regular season: 523 AB, .264 average, 37 doubles, 3 triples, 17 HR, 82 RBI, .373 OBP

2004 Postseason: 47 AB, .191 average, 3 doubles, 0 triples, 3 HR, 8 RBI, .397 OBP

2004 World Series: 10 AB, .300 average, 1 double, 0 triples, 1 HR, 4 RBI, .563 OBP

Mark Bellhorn put up some of the strangest numbers I have ever seen. I have never seen a guy with so many strikeouts, so many walks, and so many key home runs.

He tried to draw counts in his favor, and when it was, the numbers were remarkable. Bellhorn hit .264 overall, and when he was ahead in the count, he hit .344. Down in the count, he dropped to .159.

Manny Ramírez, OF

2004 World Series MVP

2004 Regular season: 568 AB, .308 average, 44 doubles, 0 triples, 43 HR, 130 RBI, .397 OBP

2004 Postseason: 60 AB, .350 average, 3 doubles, 0 triples, 2 HR, 11 RBI, .423 OBP

2004 World Series: 17 AB, .412 average, 0 doubles, 0 triples, 1 HR, 4 RBI, .412 OBP

In 2004 Manny was pretty much what Manny has been his whole career. You know you are going to get huge numbers out of him offensively. And you know that he is going to do some things that are going to drive you crazy. I think people finally accepted that in Boston. And he was helped out tremendously by having David Ortiz batting behind him.

David Ortiz, DH

2004 American League Championship Series MVP

2004 Regular season: 582 AB, .301 average, 47 doubles, 3 triples, 41 HR, 139 RBI, .380 OBP

2004 Postseason: 55 AB, .268 average, 3 doubles, 1 triple, 5 HR, 19 RBI, .515 OBP

2004 World Series: 13 AB, .308 average, 1 double, 0 triples, 1 HR, 4 RBI, .471 OBP

David Ortiz was the team's most valuable player in its championship year. At the end of 2002, this guy was not an issue in baseball; he came to Boston from Minnesota as a not-much-sought-after free agent.

Fenway Park really works for him. I think it made him a much better player because he realized he could move the ball the other way to left field and do a lot of damage with home runs and balls off the wall.

I have always said left-handed hitters who can go to the opposite field in Boston and have the strength to get the ball off the wall become much better hitters because they stay on the ball longer. He has become one of the biggest threats in the American League.

It seems like everything he does comes at the right time. He wins games, and he has got to be one of the best pickups in the club's history.

Jason Varitek, C

2004 Regular season: 463 AB, .296 average, 30 doubles, 1 triple, 18 HR, 73 RBI, .390 OBP

2004 Postseason: 53 AB, .245 average, 1 double, 1 triple, 3 HR, 11 RBI, .328 OBP

2004 World Series: 13 AB, .154 average, 0 doubles, 1 triple, 0 HR, 2 RBI, .267 OBP

Jason Varitek has become the heart and soul of the team. I have already talked about the preparation he puts in as a catcher and how he is able to put aside his offense and go back to concentrate on defense. It is not easy for anybody, but he does it better than any player I have ever seen.

I look at Varitek and I see what a baseball player should be. He plays his rear end off day in and day out, prepares well for the game, doesn't let one side of the ball affect the other side, and shuts his mouth and does what he is supposed to do.

Trot Nixon, OF

2004 Regular season: 149 AB, .315 average, 9 doubles, 1 triple, 6 HR, 23 RBI, .377 OBP

2004 Postseason: 51 AB, .255 average, 4 doubles, 0 triples, 1 HR, 8 RBI, .296 OBP

2004 World Series: 14 AB, .357 average, 3 doubles, 0 triples, 0 HR, 3 RBI, .400 OBP

Right from the start it was a tough year for Trot Nixon because of injuries; it was very frustrating for him. He appeared in only forty-eight games and got only 149 at bats. But I said during the season: If this guy can get healthy and into the postseason and do some things that are going to help the team, all that will be forgotten. That's exactly what happened.

Kevin Millar, 1B, OF

2004 Regular season: 508 AB, .297 average, 36 doubles, 0 triples, 18 HR, 57 RBI, .383 OBP

2004 Postseason: 42 AB, .238 average, 4 doubles, 0 triples, 1 HR, 6 RBI, .373 OBP

2004 World Series: 8 AB, .125 average, 1 double, 0 triples, 0 HR, 0 RBI, .364 OBP

It is no coincidence that when Kevin Millar got hot, things started to turn around for the team. Here's a guy who provided a lot of offense for Boston in 2003, but then he struggled in the first half of the 2004 season. He had to bounce around from the outfield to first base, which is not easy to do.

Then he opened up his stance, got hot, and stayed hot the rest of the year.

Bill Mueller

2004 Regular season: 399 AB, .283 average, 27 doubles, 1 triple, 12 HR, 57 RBI, .365 OBP

2004 Postseason: 56 AB, .321 average, 3 doubles, 0 triples, 0 HR, 3 RBI, .406 OBP

2004 World Series: 14 AB, .429 average, 2 doubles, 0 triples, 0 HR, 2 RBI, .556 OBP

Having the defending batting champion hitting seventh, eighth, or ninth is huge, because then there is no letup in the lineup.

Bill Mueller did so many things right. When they needed to move a guy over, he moved him over. If you needed a sacrifice fly to bring home a run, he got it done.

He was out of the lineup for the middle third of the season after knee surgery. It is not easy to come back in midseason, but you could see him get better and better as the year went on. In September, in the playoffs, and in the World Series, it was like he had never been injured.

Orlando Cabrera, SS

2004 Regular season (Montreal and Boston): 618 AB, .264 average, 38 doubles, 3 triple, 10 HR, 62 RBI, .306 OBP

2004 Postseason: 59 AB, .288 average, 4 doubles, 0 triples, 0 HR, 11 RBI, .377 OBP

2004 World Series: 17 AB, .235 average, 1 double, 0 triples, 0 HR, 3 RBI, .381 OBP

Cabrera was not a flashy defensive player but a very solid one. He had very good hands and a conventional throwing arm right over the top, and he threw strikes in the infield.

He always seemed to be in the right position and was excellent at turning the double play, just what you would like to have in a shortstop. I am sure that knowing they had a guy out there who was going to catch everything brought confidence to the pitchers.

Doug Mientkiewicz, 1B

2004 Regular season (Minnesota and Boston): 391 AB, .238 average, 24 doubles, 1 triple, 6 HR, 35 RBI, .326 OBP

2004 Postseason: 9 AB, .444 average, 1 double, 0 triples, 0 HR, 1 RBI, .444 OBP

2004 World Series: 1 AB, .000 average, 0 doubles, 0 triples, 0 HR, 0 RBI, .000 OBP

Doug Mientkiewicz was an everyday player who lost his job in Minnesota not because of his ability, but because they wanted to go with a younger player; the Red Sox were fortunate to get him. When he got here, Millar got hot again, and that cut down Mientkiewicz's playing time. But he saved many runs with his defense. It seems like every time he was in a game, he made a big play.

Kevin Youkilis, 3B

2004 Regular season: 528 AB, .260 average, 11 doubles, 0 triples, 7 HR, 35 RBI, .367 OBP

2004 Postseason: 2 AB, .000 average, 0 doubles, 0 triples, 0 HR, 0 RBI, .000 OBP

2004 World Series: Not on roster

Kevin Youkilis did a good job filling in for Mueller when he was hurt, and Youkilis became a very popular player with the fans. He only played sixty-four games at Pawtucket, so he basically made the jump from Double A ball and was thrown into a pressure cooker in Boston on a team that was supposed to win. He fit in well and played a valuable role.

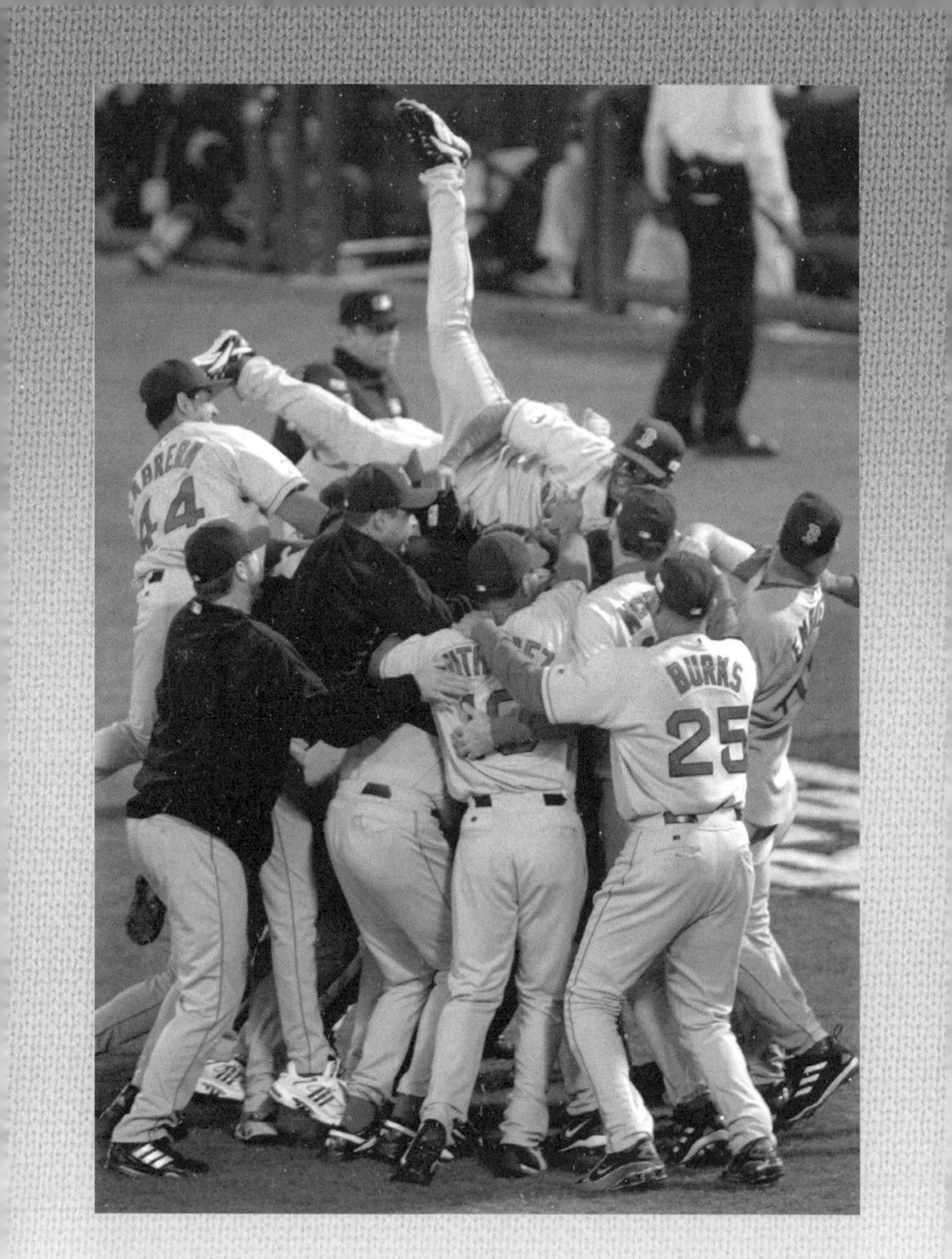

After eighty-six years of futility and near-misses, the Red Sox finally got to celebrate a 2004 World Series win at the end of a four-game sweep of the St. Louis Cardinals.

Photo courtesy AP/Mark Humphrey

CHAPTER TWENTY-NINE

The Championship Season

American League Division Series

ALDS Game 1 at Anaheim October 5, 2004

	Score by innings	R	H	E
BOSTON	100 700 010	9	11	1
Anaheim	000 100 200	3	9	1

PITCHING

	IP	H	R	ER	BB	SO	HR	ERA
BOSTON								
Schilling (W 1–0)	6.2	9	3	2	2	4	2	2.70
Embree	0.1	0	0	0	0	0	0	0.00
Timlin	2.0	0	0	0	0	3	0	0.00
ANAHEIM								
Washburn (L 0–1)	3.1	5	7	3	3	3	1	8.10
Shields	1.2	1	1	1	1	2	1	5.40
Gregg	2.0	3	0	0	1	0	0	0.00
R. Ortiz	2.0	2	2	1	1	1	0	4.50

Manny Ramírez doubled with two outs in the first inning, and the second half of baseball's best one–two punch, David Ortiz, singled him home for the lead. In the fourth inning the Sox broke the game open with seven runs that included home runs by Kevin Millar and Ramírez sandwiched around a two-run error on a Johnny Damon grounder that allowed Jason Varitek and Orlando Cabrera to score.

Meanwhile, Curt Schilling threw 6⅔ strong innings, yielding only two earned runs; Alan Embree and Mike Timlin were untouched in relief. But

Red Sox Nation grew worried when Schilling appeared to aggravate an injury to his ankle in making a fielding play.

ALDS Game 2
at Anaheim
October 6, 2004

	Score by innings	R	H	E
BOSTON	010 002 104	8	12	0
Anaheim	010 020 000	3	7	0

PITCHING

	IP	H	R	ER	BB	SO	HR	ERA
BOSTON								
Martinez (W 1–0)	7.0	6	3	3	2	6	0	3.86
Timlin (H 1)	0.1	1	0	0	0	1	0	0.00
Myers (H 1)	0.1	0	0	0	0	1	0	0.00
Foulke (S 1)	1.1	0	0	0	0	2	0	0.00
ANAHEIM								
Colon	6.0	7	3	3	3	3	1	4.50
Rodriguez (L 0–1)	2.0	2	1	1	2	2	0	4.50
Donnelly	1.0	3	4	4	2	0	0	36.00

Pedro Martínez pitched seven solid innings. He left with a slim 4–3 lead; the bull pen held the Angels in check for the remainder of the game, and the Red Sox tacked on four insurance runs in the top of the ninth to nail down the win. Trot Nixon drove in Manny Ramírez in the ninth inning, and a few batters later, Orlando Cabrera doubled with the bases loaded to score David Ortiz, Gabe Kapler, and Jason Varitek.

ALDS Game 3
at Boston
October 8, 2004

	Score by innings	R	H	E
Anaheim	000 100 500 0	6	8	2
BOSTON	002 310 000 2	8	12	0

(two outs when winning run scored in the tenth)

PITCHING

	IP	H	R	ER	BB	SO	HR	ERA
ANAHEIM								
Escobar	3.1	5	5	3	5	4	0	8.10
Shields	1.1	4	1	1	1	1	0	6.00
Donnelly	2.1	0	0	0	0	5	0	10.80
Rodriguez (L 0–2)	2.2	2	1	1	1	3	0	3.86
Washburn	0.0	1	1	1	0	0	1	10.80
BOSTON								
Arroyo	6.0	3	2	2	2	7	1	3.00
Myers	0.0	0	1	1	1	0	0	27.00
Timlin	0.2	2	3	3	1	1	1	9.00
Embree	0.2	0	0	0	1	0	0	0.00
Foulke	1.2	2	0	0	1	3	0	0.00
Lowe (W 1–0)	1.0	1	0	0	1	0	0	0.00

The Angels came back to tie the game in the top of the seventh inning off starter Bronson Arroyo and relievers Mike Myers, Mike Timlin, and Alan Embree. Keith Foulke came in to cool off Anaheim.

David Ortiz hit a two-run home run in the bottom of the tenth inning to win the game and advance the Red Sox to the American League Championship Series against the Yankees. Derek Lowe has thrown a ten-pitch top of the tenth inning, and he picked up the win, the first of his record-breaking three clinching victories.

2004 American League Divisional Series

BOSTON VERSUS ANAHEIM
Red Sox Batting

PLAYER	POS	AVG	G	AB	R	H	TB	2B	3B	HR	RBI
David Ortiz	DH	.545	3	11	4	6	11	2	0	1	4
Doug Mientkiewicz	1B	.500	3	4	0	2	2	0	0	0	1
Johnny Damon	CF	.467	3	15	4	7	8	1	0	0	0
Manny Ramírez	LF	.385	3	13	3	5	10	2	0	1	7
Bill Mueller	3B	.333	3	12	3	4	4	0	0	0	0
Kevin Millar	1B	.300	3	10	2	3	6	0	0	1	4
Trot Nixon	RF	.250	2	8	0	2	2	0	0	0	2
Gabe Kapler	OF	.200	2	5	2	1	1	0	0	0	0
Jason Varitek	C	.167	3	12	3	2	5	0	0	1	2
Orlando Cabrera	SS	.154	3	13	1	2	3	1	0	0	3
Mark Bellhorn	2B	.091	3	11	2	1	1	0	0	0	0
Pokey Reese	SS	.000	3	0	1	0	0	0	0	0	0

Dave Roberts	RF	.000	1	0	0	0	0	0	0	0	0
Kevin Youkilis	3B	.000	1	2	0	0	0	0	0	0	0
BOSTON		.302	3	116	25	35	53	6	0	4	23
ANAHEIM		.226	3	106	12	24	39	3	0	4	12

Red Sox Batting (Extended)

PLAYER	SH	SF	HP	BB	IBB	SO	SB	CS	DP	E	SLG	OBP
David Ortiz	0	0	0	5	3	2	0	0	0	0	1.000	.688
Doug Mientkiewicz	0	0	0	0	0	0	0	0	0	0	.500	.500
Johnny Damon	0	0	0	1	0	2	3	0	0	0	.533	.500
Manny Ramírez	0	2	0	1	0	4	0	0	0	0	.769	.375
Bill Mueller	0	0	0	1	0	1	0	0	0	0	.333	.385
Kevin Millar	0	0	0	1	0	1	0	0	0	0	.600	.364
Trot Nixon	0	0	0	2	1	1	0	0	1	0	.250	.400
Gabe Kapler	0	0	0	0	0	0	0	0	0	0	.200	.200
Jason Varitek	0	0	1	2	2	5	0	0	1	0	.417	.333
Orlando Cabrera	0	0	0	2	0	2	0	0	0	0	.231	.267
Mark Bellhorn	0	0	0	5	0	4	0	0	0	0	.091	.375
Pokey Reese	0	0	0	0	0	0	0	0	0	0	.000	.000
Dave Roberts	0	0	0	0	0	0	0	0	0	0	.000	.000
Kevin Youkilis	0	0	0	0	0	1	0	0	0	0	.000	.000
BOSTON	0	2	1	20	6	23	3	0	2	1	.457	.403
ANAHEIM	1	0	2	11	1	28	1	1	0	3	.368	.311

Red Sox Pitching

PITCHER	R/L	W	L	ERA	G	GS	CG	GF	SHO	SV
Bronson Arroyo	R	0	0	3.00	1	1	0	0	0	0
Alan Embree	L	0	0	0.00	2	0	0	0	0	0
Keith Foulke	R	0	0	0.00	2	0	0	1	0	1
Derek Lowe	R	1	0	0.00	1	0	0	1	0	0
Pedro Martinez	R	1	0	3.86	1	1	0	0	0	0
Mike Myers	L	0	0	27.00	2	0	0	0	0	0
Curt Schilling	R	1	0	2.70	1	1	0	0	0	0
Mike Timlin	R	0	0	9.00	3	0	0	1	0	0
BOSTON		3	0	3.54	3	3	0	3	0	1
ANAHEIM		0	3	5.86	3	3	0	3	0	0

Red Sox Pitching (Extended)

PITCHER	IP	H	R	ER	HR	HB	BB	IBB	SO	WP	BK	OPP AVG
Bronson Arroyo	6.0	3	2	2	1	1	2	0	7	0	0	.143
Alan Embree	1.0	0	0	0	0	0	1	0	0	0	0	.000
Keith Foulke	3.0	2	0	0	0	0	1	1	5	0	0	.182
Derek Lowe	1.0	1	0	0	0	0	1	0	0	0	0	.333

Pedro Martinez	7.0	6	3	3	0	1	2	0	6	0	0	.240
Mike Myers	0.1	0	1	1	0	0	1	0	1	0	0	.000
Curt Schilling	6.2	9	3	2	2	0	2	0	4	0	0	.300
Mike Timlin	3.0	3	3	3	1	0	1	0	5	0	0	.250
BOSTON	28.0	24	12	11	4	2	11	1	28	0	0	.226
ANAHEIM	27.2	35	25	18	4	1	20	6	23	4	0	.302

American League Championship Series

ALCS Game 1
at New York
October 12, 2004

	Score by innings	R	H	E
Boston	000 000 520	7	10	0
NEW YORK	204 002 02x	10	14	0

PITCHING

	IP	H	R	ER	BB	SO	HR	ERA
BOSTON								
Schilling (L 0–1)	3.0	6	6	6	2	1	0	18.00
Leskanic	1.0	0	0	0	2	1	0	0.00
Mendoza	1.0	1	0	0	0	0	0	0.00
Wakefield	1.0	3	2	2	0	1	1	18.00
Embree	1.0	1	0	0	0	0	0	0.00
Timlin	0.2	3	2	2	0	0	0	27.00
Foulke	0.1	0	0	0	0	0	0	0.00
NEW YORK								
Mussina (W 1–0)	6.2	4	4	4	0	8	0	5.40
Sturtze	0.1	1	1	1	0	1	1	27.00
Gordon (H 1)	0.2	3	2	2	0	1	0	27.00
Rivera (S 1)	1.1	2	0	0	0	0	0	0.00

The hopes of Boston were on Curt Schilling as the American League Championship Series began, but it was apparent from the start of the game that something was wrong; his right ankle, which had been troublesome for much of the second half of the season, was causing him pain and not allowing him to drive off the rubber with power. By the end of the third inning, the Yankees held a 6–0 lead and Schilling was out of the game, the shortest postseason appearance of his career. New York tacked on two more runs in the sixth inning off Tim Wakefield, and the game looked to be out of reach.

Meanwhile, New York's Mike Mussina carried a perfect game into the seventh inning. Mark Bellhorn broke the string with a one-out double. Successive hits by David Ortiz, Kevin Millar, and Trot Nixon brought in three runs and chased Mussina; Jason Varitek greeted reliever Tanyon Sturtze with a two-run homer.

In the eighth inning Ortiz drove a ball to center field that just missed clearing the fence; the big man rumbled into third with a two-run triple, and the Red Sox were down just one, at 8–7.

Mariano Rivera, who had returned to the team in the middle of the game after flying back from a family funeral in Panama, came in to get the final five outs and the save; in the bottom of the eighth, the Yankees picked up two insurance runs off Mike Timlin.

After the game Schilling wondered aloud whether he would be able to come back to pitch again in the postseason.

ALCS Game 2
at New York
October 13, 2004

	Score by innings	R	H	E
Boston	000 000 010	1	5	0
NEW YORK	100 020 00x	3	7	0

PITCHING

	IP	H	R	ER	BB	SO	HR	ERA
BOSTON								
Martinez (L 0–1)	6.0	4	3	3	4	7	1	4.50
Timlin	0.2	1	0	0	0	0	0	13.50
Embree	0.2	2	0	0	0	0	0	0.00
Foulke	0.2	0	0	0	1	1	0	0.00
NEW YORK								
Lieber (W 1–0)	7.0	3	1	1	1	3	0	1.29
Gordon (H 2)	0.2	1	0	0	0	0	0	13.50
Rivera (S 2)	1.1	1	0	0	0	3	0	0.00

While Yankee Stadium rocked with chants of "Who's your daddy?" Pedro Martínez pitched well—just 3 runs on 4 hits and 7 strikeouts over six innings—but not quite as well as Jon Lieber, who yielded only one run on three hits in seven innings.

Boston tried to mount a rally in the eighth inning. With Lieber still on the mound, Trot Nixon singled. The Yankees brought in Tom Gordon, who was greeted by a Jason Varitek double that moved Nixon to third. Orlando Cabrera brought Nixon home on a groundout. With two outs in the inning, the Yankees once again called on Mariano Rivera, who got the last four outs for his second save in two games.

ALCS Game 3
at Boston
October 16, 2004

	Score by innings	R	H	E
NEW YORK	303 520 402	19	22	1
Boston	042 000 200	8	15	0

PITCHING

	IP	H	R	ER	BB	SO	HR	ERA
NEW YORK								
Brown	2.0	5	4	3	2	1	1	13.50
Vazquez (W 1–0)	4.1	7	4	4	2	4	1	8.31
Quantrill	1.2	2	0	0	0	2	0	0.00
Gordon	1.0	1	0	0	0	1	0	7.71
BOSTON								
Arroyo	2.0	6	6	6	2	0	2	27.00
Mendoza (L 0-1)	1.0	1	1	1	0	1	0	4.50
Leskanic	0.1	2	3	3	1	0	1	20.25
Wakefield	3.1	5	5	5	2	1	0	14.54
Embree	0.1	3	2	2	0	0	0	9.00
Myers	2.0	5	2	2	0	3	1	9.00

After a rainout the day before, hopes were high as the Red Sox came home to Fenway Park. The outcome, though, was not what players and fans had dreamed: a 19–8 massacre in Boston. Neither starting pitcher—Kevin Brown for New York and Bronson Arroyo for Boston—was effective and the score was tied at 6–6 after three innings.

From there the game fell into a slow-motion four-hour, twenty-minute torture. The Yankees scored 19 runs on 22 hits, including 4 home runs, 1 triple, and 8 doubles. The Red Sox stood there and took the pummeling, with the exception of a Jason Varitek two-run homer in the seventh inning.

Perhaps more important, the always-versatile Tim Wakefield—who had been scheduled as the Game 4 starter—instead came in to eat up the middle three innings of the game and rest Mike Timlin and Keith Foulke. More bad news: The Yankee assault allowed them to give closer Mariano Rivera the night off.

The Red Sox, who had come into the ALCS favored to beat the Yankees and avenge 2003's heartbreaking loss, instead were in danger of being swept. Every news report the next morning included some variation of this daunting line: No team in baseball history has ever come back from an 0–3 deficit in a seven-game playoff or World Series.

ALCS Game 4
at Boston
October 17, 2004

	Score by innings	R	H	E
New York	002 002 000 000	4	12	1
BOSTON	000 030 001 002	6	8	0

PITCHING

	IP	H	R	ER	BB	SO	HR	ERA
NEW YORK								
Hernandez	5.0	3	3	3	5	6	0	5.40
Sturtze (H 1)	2.0	1	0	0	0	1	0	3.86
Rivera (BS 1)	2.0	2	1	1	2	2	0	1.93
Gordon	2.0	0	0	0	1	1	0	4.15
Quantrill (L 0–1)	0.0	2	2	2	0	0	1	10.80
BOSTON								
Lowe	5.1	6	3	3	0	3	1	5.06
Timlin (BS 1)	1.0	3	1	1	3	0	0	11.57
Foulke	2.2	0	0	0	2	3	0	0.00
Embree	1.2	2	0	0	1	0	0	4.91
Myers	0.0	0	0	0	1	0	0	9.00
Leskanic (W 1–0)	1.1	1	0	0	0	1	0	10.13

Derek Lowe, whose uneven performance at the end of the regular season had knocked him out of the starting rotation, got the call to start Game 4 and give the Red Sox a chance to salvage a sliver of dignity.

Boston received a strong performance from Lowe, although hometown hearts sank in the third inning when he gave up a two-run homer to Alex Rodríguez.

The Red Sox took the lead in the fifth on walks by Millar and Bellhorn, an RBI hit by Orlando Cabrera, and a two-run, two-out single by David Ortiz.

Lowe pitched into the top of the sixth inning holding a 3–2 lead until Hideki Matsui walloped a triple to deep center with one out. Mike Timlin came in to relieve and blew the save, with an infield single by Bernie Williams to tie the game, and a wild pitch, a walk, a passed ball, and an infield single by Tony Clark that put the Yankees ahead by a 4–3 score.

The great closer Mariano Rivera came into the game in the eighth inning and shut down the Red Sox in that frame; he was on the mound once more in the ninth, and Boston stood three outs away from a humiliating loss and a sweep at the hands of the Yankees. Instead Kevin Millar worked a walk to lead off the ninth. Dave Roberts came in as a pinch runner, and everybody watching knew that his job was to steal second base; that's just what he did, despite a fine throw from Jorge Posada. Bill Mueller capitalized with a single to center that tied the game 4–4 and blew the save for Rivera.

The Red Sox almost won the game right there. Doug Mientkiewicz sacrificed Mueller to second base. Johnny Damon reached on an error by first baseman Clark, and Manny Ramírez walked. That brought David Ortiz up to bat with the bases loaded and two outs; his moment as hero was yet to come—he popped out to second to send the game into extra innings.

The Yankees threatened in the top of the eleventh, loading the bases with two outs, but Curtis Leskanic came in to end the inning with a fly ball to center by Bernie Williams.

In the bottom of the twelfth, Paul Quantrill replaced Tom Gordon for the Yankees. He was greeted with a single by Ramírez to left, and then there stood David Ortiz. Boom, a two-run home run to right field for a walk-off win early Monday morning, after five hours and two minutes of baseball.

ALCS Game 5
at Boston
October 18, 2004

	Score by innings	R	H	E
New York	010 003 000 000 00	4	12	1
BOSTON	200 000 020 000 01	5	13	1

PITCHING

	IP	H	R	ER	BB	SO	HR	ERA
NEW YORK								
Mussina	6.0	6	2	2	2	7	0	4.26
Sturtze (H 2)	0.1	0	0	0	1	0	0	3.38
Gordon (H 3)	0.2	2	2	2	1	0	1	7.20
Rivera (BS 2)	2.0	1	0	0	0	1	0	1.35
Heredia	0.1	1	0	0	0	1	0	0.00
Quantrill	1.0	2	0	0	0	0	0	6.75
Loaiza (L 0–1)	3.1	1	1	1	3	3	0	2.70
BOSTON								
Martinez	6.0	7	4	4	5	6	1	5.25
Timlin	1.2	2	0	0	1	1	0	6.75
Foulke	1.1	1	0	0	1	0	0	0.00
Arroyo	1.0	0	0	0	0	2	0	18.00
Myers	0.1	0	0	0	0	1	0	7.71
Embree	0.2	1	0	0	0	2	0	4.15
Wakefield (W 1–0)	3.0	1	0	0	1	4	0	8.59

Later that same day . . . the Red Sox received solid pitching from Pedro Martínez, this time throwing in front of a faithful hometown crowd, but that was only the opening act in a long, long thriller.

Boston scored a pair of runs in the first inning: Orlando Cabrera singled, Manny Ramírez singled, David Ortiz singled to score Cabrera, and Kevin Millar walked to load the bases. Trot Nixon grounded into a frustrating fielder's choice with Ramírez out at home plate, but Jason Varitek worked a walk with the bases loaded to bring home the second run.

The Yankees got one run back in the second on a home run by Bernie Williams, and then went ahead with three runs in the sixth inning. After Martínez gave up singles to Jorge Posada and Ruben Sierra, Pedro hit Miguel Cairo to load the bases. With two outs Derek Jeter doubled to right, clearing the bases. Pedro got the last out of the inning, but left the game, once again roughed up by the Yankees and this time trailing 4–2.

In the eighth inning the Red Sox evened the score. Ortiz once again came up huge with a leadoff home run to bring Boston within a run. Millar followed with a walk; Dave Roberts came in as pinch runner. Nixon singled to center and the speedy Roberts moved to third base. The Yankees once again called on Mariano Rivera to save the day, but Varitek lifted a sacrifice fly to center field bringing Roberts home with the tying run.

The Red Sox bull pen, which had worked into the twelfth inning the night before, managed to shut down the Yankees for the next eight innings: Mike Timlin, Keith Foulke, Bronson Arroyo, Mike Myers, and Alan Embree scattered four hits in five frames, and Tim Wakefield came in for three superb innings, giving up just a single hit and striking out four.

In the bottom of the fourteenth inning, with Esteban Loaiza in his fourth inning of relief, Johnny Damon walked with one out. Cabrera struck out for the second out of the inning, and then Ramírez drew a walk. Up came Ortiz: a single to center scored Damon. The five-hour, forty-nine-minute game had begun in the late afternoon and ended before midnight: Ortiz thus had his second game-winning walk-off hit in the same day.

ALCS Game 6
at New York
October 19, 2004

	Score by innings	R	H	E
BOSTON	000 400 000	4	11	0
New York	000 000 110	2	6	0

PITCHING

	IP	H	R	ER	BB	SO	HR	ERA
BOSTON								
Schilling (W 1–1)	7.0	4	1	1	0	4	1	6.30
Arroyo (H 1)	1.0	2	1	1	0	1	0	15.75
Foulke (S 1)	1.0	0	0	0	2	2	0	0.00
NEW YORK								
Lieber (L 1–1)	7.1	9	4	4	0	2	1	3.14
Heredia	0.1	0	0	0	0	0	0	0.00
Quantrill	0.2	2	0	0	0	0	0	5.40
Sturtze	0.2	0	0	0	1	0	0	2.70

Because of the rainout before Game 3 in Boston, there was no off-day between the end of the second consecutive extra-inning game and the return to New York. Both teams came into Game 6 with their bull pens running on fumes; twenty-six innings within twenty-four hours will do that.

One of the pregame stars for Boston was the medical staff. The Red Sox called on their stalwart, Curt Schilling, to take the mound. In an apparently unique bit of surgery, doctors sutured the skin around the dislocated tendon in his ankle to relieve discomfort and give him a bit more support. When he began the game, no one knew how well he could throw.

The answer came quickly: Schilling dominated the Yankees over seven innings in a cold drizzle, yielding just one run—on a bases-empty home run by Bernie Williams in the last inning he pitched—giving up just four hits, walking none, and striking out four. Television zoom lenses focused in on his right ankle where a small circle of blood colored his white sock.

Bronson Arroyo came in for the eighth inning, giving up a second run on a double by Miguel Cairo and a single by Derek Jeter. Then came one of those weird plays that seem to pop up only in the most important of games—like a Red Sox–Yankees playoff. Alex Rodríguez hit an easy grounder to the right of the mound that was fielded by Arroyo, who ran toward first base. Just short of the bag, Arroyo reached out to tag A-Rod.

In a play that was examined over and over from every angle by television broadcasters, the Yankee third baseman appeared to swing his arm at Arroyo's glove, knocking the ball loose. Jeter continued running and came all the way around from first to score, which would have brought the Yankees within one run of the Red Sox.

The first-base umpire, who was watching the play as it came toward him, ruled A-Rod safe. But Boston manager Terry Francona protested the call, and all six field umpires gathered to discuss the event. After a minute the umps decided that Rodriguez had violated section 6.1 of the umpire's manual, which states that although contact may occur between a fielder and runner during a tag attempt, "a runner is not allowed to use his hands or arms to commit an obviously malicious or unsportsmanlike act . . . such as grabbing, tackling, intentionally slapping at the baseball, punching, kicking, flagrantly using his arms or forearms . . . to commit an intentional act of interference unrelated to running the bases."

Bottom line: A-Rod was called out and Jeter was required to return all the way to first base. Gary Sheffield fouled out to the catcher to end the inning, and once again Keith Foulke was called on to save the game.

(Ironically, it was Arroyo who hit Rodríguez with a pitch on July 24, 2004, setting off a brawl between A-Rod and Jason Varitek and both teams; some point to that first incident as one that fired up the Red Sox for their second-half stretch run.)

And it was not the first time in that game that the umpires had reversed a ruling to the benefit of Boston. The Red Sox scored all four of their runs in the fourth inning. With two outs Kevin Millar had doubled and moved to third on a wild pitch by Jon Lieber. Varitek singled Millar home; Orlando Cabrera followed with another single. Then Mark Bellhorn hit a long fly ball that was at first ruled a double off the wall; after the umpires gathered they decided that the ball had actually cleared the wall and bounced off a fan in the stands, making it a three-run homer. Television replays confirmed that the second ruling was correct.

After the game A-Rod had two comments. First he said, "I know that the line belongs to me. Looking back, maybe I should have run him over." And, he added, "I don't want those umpires meeting anymore. Every time they have a meeting, they make a call against the Yankees."

In any case the Red Sox had accomplished the nearly impossible: coming back from an 0–3 deficit to tie the playoffs at 3–3, setting the stage for a classic Game 7.

ALCS Game 7
at New York
October 20, 2004

	Score by innings	R	H	E
BOSTON	240 200 011	10	13	0
New York	001 000 200	3	5	1

PITCHING

	IP	H	R	ER	BB	SO	HR	ERA
BOSTON								
Lowe (W 1–0)	6.0	1	1	1	1	3	0	3.18
Martinez	1.0	3	2	2	0	1	0	6.23
Timlin	1.2	1	0	0	1	1	0	4.76
Embree	0.1	0	0	0	0	0	0	3.86

NEW YORK							
Brown (L 0–1)	1.1	4	5	5	2	1	1	21.60
Vazquez	2.0	2	3	3	5	2	2	9.95
Loaiza	3.0	4	0	0	0	2	0	1.42
Heredia	0.2	0	0	0	0	0	0	0.00
Gordon	1.2	3	2	2	0	0	1	8.10
Rivera	0.1	0	0	0	0	0	0	1.29

After the incredible difficulties of the first six games of the ALCS, the seventh game turned into a laugher. Not to say that Red Sox fans weren't nervous all the way through the bottom of the ninth.

In the first inning Johnny Damon singled to left and then stole second. With one out Manny Ramírez singled to left of center and Damon was thrown out at home plate. But Big Papi—David Ortiz—took care of business with a two-run home run to right.

There were four more runs for Boston in the second inning: a Damon grand slam off newly installed reliever Javier Vazquez, bringing home Kevin Millar, Bill Mueller, and Orlando Cabrera, who had reached base against Kevin Brown. It was 6–0 Red Sox after two innings.

The Red Sox were cruising behind the superb pitching of Derek Lowe, who had fought his way back into the starting rotation with his earlier work. He threw six innings of one-hit ball; the Yankees nicked him for a single run in the third inning after Miguel Cairo was hit by a pitch, stole second, and came around on a Derek Jeter single.

Boston answered back in the fourth inning when Damon hit his second home run off Lieber, bringing home Cabrera, who had reached on a walk.

For the record New York picked up two runs in the seventh inning on a pair of doubles by Hideki Matsui and Bernie Williams and a single by Kenny Lofton off Pedro Martínez, who was brought in as a reliever. That was the end of scoring for the Yankees, but the Red Sox put the icing on the American League championship—and the champagne on ice—with a run in the eighth on a Mark Bellhorn home run, and another in the ninth on singles by Trot Nixon and Doug Mientkiewicz and a sacrifice fly by Cabrera. Final score: Boston 10, New York 3.

The "Curse," if there ever was one, was now officially "Reversed." In the process the Red Sox had accomplished what may have been the most amazing comeback in baseball history: from 0–3 to 4–3 in the league championship.

2004 American League Championship Series

BOSTON VERSUS NEW YORK
Red Sox Batting

PLAYER	POS	AVG	G	AB	R	H	TB	2B	3B	HR	RBI
David Ortiz	DH	.387	7	31	6	12	23	0	1	3	11
Orlando Cabrera	SS	.379	7	29	5	11	13	2	0	0	5
Jason Varitek	C	.321	7	28	5	9	16	1	0	2	7
Manny Ramírez	LF	.300	7	30	3	9	10	1	0	0	0
Bill Mueller	3B	.267	7	30	4	8	9	1	0	0	1
Kevin Millar	1B	.250	7	24	4	6	9	3	0	0	2
Trot Nixon	RF	.207	7	29	4	6	10	1	0	1	3
Mark Bellhorn	2B	.192	7	26	3	5	13	2	0	2	4
Johnny Damon	CF	.171	7	35	5	6	12	0	0	2	7
Doug Mientkiewicz	1B	.500	4	4	0	2	3	1	0	0	0
Gabe Kapler	RF	.333	2	3	0	1	1	0	0	0	0
Doug Mirabelli	C	.000	1	1	0	0	0	0	0	0	0
Pokey Reese	SS	.000	3	1	0	0	0	0	0	0	0
Dave Roberts	RF	.000	2	0	2	0	0	0	0	0	0
BOSTON		.277	7	271	41	75	119	12	1	10	40
NEW YORK		.282	7	277	45	78	130	21	2	9	44

Red Sox Batting (Extended)

PLAYER	SH	SF	HP	BB	IBB	SO	SB	CS	DP	E	SLG	OBP
David Ortiz	0	0	0	4	0	7	0	1	0	0	.742	.457
Orlando Cabrera	0	1	0	3	0	5	1	0	1	0	.448	.424
Jason Varitek	0	1	0	2	0	6	0	0	0	0	.571	.355
Manny Ramírez	0	0	0	5	0	4	0	0	1	1	.333	.400
Bill Mueller	0	0	1	2	0	1	0	0	3	0	.300	.333
Kevin Millar	0	0	0	5	0	4	0	0	1	0	.375	.379
Trot Nixon	0	0	0	0	0	5	0	0	0	0	.345	.207
Mark Bellhorn	0	0	0	5	0	11	0	0	1	0	.500	.323
Johnny Damon	0	0	0	2	0	8	2	1	1	0	.343	.216
Doug Mientkiewicz	1	0	0	0	0	1	0	0	0	0	.750	.500
Gabe Kapler	0	0	0	0	0	0	0	0	0	0	.333	.333
Doug Mirabelli	0	0	0	0	0	0	0	0	0	0	.000	.000
Pokey Reese	0	0	0	0	0	1	0	0	0	0	.000	.000
Dave Roberts	0	0	0	0	0	0	1	0	0	0	.000	.000
BOSTON	1	2	1	28	0	53	4	2	8	1	.439	.344
NEW YORK	3	1	7	33	3	51	3	0	3	4	.469	.371

Red Sox Pitching

PITCHER	R/L	W	L	ERA	G	GS	CG	GF	SHO	SV
Bronson Arroyo	R	0	0	15.75	3	1	0	0	0	0
Alan Embree	L	0	0	3.86	6	0	0	1	0	0
Keith Foulke	R	0	0	0.00	5	0	0	3	0	1
Curt Leskanic	R	1	0	10.12	3	0	0	1	0	0
Derek Lowe	R	1	0	3.18	2	2	0	0	0	0
Pedro Martinez	R	0	1	6.23	3	2	0	0	0	0
Ramiro Mendoza	R	0	1	4.50	2	0	0	0	0	0
Mike Myers	L	0	0	7.71	3	0	0	1	0	0
Curt Schilling	R	1	1	6.30	2	2	0	0	0	0
Mike Timlin	R	0	0	4.76	5	0	0	0	0	0
Tim Wakefield	R	1	0	8.59	3	0	0	1	0	0
BOSTON		4	3	5.87	7	7	0	7	0	1
NEW YORK		3	4	5.17	7	7	0	7	0	2

Red Sox Pitching (Extended)

PITCHER	IP	H	R	ER	HR	HB	BB	IBB	SO	WP	BK	OPP AVG
Bronson Arroyo	4.0	8	7	7	2	0	2	0	0	0	0	.421
Alan Embree	4.2	9	2	2	0	0	1	1	2	0	0	.409
Keith Foulke	6.0	1	0	0	0	1	6	0	6	0	0	.053
Curt Leskanic	2.2	3	3	3	1	0	3	0	0	0	0	.300
Derek Lowe	11.1	7	4	4	1	1	1	0	6	0	0	.175
Pedro Martinez	13.0	14	9	9	2	2	9	0	14	0	0	.269
Ramiro Mendoza	2.0	2	1	1	0	2	0	0	0	0	1	.250
Mike Myers	2.1	5	2	2	1	0	1	0	0	0	0	.455
Curt Schilling	10.0	10	7	7	1	0	2	0	5	0	0	.256
Mike Timlin	5.2	10	3	3	0	0	5	0	2	1	0	.400
Tim Wakefield	7.1	9	7	7	1	0	3	2	6	0	0	.281
BOSTON	69.0	78	45	45	9	6	33	3	53	1	1	.278
NEW YORK	69.2	75	41	40	10	1	28	0	51	2	0	.282

2004 World Series

World Series Game 1
at Boston
October 23, 2004

	Score by innings	R	H	E
St. Louis	011 302 020	9	11	1
BOSTON	403 000 22x	11	13	4

PITCHING

	IP	H	R	ER	BB	SO	HR	ERA
ST. LOUIS								
Williams	2.1	8	7	7	3	1	1	27.00
Haren	3.2	2	0	0	3	1	0	0.00
Calero	0.1	1	2	2	2	0	0	54.00
King	0.1	1	0	0	0	0	0	0.00
Eldred	0.1	0	0	0	0	1	0	0.00
Tavarez (L 0–1)	1.0	1	2	1	0	0	1	9.00
BOSTON								
Wakefield	3.2	3	5	5	5	2	1	12.27
Arroyo	2.1	4	2	2	0	4	0	7.71
Timlin	1.1	1	1	1	0	0	0	6.75
Embree	0.0	1	1	0	0	0	0	0.00
Foulke (BS 1, W 1–0)	1.2	2	0	0	1	3	0	0.00

Johnny Damon led off the Red Sox march to the championship in the first inning with a double to left. Orlando Cabrera was hit by a pitch. Manny Ramírez hit a fly ball out, but David Ortiz took care of business with a glorious three-run homer to right. Another run scored after Kevin Millar doubled and Bill Mueller singled him home.

Tim Wakefield's knuckleball wasn't knuckling all that well, though, and St. Louis picked up single runs in the second and third innings.

In the bottom of the third, Boston put up three more runs. Mueller walked, Doug Mirabelli singled, and Mark Bellhorn walked to load the bases for Damon. Johnny singled to right, scoring Mueller and reloading the bases. With Danny Haren in relief, Cabrera singled, scoring Mirabelli and once again putting a man on every base. Ramírez could produce only a grounder to short, but Bellhorn scored on a fielder's choice.

Wakefield could not hold the lead in the top of the fourth, suddenly losing the ability to throw a strike. He walked the first batter, threw a passed ball, and then walked the next two Cardinals. Then the Red Sox defense went cold. Mike Matheny drove in a run with a fly ball to right and a second run scored on Millar's throwing error. A third run came in on a ground out. Bronson Arroyo came in to stop the bleeding, with the Red Sox holding on to a slim 7–5 lead.

In the sixth St. Louis tied the game off Arroyo. So Taguchi singled to the pitcher and took second on Arroyo's throwing error. Edgar Rentería and Larry Walker each doubled to score two runs. An inning later, the Red Sox took back the lead with a pair of runs: Ramírez singled to bring home Bellhorn (who had, of course, gotten on base with a walk), and Ortiz singled in Cabrera to put Boston ahead 9–7.

In the eighth inning Mike Timlin and Alan Embree each gave up a single. Red Sox closer Keith Foulke came in with one out and hopes of extinguishing the fire, but the Cardinals came back to tie the score at 9–9 on two consecutive errors by Manny Ramírez. He bobbled a single by Rentería and then tried to make a diving catch on a fly ball by Walker that instead glanced off his glove as he tumbled.

With the Cardinals effective setup man Julián Tavárez on the mound in the bottom of the eighth, Jason Varitek reached first on an error by shortstop Rentería. Mark Bellhorn put the Sox back on top with a home run to right field.

Foulke made it interesting again in the ninth, giving up a double to Marlon Anderson before striking out Roger Cedeño to end the game.

The Red Sox tied a World Series record with four errors. It wasn't pretty and it wasn't easy, but it was a win.

World Series Game 2
at Boston
October 24, 2004

	Score by innings	R	H	E
St. Louis	000 100 010	2	5	0
BOSTON	200 202 00x	6	8	4

PITCHING

	IP	H	R	ER	BB	SO	HR	ERA
ST. LOUIS								
Morris (L 0–1)	4.1	4	4	4	4	3	0	8.31
Eldred	1.1	4	2	2	0	1	0	10.80
King	0.1	0	0	0	0	1	0	0.00
Marquis	1.0	0	0	0	2	0	0	0.00
Reyes	1.0	0	0	0	0	0	0	0.00
BOSTON								
Schilling (W 1–0)	6.0	4	1	0	1	4	0	0.00
Embree	1.0	0	0	0	0	3	0	0.00
Timlin	0.2	1	1	1	1	0	0	9.00
Foulke	1.1	0	0	0	0	3	0	0.00

Curt Schilling was almost unable to take the mound because of pain in his temporarily repaired ankle; a suture touching a nerve was removed before the game, and he gave Boston six strong innings, allowing no earned runs.

The Red Sox took the lead in the first inning after Jason Varitek tripled to center field, scoring Manny Ramírez and David Ortiz, who had each reached with walks.

In the fourth inning they gave back one of the runs on the second error of the game by Bill Mueller, allowing Albert Pujols to score. When the Red Sox came up to bat in the bottom of that inning, they scored two more on Mark Bellhorn's double to center, scoring Kevin Millar and Mueller, giving them a 4–1 lead.

In the sixth inning Mueller tied an ancient World Series record when he made his third error of the game; on the next play Bellhorn committed a fourth error to allow the team to set an unmatched record: No team had ever made more than seven errors in the first two games of the World Series. But Schilling managed to get the third out of the inning without any runs crossing the plate.

In the bottom of the sixth, Trot Nixon singled, and with two outs Johnny Damon got a base hit to left. Orlando Cabrera drove them both home with another single, and the Red Sox had a 6–1 lead. Mike Timlin gave up a run in the eighth on a walk, single, and sacrifice fly before Keith Foulke came in to get the last four batters out and secure the second win of the World Series in the last game of the season played in Boston.

World Series Game 3
at St. Louis
October 26, 2004

	Score by innings	R	H	E
BOSTON	100 120 000	4	9	0
St. Louis	000 000 001	1	4	0

PITCHING

	IP	H	R	ER	BB	SO	HR	ERA
BOSTON								
Martinez (W 1–0)	7.0	3	0	0	2	6	0	0.00
Timlin	1.0	0	0	0	0	1	0	6.00
Foulke	1.0	1	1	1	0	2	1	2.25

ST. LOUIS								
Suppan (L 0-1)	4.2	8	4	4	1	4	1	7.71
Reyes	0.1	0	0	0	0	0	0	0.00
Calero	1.0	1	0	0	2	0	0	13.50
King	2.0	0	0	0	1	0	0	0.00
Tavarez	1.0	0	0	0	0	1	0	4.50

Pedro Martínez pitched like the Pedro of old, throwing seven innings of three-hit scoreless ball in his first appearance in a World Series game. Mike Timlin pitched a perfect eighth inning. Keith Foulke was almost perfect in the ninth, allowing a bases-empty home run by Larry Walker.

Boston once again scored in the first inning, this time on a massive home run to left field by Manny Ramírez. Bill Mueller doubled, and Trot Nixon drove him in with a single in the fourth inning. In the fifth Johnny Damon doubled, Orlando Cabrera singled, and Ramírez singled for one run; Mueller drove in a second run with a single.

For the Red Sox it was a cleanly played game including a very nice throw by Ramírez to cut down Walker at home in the bottom of the first. On the St. Louis side, the game may best be remembered for the baserunning adventures of pitcher Jeff Suppan in the third inning. He began by reaching first on a surprise bunt down the third base line, and was moved over to third on a double to the warning track by Edgar Rentería. With nobody out, the Red Sox were playing back, willing to concede a run to get an out. Larry Walker hit an easy grounder to Mark Bellhorn at second, who threw to first. But for some reason, Suppan failed to come home; worse, he see-sawed back and forth a few times and David Ortiz ran a few steps toward him from first base and then threw behind him to Mueller for a truly bizarre 4–3–5 double play that ruined a Cardinals rally in a close game.

World Series Game 4
At St. Louis
Wednesday, October 27, 2004

	Score by Innings	R	H	E
BOSTON	102 000 000	3	9	0
St. Louis	000 000 000	0	4	0

PITCHING

	IP	H	R	ER	BB	SO	HR	ERA
BOSTON								
Lowe (W 1-0)	7.0	3	0	0	1	4	0	0.00
Arroyo (H 1)	0.1	0	0	0	1	0	0	6.75
Embree (H 1)	0.2	0	0	0	0	1	0	0.00
Foulke (S 1)	1.0	1	0	0	0	1	0	1.80
ST. LOUIS								
Marquis (L 0-1)	6.0	6	3	3	5	4	1	3.86
Haren	1.0	2	0	0	0	1	0	0.00
Isringhausen	2.0	1	0	0	1	2	0	0.00

Johnny Damon homered to right field to lead off the game, the only run Derek Lowe and the Red Sox would need to win the game. Boston picked up two more runs in the third inning after Manny Ramírez singled to left and David Ortiz doubled to right. With runners on second and third, Jason Varitek grounded into a fielder's choice with Ramírez tagged out at home. Bill Mueller walked to load the bases and Trot Nixon doubled to center, scoring Ortiz and Varitek.

Lowe needed only eighty-five pitches to get through seven innings. Bronson Arroyo and Alan Embree preserved the shutout in the eighth, setting up the eleventh appearance by closer Keith Foulke in the fourteen postseason games.

In a sign from above, in the eighth inning there was a total lunar eclipse; rumors of a place well down below freezing over were unconfirmed.

In the ninth inning, Edgar Rentería grounded back to the mound and Foulke grabbed the ball and tossed it ever so carefully to Doug Mientkiewicz at first base. And the Boston Red Sox were "World Champions."

2004 World Series

BOSTON VERSUS ST. LOUIS
Red Sox Batting

PLAYER	POS	AVG	G	AB	R	H	TB	2B	3B	HR	RBI
Bill Mueller	3B	.429	4	14	3	6	8	2	0	0	2
Manny Ramírez	LF	.412	4	17	2	7	10	0	0	1	4
Trot Nixon	RF	.357	4	14	1	5	8	3	0	0	3
Doug Mirabelli	C	.333	1	3	1	1	1	0	0	0	0
David Ortiz	DH/1B	.308	4	13	3	4	8	1	0	1	4

Mark Bellhorn	2B	.300	4	10	3	3	7	1	0	1	4
Johnny Damon	CF	.286	4	21	4	6	13	2	1	1	2
Orlando Cabrera	SS	.235	4	17	3	4	5	1	0	0	3
Jason Varitek	C	.154	4	13	2	2	4	0	1	0	2
Kevin Millar	1B	.125	4	8	2	1	2	1	0	0	0
Gabe Kapler	OF	.000	4	2	0	0	0	0	0	0	0
Derek Lowe	P	.000	1	2	0	0	0	0	0	0	0
Pedro Martinez	P	.000	1	2	0	0	0	0	0	0	0
Doug Mientkiewicz	1B	.000	4	1	0	0	0	0	0	0	0
Pokey Reese	2B	.000	4	1	0	0	0	0	0	0	0
Dave Roberts	PR	.000	0	0	0	0	0	0	0	0	0
Kevin Youkilis	3B	.000	0	0	0	0	0	0	0	0	0
BOSTON		.283	4	138	24	39	66	11	2	4	24
ST. LOUIS		.190	4	126	12	24	38	8	0	2	8

Red Sox Batting (extended)

PLAYER	SH	SF	HP	BB	IBB	SO	SB	CS	DP	E	SLG	OBP
Bill Mueller	0	0	0	4	0	0	0	0	1	3	.571	.556
Manny Ramírez	0	0	0	3	0	3	0	0	0	2	.588	.500
Trot Nixon	0	0	0	1	0	1	0	0	0	0	.571	.400
Doug Mirabelli	0	0	0	0	0	1	0	0	0	0	.333	.333
David Ortiz	0	0	0	4	0	1	0	0	0	0	.615	.471
Mark Bellhorn	0	0	1	5	1	2	0	0	1	1	.700	.563
Johnny Damon	0	0	0	0	0	1	0	0	1	0	.619	.286
Orlando Cabrera	0	0	1	3	0	1	0	0	0	0	.294	.381
Jason Varitek	0	0	1	1	0	4	0	0	0	0	.308	.267
Kevin Millar	0	0	1	2	0	2	0	0	0	1	.250	.364
Gabe Kapler	0	0	0	0	0	1	0	0	0	0	.000	.000
Derek Lowe	1	0	0	0	0	1	0	0	0	0	.000	.000
Pedro Martinez	0	0	0	1	0	2	0	0	0	0	.000	.333
Doug Mientkiewicz	0	0	0	0	0	0	0	0	0	0	.000	.000
Pokey Reese	0	0	0	0	0	0	0	0	0	0	.000	.000
Dave Roberts	0	0	0	0	0	0	0	0	0	0	.000	.000
Kevin Youkilis	0	0	0	0	0	0	0	0	0	0	.000	.000
BOSTON	1	0	4	24	1	20	0	0	3	8	.478	.404
ST. LOUIS	2	3	1	12	1	32	1	0	2	1	.302	.261

Red Sox Pitching

PITCHER	R/L	W	L	ERA	G	GS	CG	GF	SHO	SV
Keith Foulke	R	1	0	1.80	4	0	0	4	0	1
Derek Lowe	R	1	0	0.00	1	1	0	0	0	0
Pedro Martinez	R	1	0	0.00	1	1	0	0	0	0
Curt Schilling	R	1	0	0.00	1	1	0	0	0	0
Bronson Arroyo	R	0	0	6.75	2	0	0	0	0	0
Alan Embree	L	0	0	0.00	3	0	0	0	0	0
Curtis Leskanic	R	0	0	—	0	0	0	0	0	0
Mike Myers	L	0	0	—	0	0	0	0	0	0
Mike Timlin	R	0	0	6.00	3	0	0	0	0	0
Tim Wakefield	R	0	0	12.27	1	1	0	0	0	0
BOSTON		4	0	2.50	4	4	0	4	1	1
ST. LOUIS		0	4	6.09	4	4	0	4	0	0

Red Sox Pitching (extended)

PITCHER	IP	H	R	ER	HR	HB	BB	IBB	SO	WP	BK	AVG[a]
Keith Foulke	5.0	4	1	1	1	0	1	1	8	0	0	.200
Pedro Martinez	7.0	3	0	0	0	0	2	0	6	0	0	.136
Curt Schilling	6.0	4	1	0	0	0	1	0	4	0	0	.174
Bronson Arroyo	2.2	4	2	2	0	0	1	0	4	0	0	.333
Alan Embree	1.2	1	1	0	0	0	0	0	4	0	0	.167
Curtis Leskanic	0.0	0	0	0	0	0	0	0	0	0	0	.000
Mike Myers	0.0	0	0	0	0	0	0	0	0	0	0	.000
Mike Timlin	3.0	2	2	2	0	0	1	0	0	0	0	.200
Tim Wakefield	3.2	3	5	5	1	1	5	0	2	0	0	.300
BOSTON	36.0	24	12	10	2	1	12	1	32	1	0	.190
ST. LOUIS	34.0	39	24	23	4	4	24	1	20	0	0	.283

[a]AVG: Opposing team batting average

PART ELEVEN

Return to the Promised Land

Josh Beckett had a superb season in 2007, leading Boston to the Promised Land. If the voting for the Cy Young Award had come after the postseason, there is no doubt he would have had that trophy as well as a World Series ring.

Photo by Brita Meng Outzen

CHAPTER THIRTY

2007: Solid All the Way

The Red Sox played like champions for the entire 2007 season. They moved into first place two weeks after opening day and never gave it up for the remaining 166 days of the season.

In spring training I thought that the Yankees and the Red Sox would once again be the two best teams in the division. If anything, I thought the Yankees might have had a slight edge because of their offense—it turned out to be the best in the league—and I thought that perhaps they could squeeze out one more decent year from some of their veteran pitchers like Andy Pettite and Mike Mussina.

But coming out of the chute the Yankees had one after another injury with their pitchers. They were starting kids from Double A and Triple A.

In Boston, the Red Sox had strong pitching and very good luck when it came to injuries. Never once after they built a lead over the Yankees did I feel that they were in jeopardy of not making the playoffs. And I really didn't fear they would lose grip of first place.

The Yankees Rise from the Dead

Everybody was aware that at some point the Yankees were going to make a run. They were too good; once they got people healthy you knew that was coming.

I know a little bit about that myself; I experienced it when I played for the Red Sox in 1978. In that year we owned the league for half the season. On July 19 we were 9 games over the Milwaukee Brewers, 12½ above Baltimore, and 14 above the Yankees. New York was in great turmoil on the field and in the clubhouse. Jim Rice was having his MVP season, ending up with 46 home runs, 139 RBIs, and a .315 batting average.

But somehow in 1978, the Yankees put it together and by the beginning of September, they were breathing down our necks, down only four games, and after they swept us in four games at Fenway, we ended up dead even on the last day of the season. We faced them in a one-game playoff, and well, we lost.

But back to 2007: The Red Sox were a model of consistency all year long, mostly because of their starting pitching and the bull pen. As we got to the last three weeks of the season, the Yankees were closing the gap, but I didn't see panic anywhere in the organization.

The low point was the three games the Sox lost up in Toronto. They got swept in mid-September and the Yankees closed to within 1½ games. Then we went back to Tampa and got well again. That was the closest the Yankees got to first place at the end of the season.

This is where the Wild Card has had an impact on baseball. The Red Sox knew they were going to be in the playoffs one way or another, so they could rest some of their players. Getting people healthy and ready for postseason play was the most important thing.

All Champagne Tastes Sweet

To me it doesn't matter whether you get to the playoffs as division champion or by winning the Wild Card; remember, the Red Sox got to the 2004 World Championship—the one that ended the eighty-six-year drought—as the Wild Card team, and I don't recall anyone complaining about it.

In 2007 it was sweet because they hadn't won a division in so long and they finally finished ahead of New York, but the goal is to win the World Series. Whoever pitches the best and whoever gets hot at the end is going to win.

There was some panic in the streets that the Red Sox were in a slide and that they were going to finish second. But they had a plan. For example, nobody could have predicted Manny Ramírez's injury late in the season, but they focused on getting him back in the lineup by the last week of the season so he would be ready for postseason.

Many fans and reporters focus on the day-by-day goings-on with the team. While they are thinking small picture, management is thinking big picture. The big picture is winning the World Championship; they played it very smart.

For example, Hideki Okajima—one of the season's heroes—began to struggle after throwing many more innings than he had been used to throwing in Japan. So they shut him down for about ten days to give him some time off; they hoped he would be able to bounce back and be the pitcher he was in the first half of the year. And so he did.

You have to give credit to the front office, including Theo Epstein and his crew and to Terry Francona for doing that, even with the immense pressure that was on them from outside to finish first.

In the end it could not have worked out better. They were able to line up their pitching for every single series. They had Josh Beckett ready to start the first game of every series.

Boston Builds Its Base

A second World Series trophy in four years proves that Boston now has a very solid organization.

It wasn't easy. In my opinion, this new ownership group—which took over in 2002—has three times been on the brink of disaster.

In 2004 they fell behind the Yankees three games to none in the American League Championship Series; if the Red Sox had been swept there it would have been a second consecutive heartbreak loss to New York. But they came back from the brink, winning four in a row and went on to win the World Series.

The fans loved the team in 2004, but like generations before they expected bad things to happen. The comeback changed the whole culture for today's Red Sox rooters. It was the perfect cure.

The second test came after the 2005 season when Theo Epstein resigned as general manager; that could have been a disaster. But Epstein and the front office worked out a new arrangement and he was back in January of 2006.

And then there were the final six weeks of the 2006 season when the Red Sox fell out of the race because of injuries. There was lack of interest at the ballpark, the media lost interest, and they knew they had to do something. They made a big splash going out to get Daisuke Matsuzaka from Japan.

Management has shown itself to be pretty smart; when things seem to be heading in a bad direction, the organization goes out and does something about it.

In 2007 the Red Sox came back from a 3–1 games deficit against the Indians in the ALCS; again they were just one loss away from elimination. But in 2007 the fans had changed: fans now expect good things to happen.

And the players don't have to hear about how Boston hasn't won a championship in eighty-six years. They are champions, twice over.

Enough about the Yankees, Already

As the 2007 playoffs began we wondered whether the Red Sox would have to face the Yankees once again in the ALCS. The Cleveland Indians took care of that problem for us, and I can't say I was disappointed.

The Yankees are a little tiring. The Red Sox play them nineteen times in the regular season and they are all brutal battles, like nineteen World Series games. I was a little tired of seeing the Yankees myself.

We have already been through the Bronx. As far as the players and ownership were concerned, the only thing that mattered was winning a championship. That said, I felt that the Indians would give the Red Sox a

Remy Says: Watch This

Invasion of the Midges

One of the memorable moments of the New York-Cleveland ALDS in 2007 was the invasion of the Yankee-hating midges in the late innings of the second game.

This sort of thing happened to us a few times in the old parks in Cleveland and Minnesota. You used to have to spray yourself down from head to toe before a game.

In 2007 it seemed like it affected Yankee rookie Joba Chamberlain a little bit. It was weird, but even stranger was that this was the kind of thing that used to happen to the Red Sox and this time it was affecting the Yankees—so you know that's a good thing.

bigger challenge than the Yankees would, and the series against Cleveland proved that.

But Cleveland lost because their two big starters, C. C. Sabathia and Fausto Carmona—two of the best pitchers in baseball—couldn't win a game against Boston.

The 2007 World Champion Roster

Wire to wire, the Red Sox showed they had what it took to win. Josh Beckett had a Cy Young Award-like year. Hideki Okajima and Jonathan Papelbon showed the rest of both leagues how a great bullpen worked. Dustin Pedroia swung out of his shoes for a Rookie of the Year season. And old pro Mike Lowell and newly proven Kevin Youkilis anchored the corners. These are the strengths that built the foundation for a trip to the promised land.

Josh Beckett, SP

American League Championship Series MVP

2007 Regular season: W–L 20–7, 3.27 ERA, 200.2 IP, 194 K, 40 BB, 1.14 WHIP

2007 Postseason: W–L 4–0, 1.20 ERA, 30.0 IP, 35 K, 2 BB, 0.70 WHIP

2007 World Series: W–L 1–0, 1.29 ERA, 7.0 IP, 9 K, 1 BB, 1.00 WHIP

Josh Beckett had a superb season in his second year as a member of the Red Sox, winning 20 games and coming in second in the voting for the Cy Young Award; if the ballots had been cast after the postseason, he almost certainly would have been the winner.

Beckett was locked in all year. There were times when I couldn't figure out how anyone was getting any hits at all off him.

When he came to the team in 2006, Beckett had that Texas mentality: I am going to blow you away. I think he realized that he couldn't get by in the American League just throwing fastballs. He was convinced to use his curveball and his changeup more, and from day one in spring training for the 2007 season, he never wavered. That shows both a physical gift and a mental toughness.

He kept mixing his pitches and became one of the top pitchers in the game. He didn't have a bad streak all year, and he was lights out in the playoffs.

Daisuke Matsuzaka, SP

2007 Regular season: W–L 15–12, 4.40 ERA, 204.2 IP, 201 K, 80 BB, 1.32 WHIP

2007 Postseason: W–L 2–1, 5.03 ERA, 19.2 IP, 17 K, 8 BB, 1.53 WHIP

2007 World Series: W–L 1–0, 3.38 ERA, 5.1 IP, 5 K, 3 BB, 1.13 WHIP

I still haven't quite figured Matsuzaka out; all through the 2007 season, I felt that he didn't use his fastball enough, but pitching coach John Farrell said that sometimes he used it too much. But what I don't know about pitching could fill a book.

For part of his first season, he became a cut fastball pitcher. They called him a power nibbler: a guy who strikes out a lot of batters but nibbles at the strike zone instead of challenging hitters.

But how can you complain about 15 wins in his first season?

When I first saw him in spring training, I said he was something special. But I also knew that he had never faced the kind of competition that he faced day in and day out in the American League. And add to that the travel and the adjustment to a new culture.

I think that Matsuzaka, like Beckett before him, has to figure out what is his best stuff. He has a good fastball, breaking ball, and curveball. He also has a very good split and changeup. I think he is going to get better in years to come as he adjusts.

I never really spoke with him, just exchanged a couple of bows. He seems like a good kid and the players accepted him very well.

He worked very hard all season long. He was so used to throwing complete games that he was stunned early in the year when Francona came to the mound to take him out in the seventh inning. He couldn't believe it. But pitchers are treated differently here because of the huge financial investment the team makes in them.

Curt Schilling, SP

2007 Regular season: W–L 9–8, 3.87 ERA, 151.0 IP, 101 K, 23 BB, 1.25 WHIP

2007 Postseason: W–L 3–0, 3.00 ERA, 24.0 IP, 16 K, 3 BB, 1.17 WHIP

2007 World Series: W–L 1–0, 1.69 ERA, 5.1 IP, 4 K, 2 BB, 1.13 WHIP

Curt Schilling is one of a kind, and Boston really is the perfect spot for him. In Baltimore he was a kid, in Philadelphia he was a good pitcher on a terrible team, and in Arizona nobody cared.

He signed what he says will be his last pitching contract to come back for the 2008 season; he began it on the disabled list. He has won two championships since coming here and has a chance for a third.

He loves the attention and the passion of the fans in Boston. And he loves baseball.

Schilling goes out there every day and gives you the best that he has. Being in the playoffs doesn't faze him. He has been there and he has been very successful. That knowledge has to rub off on other pitchers and players in the clubhouse.

He got a wakeup call in 2007. He pitched a game in Atlanta on a warm day and he was out of gas. They told him he had to get himself into better shape. They sat him down for a while; they said his elbow or shoulder was bothering him, but basically they gave him time off to get into shape.

He came back after that and people talked about Schilling reinventing himself because he wasn't throwing 96 or 97 miles per hour anymore. Well, he hadn't thrown that hard in a couple of years; he was throwing somewhere between 88 and 92 miles per hour or so.

What's most important is that Schilling knows how to pitch. It doesn't matter if he is throwing 88 or 98. He is still a great control pitcher; he has been his whole career.

For Schilling, everything works off his fastball. He still has a very good split and he threw a few more curveballs in 2007 than he used to. When he is able to locate his fastball, he is going to win. It is that plain and simple, because he can outthink hitters.

So when they say he reinvented himself, it is really that he went to more pitches than he has in the past: changeups, curveballs, splitters, and cutters to go along with this fastball. It gave hitters something else to look for.

And then came the postseason and he was rested and healthy and did his thing. He went out and won three of the eleven postseason games the Red Sox needed to get the World Series trophy again.

Tim Wakefield, SP

2007 Regular season: W–L 17–12, 4.76 ERA, 189.0 IP, 110 K, 64 BB, 1.35 WHIP

2007 Postseason: W–L 0–1, 9.64 ERA, 4.2 IP, 7 K, 2 BB, 1.50 WHIP

2007 World Series: Not on roster

As a knuckleball pitcher, Tim Wakefield gives the Red Sox pitching staff a lot of different styles to show other teams.

It is tough to manage a knuckleball pitcher because he could be flying along and all of a sudden he gives up a three-run home run and you don't have time to get a guy up in the bull pen.

A coach can look at a fastball pitcher and see that his location is off tonight or his velocity is down, but what do you say to a knuckleball pitcher? There are certain fundamentals that he may be doing right or wrong, but when the ball leaves his fingers, nobody knows where it is going.

I don't think Wakefield knows what is going to happen from pitch to pitch, much less from inning to inning.

Some people made a big deal about slotting Wakefield in the rotation between fastball pitchers like Beckett or Matsuzaka. I don't think that makes a big difference. I faced knuckleball pitchers when I played; it might have had an effect on me in the middle of the game when a knuckleballer leaves and the next guy you see throws 98 miles an hour.

Let's say Wakefield goes seven strong innings and they bring in a guy like Papelbon; that's a little bit of a shock. But when it comes to the next night, there is no hangover effect at all.

Jonathan Papelbon, RP

2007 Regular season: W–L 1–3, 37 saves, 1.85 ERA, 58.1 IP, 84 K, 15 BB, 0.77 WHIP

2007 Postseason: W–L 1–0, 4 saves, 0.00 ERA, 10.2 IP, 7 K, 4 BB, 0.84 WHIP

2007 World Series: W–L 0–0, 3 saves, 0.00 ERA, 4.1 IP, 3 K, 0 BB, 0.46 WHIP

Every pitcher starts out wanting to be a starter and so did Jonathan Papelbon, but now he loves his role as closer.

He has the perfect mentality for a closer. He loves the competition. You have to be a little bit goofy to thrive in that job, and he certainly is. He is a fun kid and it is all genuine. It is not phony.

The Red Sox did a perfect job in handling him in 2007. There was no way they were going to allow this guy to be overworked. He was given plenty of time off. He was healthy and as free and strong as he could be entering the playoffs.

Right now Papelbon is one of the top closers in the league. When he comes in throwing fastballs at 95 to 98 miles per hour, plus a nasty splitter and an average slider, he is lights out.

Papelbon saved three of the Red Sox's four wins in their World Series sweep of the Rockies, and he came in for the final five outs of the last game. He, and Hideki Okajima, had nothing left in the tank. Actually that should have been a night off for both of them, but when you have a chance to wrap up the World Series, you go for it.

Even if you are on fumes, you find something a little extra and he did.

Hideki Okajima, RP

2007 Regular season: W–L 3–2, 5 saves, 2.22 ERA, 69.0 IP, 63 K, 17 BB, 0.97 WHIP

2007 Postseason: W–L 0–0, 0 saves, 2.45 ERA, 11.0 IP, 11 K, 3 BB, 1.09 WHIP

2007 World Series: W–L 0–0, 0 saves, 7.36 ERA, 3.2 IP, 6 K, 0 BB, 1.09 WHIP

The Red Sox had scouted Hideki Okajima in Japan. They probably figured he might be a complementary left-hander out of the bull pen and some thought he was hired to give Daisuke Matsuzaka someone to talk with close up. I am sure that they didn't think they were getting what they ended up with.

I watched him when he arrived for spring training in 2007 and I didn't see anything that impressive. I didn't see any success for him.

He throws about 88 miles an hour, and his curveball was only average; that was supposed to have been his big pitch in Japan. But then they came up with this little split-finger fastball that turned his whole year around and turned out to be very, very important to the success of the Red Sox, especially in the first half of the season.

All of a sudden he became the most valuable pitcher out of the bull pen because he made it so easy to get to the closer, Jonathan Papelbon.

Okajima showed he could get both right-handers and left-handers out. Francona didn't have to mix and match when he got to the seventh or eighth; Okajima would come in and get it done.

It all started out a bit scary; Okajima gave up a home run on the first pitch he threw in the major leagues on April 2, against Kansas City. Catcher John Buck turned around a flat fastball and deposited it over the centerfield fence. "First pitch didn't go as we planned," Terry Francona said after the game.

But just over two weeks later, on April 20, the Red Sox roared back with five runs against Luis Vizcaíno and Mariano Rivera in the bottom of the eighth inning to take a 7–6 lead over the New York Yankees. And then Francona handed the ball to Okajima to close the ninth inning; Papelbon had closed out the two previous games in Toronto and was not available.

Okajima set down the Yankees, including Alex Rodríguez—already 3 for 4 with two homers in the game—and earned his first major league save. It was his coming out, and a huge confidence builder for him.

That changed it all around for him. There are so few good pitchers at that stage of the game to hold that lead until you get to your closer, and he did it better than anybody this year.

His workload was much more than he had ever pitched in his career, the same kind of experience that Matsuzaka had, and late in the season, Okajima needed to be shut down for a few weeks because he was getting really tired. It worked out perfectly because he pitched great in the playoffs.

Jon Lester, SP/RP

2007 Regular season: W–L 4-0, 4.57 ERA, 63.0 IP, 50 K, 31 BB, 1.46 WHIP

2007 Postseason: W–L 1–0, 1.93 ERA, 9.1 IP, 8 K, 4 BB, 1.07 WHIP

2007 World Series: W–L 1–0, 0.00 ERA, 5.2 IP, 3 K, 3 BB, 1.06 WHIP

Jon Lester was the winning pitcher in Game 4 of the World Series as the Red Sox swept the Rockies; a year before he was out of baseball, going through chemotherapy.

The Red Sox considered him a higher prospect in the minors than Jonathan Papelbon, which is pretty impressive. We haven't seen that level of performance yet, but he is still a kid and he has had to deal with serious off-field problems.

And now he is going to be able to concentrate on getting himself strong. I don't think we've seen the best of him yet.

Manny Delcarmen, RP

2007 Regular season: W–L 0–0, 1 save, 2.05 ERA, 44.0 IP, 41 K, 17 BB, 1.02 WHIP

2007 Postseason: W–L 0–0, 0 saves, 8.31 ERA, 4.1 IP, 5 K, 3 BB, 2.31 WHIP

2007 World Series: W–L 0–0, 0 saves, 6.75 ERA, 1.1 IP, 1 K, 1 BB, 3.00 WHIP

Manny Delcarmen had a breakout year in 2007. All of a sudden he was throwing strikes, something he hadn't been able to do when he first came up, and he was bringing it at 97 or 98 miles per hour. He also had a very good change and good breaking ball.

He has a great arm and you could see his confidence grow in the second half of the season.

Clay Buchholz, SP/RP

2007 Regular season: W–L 3–1, 1.59 ERA, 22.2 IP, 22 K, 10 BB, 1.06 WHIP

2007 Postseason: Not on roster

2007 World Series: Not on roster

Another great story in 2007 was Clay Buchholz, a kid who threw a no-hitter in his second start.

You can tell he has good stuff, but as with any young player we'll need to see more. But what I've seen so far I like a lot. He has an over-the-top fastball and curveball and a very good change up. He looks like he can win.

A no-hitter is kind of a freak thing in baseball. It is not something everybody expects every time you pitch. If you do it once in your career, that's great. It's not the same as coming up in your first year and winning 18 games and now you are expected to be an 18-game winner next year.

There was real concern in the front office about having Buchholz throw too many innings, or too many pitches in one game. But I think there would have been a riot at Fenway Park if Francona had taken Buchholz out of the game while he still had a no-hitter going.

The Red Sox are very conscious of protecting their young pitchers. I understand that. But when someone is pitching a no-hitter you don't pull him. I don't care if it is another forty pitches. You got to leave him out there.

What we need to see now is consistency. It was a good no-hitter, and I think he is going to be a good pitcher.

Julian Tavárez, SP/RP

2007 Regular season: W–L 7–11, 5.15 ERA, 134.2 IP, 77 K, 51 BB, 1.50 WHIP

2007 Postseason: Not on roster

2007 World Series: Not on roster

Julian Tavárez did a decent job in the roles they gave him.

Yo-Yo was a lot of fun to watch on the field; you never quite knew what he was going to do. I remember when he rolled a couple of balls at Youkilis instead of throwing them to make an out.

He is one of those rare guys who can sit around for a week and not do anything and then go out and pitch on a moment's notice. He loves baseball and I was a little sad for him when he wasn't on the postseason roster because he made some contributions during the season.

Dustin Pedroia, 2B

American League Rookie of the Year

2007 Regular season: 520 AB, .317 average, 39 doubles, 1 triple, 8 HR, 50 RBI, .380 OBP

2007 Postseason: 60 AB, .283 average, 6 doubles, 0 triples, 2 HR, 10 RBI, .348 OBP

2007 World Series: 18 AB, .278 average, 1 double, 0 triples, 0 HR, 4 RBI, .350 OBP

When Pedroia came up for a look-see at the end of 2006 and then was in the lineup at the start of the 2007 season, I didn't think he was ready for prime time; I wasn't even sure he was a big league player.

But the front office felt very strongly that if they stayed with the kid, he would survive the way he has his whole life. And all of a sudden things started to click for him. And it became one of the nice stories of the year. On May 1, he was batting .182, and by the end of the season, he was chosen as AL Rookie of the Year.

He is a classic overachiever. He has been that way his whole life. He is not big in stature and he has to work harder than everybody else. He is very confident in himself, almost to the point of being cocky.

He was well received by his teammates because of his attitude and he got a lot of support from veteran players on the team, which is unusual in baseball. He surprised a lot of people except probably himself.

I guess that almost everything that I've just said about Pedroia could probably have been fairly said about me when I first came up from the minors. I know what he is going through because I had to do the same thing. It took a while to figure what my game was. It probably took me until I got to Boston really to figure out what kind of player I was going to be. And I think Pedroia is still figuring it out for himself.

It was a great rookie year for him, but I don't get too excited until I see it over and over and over again. I don't mean to take anything away from him; it's just that you want to see consistency and that takes a while to build up.

He does have tremendous hand-eye coordination. It is pretty unique to see a guy that small swinging as hard as he does. He uses a pretty light bat, gets good bat speed, doesn't strike out, and gets the bat on the ball.

He is a dead fastball hitter. Sometimes I wonder why a pitcher would ever throw him a fastball.

Jacoby Ellsbury, OF

2007 Regular season: 116 AB, .353 average, 7 doubles, 1 triple, 3 HR, 18 RBI, .394 OBP

2007 Postseason: 25 AB, .360 average, 4 doubles, 0 triples, 0 HR, 3 RBI, .429 OBP

2007 World Series: 16 AB, .438 average, 4 doubles, 0 triples, 0 HR, 3 RBI, .500 OBP

Here's another great story; there's no question about the level of excitement Jacoby Ellsbury brought to the team with his tremendous speed.

He is one of the fastest Red Sox in memory, up there with Otis Nixon and Tommy Harper. I think before my knees went bad, I could have been there with him.

He reminds me a bit of Johnny Damon when he was younger. We'll have to see how he performs over time, after he gets 500 at bats; I think the results are going to be pretty good.

His speed makes him an impact player immediately. Now we will have to see how he hits. Other teams are going to try and figure a way to get him out, and I think I know how they are going to do that. And then he will have to adjust to that.

When it comes to defense in the outfield, he is still learning. He was good, but not at the level of Coco Crisp.

And it's also interesting to learn that he may be the first Navajo to play major league baseball. He was born and grew up in Oregon, but he is a member of the Colorado River Indian Tribes in Arizona.

It is going to be fun to watch him grow. I do see things that could make him very special.

Kevin Youkilis, 1B

American League Gold Glove winner

2007 Regular season: 528 AB, .288 average, 35 doubles, 2 triples, 16 HR, 83 RBI, .390 OBP

2007 Postseason: 49 AB, .388 average, 4 doubles, 1 triple, 4 HR, 10 RBI, .475 OBP

2007 World Series: 9 AB, .222 average, 2 doubles, 0 triples, 0 HR, 1 RBI, .417 OBP

Kevin Youkilis played his first full season at first base in 2007 and he was perfect for the year; he won the Gold Glove. This is a guy who started as a catcher in the minor leagues and came up to the majors as a third baseman.

It was like he was made for first base. He was really good over there. He saved a lot of errors for his infielders taking balls out of the dirt. He was excellent on bunt plays. And to go a whole year without making an error at first base is remarkable with all the balls you have to handle. Good plays save runs and he was so very solid.

At the plate he is such a patient hitter, almost never swinging at bad pitches. He tries to work counts; he was that way all through the minor leagues. That's why the Red Sox loved him; he fit right in to what they were trying to do as an offensive team, and that is to wear pitchers down.

I don't know if you can teach that. Some guys are aggressive and some guys can be very patient.

David Ortiz, DH

2007 Silver Slugger winner

2007 Regular season: 549 AB, .332 average, 52 doubles, 1 triple, 35 HR, 117 RBI, .445 OBP

2007 Postseason: 46 AB, .370 average, 6 doubles, 0 triples, 3 HR, 10 RBI, .508 OBP

2007 World Series: 15 AB, .333 average, 3 doubles, 0 triples, 0 HR, 4 RBI, .412 OBP

This may have been David Ortiz's best all-around year. His home run numbers were down to a mere 35, but his batting average was way up, and he led the major leagues with a .445 on-base percentage.

When you hit 54 home runs the year before, you think you've got to do it again, and that doesn't always happen. All through the season, other teams pitched him very carefully and I think that hurt some of his pop.

For the first half of the year, his knees were bothering him, which affected his legs; most of a hitter's power comes from his legs. In the second half he was a little healthier and you could see his swing was better. He went in for knee surgery a few days after the World Series parade.

Through it all, he ended up batting .332 for the season and got 52 doubles and even a triple, although he couldn't run a lick and he had to hit through defensive shifts. That's pretty impressive.

Manny Ramírez, who batted behind him most of the year, put up lesser numbers than he has in recent years. But that didn't mean that there were many teams that pitched around Ortiz to get to Manny.

There are still not that many managers who want to see Manny come to the plate, choosing to take their chances with Ortiz. It is "pick your poison" when Ortiz and Ramírez are swinging the bat well.

Manny Ramírez, OF

2007 Regular season: 483 AB, .295 average, 33 doubles, 1 triple, 20 HR, 88 RBI, .388 OBP

2007 Postseason: 46 AB, .348 average, 2 doubles, 0 triples, 4 HR, 16 RBI, .508 OBP

2007 World Series: 16 AB, .250 average, 1 double, 0 triples, 0 HR, 2 RBI, .333 OBP

There were a couple of games early in the season when Manny Ramírez hit balls that I thought were gone. But each time the wind was blowing in, and he was robbed of a home run. He could have had at least five in the first month or two taken away from him by weather conditions or good plays. That's huge when you think of the final total.

Sometimes a player gets on a roll hitting home runs and it keeps going and going. And then when you are not hitting them, you start pressing and that usually doesn't work.

Manny didn't speak with reporters for the entire season, but in the playoffs all of a sudden he became the most quotable guy in town. Of course, Manny being Manny, he made those comments just after he beat the Angels in the bottom of the ninth inning of the second game of the ALDS, hitting the first walkoff home run of his fabulous Red Sox career, a moon shot off Francisco Rodríguez that cleared the Coke bottles and was last seen headed for the Mass Pike.

The suddenly talkative Ramírez told reporters that Rodriguez was one of the greatest closers in the game and that he was one of the best hitters.

It wasn't a typical Manny Ramírez year, but I didn't see any decline in his bat speed or ability. And he seemed to benefit from the time he took off to recover from a strained left oblique muscle late in the season.

Manny can turn it on any time.

Mike Lowell, 3B

World Series MVP

2007 Regular season: 589 AB, .324 average, 37 doubles, 2 triples, 21 HR, 120 RBI, .378 OBP

2007 Postseason: 51 AB, .353 average, 7 doubles, 0 triples, 2 HR, 15 RBI, .410 OBP

2007 World Series: 15 AB, .400 average, 3 doubles, 0 triples, 1 HR, 4 RBI, .500 OBP

Lowell was my MVP for the whole season. He was in the perfect position behind Ortiz and Ramírez. It doesn't get any better than that. He had men on base all the time for him.

Lowell was a model of consistency all year, hitting for average, driving in runs, getting two-out hits to the opposite field to drive in runs. He put up the best numbers of his career in batting average, hits, RBIs, and on-base percentage.

Day in and day out, he was a true professional. He never gets too high or too low and he was great with the guys in the clubhouse.

J. D. Drew, OF

2007 Regular season: 466 AB, .270 average, 30 doubles, 4 triples, 11 HR, 64 RBI, .373 OBP

2007 Postseason: 51 AB, .314 average, 3 doubles, 0 triples, 1 HR, 11 RBI, .352 OBP

2007 World Series: 15 AB, .333 average, 2 doubles, 0 triples, 0 HR, 2 RBI, .412 OBP

I didn't know very much about J. D. Drew because he had spent his entire career in the National League. But when I got to spring training and I saw him play I said, "This is a talented guy."

He had a difficult year, and I think part of it had to do with family issues off the field; some guys handle that better than others. I think he also had some difficulty because he did not know the American League; some of the better games he had were against National League teams.

I think he finally realized that if you are a left-handed hitter at Fenway Park and have some power, left field is a nice place to go. Toward the end of the year, he started to use the opposite field and that helped him.

In the end I think he got a mulligan from the fans because he hit well in the playoffs.

Jason Varitek, C

2007 Regular season: 435 AB, .255 average, 15 doubles, 3 triples, 17 HR, 68 RBI, .367 OBP

2007 Postseason: 52 AB, .269 average, 5 doubles, 0 triples, 1 HR, 10 RBI, .310 OBP

2007 World Series: 15 AB, .333 average, 1 double, 0 triples, 0 HR, 5 RBI, .333 OBP

Jason Varitek is the general. The confidence he brings to the pitchers is tremendous. They know when he is catching, they are going to have a pretty good plan of attack against the guys they are facing.

He has tremendous knowledge of the league. He deals with his pitching staff every day; he knows what is good for them, what is bad for them, and makes adjustments through the season and each game.

He is getting up there a little bit in age, and you have to start to be concerned about that, especially for a catcher. But players today work hard so they can get those extra four or five years they didn't get years ago.

Julio Lugo, SS

2007 Regular season: 570 AB, .237 average, 36 doubles, 2 triples, 8 HR, 73 RBI, .294 OBP

2007 Postseason: 48 AB, .271 average, 3 doubles, 0 triples, 0 HR, 3 RBI, .340 OBP

2007 World Series: 13 AB, .385 average, 1 double, 0 triples, 0 HR, 1 RBI, .500 OBP

Julio Lugo was a pretty good offensive player at Tampa Bay, but when he came to Boston in 2007, he started off the season in a terrible slump. He wasn't a disaster, though. He had some big hits and even when he was not hitting well, he was still driving in runs; he ended up with 73 RBIs, fifth highest on the team.

Defensively he was better than I thought he was going to be. When he played for Tampa, many of his errors were on throws; he always had decent hands and range. Luis Alicea, Boston's first-base coach who was a former infielder, worked hard with him on footwork and getting into good position to make throws and it paid off.

Coco Crisp, OF

2007 Regular season: 526 AB, .268 average, 28 doubles, 7 triples, 6 HR, 60 RBI, .330 OBP

2007 Postseason: 33 AB, .182 average, 1 double, 0 triples, 0 HR, 2 RBI, .206 OBP

2007 World Series: 2 AB, .500 average, 0 doubles, 0 triples, 0 HR, 0 RBI, .500 OBP

Coco Crisp didn't win the Gold Glove in 2007, coming in behind Grady Sizemore of Cleveland, but as far as I am concerned I don't think anybody played a better defensive center field. He doesn't throw very well, but he gets a great jump on the ball and he is fearless. He will dive for everything.

As we've already talked about in this book, center fielders get the best look at the pitches so they get the best jumps. In addition Crisp learned how to play the wall, how to play the triangle, and how to play the bull pen area—all of these are essentials in the tricky Boston outfield.

Alex Cora, IF

2007 Regular season: 207 AB, .246 average, 10 doubles, 5 triples, 3 HR, 18 RBI, .298 OBP

2007 Postseason: 0 AB, .000 average, 0 doubles, 0 triples, 0 HR, 0 RBI, .000 OBP

2007 World Series: No plate appearances

Alex Cora was perfect for his role with the team. Everybody wants to play every day, but the Red Sox had the luxury of veteran guys like him on the bench.

It's not an easy job to be a backup player. You don't get to keep your timing sharp like you can when you play every day; you have to make the most of pregame practice and stay in condition.

The Red Sox also had veterans like Eric Hinske, who was an everyday

Powerhouse Pitching in 2007

Among the great pitching accomplishments of 2007 was Clay Buchholz throwing a no-hitter on his second start in the major leagues, forty-year-old veteran Curt Schilling coming within one out of doing the same, and Josh Beckett's lights-out pitching down the stretch and into the postseason.

To me Beckett's season would absolutely come in first. Even if he didn't get the award, he had a Cy Young year.

Schilling will remember for the rest of his life that he shook off Varitek's pitch call; you don't get many chances for no-hitters. Clay Buchholz's game was even better, but in the long haul they don't compare with what Beckett did all year.

player before he came over, and Bobby Kielty, who arrived late in the year. I guess when you are on a team like the Red Sox, you figure you have a chance to win a World Series and that makes it easier to accept those roles.

But I love veterans like Cora because nothing fazed him. He could sit out a week, come in and do a decent job defensively, and stick a hit every once in a while.

I was so used to being an everyday player I couldn't have done it. Not that I was a great player, but I don't think I could have accepted it.

Bobby Kielty, OF

2007 Regular season: 87 AB, .218 average, 3 doubles, 0 triples, 1 HR, 12 RBI, .287 OBP

2007 Postseason: 6 AB, .500 average, 0 doubles, 0 triple, 1 HR, 2 RBI, .667 OBP

2007 World Series: 1 AB, 1.000 average, 0 doubles, 0 triples, 1 HR, 1 RBI, 1.000 OBP

Another great story from the 2007 season: Bobby Kielty gets one at bat in the World Series in the eighth inning of the final game. He sees one pitch, swings, and hits a home run that turns out to be the deciding run.

You can't predict that stuff. The first thing I thought was, suppose Wily Mo Peña had been in that spot; he probably would have struck out.

Kielty had been released by the Oakland Athletics on July 31, and the Red Sox signed him to a minor league deal a week later. On August 18, he was called up from Pawtucket after Wily Mo Peña was traded to the Washington Nationals.

It turned out that the move the front office made to get Kielty was a good one. It worked out perfectly for that one hit. They knew he was a pretty decent outfielder and as a batter he was better from the right side than the left.

He had to walk away from the World Series with a great feeling. He went from being released to joining a team that was going to the postseason, and then hitting a home run in the World Series. It's like heaven.

Dustin Pedroia, the surprise Rookie of the Year for the 2007 season, takes to the air in the arms of David Ortiz. Pedroia became only the second player in World Series history to lead off the first inning of Game 1 with a home run. Big Papi eventually gently returned little Pedroia to earth.

Photo by Brita Meng Outzen

CHAPTER THIRTY-ONE

We Don't Need No Stinkin' Wild Card

Let's start with one essential fact about the 2007 regular season: The Boston Red Sox won the American League East. They did not enter the playoffs with the Wild Card the way they did in 2005, 2004, 2003, 1999, and 1998. They were the champions of their division, two solid games ahead of the New York Yankees.

Any way you can get into the playoffs is good, but when you're in the same division as those guys from New York, it's a triumph. Boston holds the record for the most Wild Card appearances in major league baseball, with five entries.

But right from the start of the 2007 season, the Red Sox showed they were going to be in the hunt. Boston claimed the top spot two weeks after opening day, on April 18, and did not let go for the remaining 166 days of the season.

New York stumbled out of the gate, and by the end of May, they were competing with the Tampa Bay Devil Rays for last place. The Red Sox were winning steadily and put some distance between themselves and Toronto and Baltimore.

On May 29, the Red Sox floated an amazing 14½ games above the Yankees. As bad as they were in the first few months, New York put on an amazing run in the second half. As the teams came down the stretch, a stumble by Boston could have dropped them into second place and completely out of the playoffs.

To add to the sense of dread in Red Sox Nation, manager Terry Francona had to deal with injuries and fatigue that struck key players. Manny Ramírez sat for a few weeks with a muscle strain. Starting warhorse Curt Schilling and stellar setup man Hideki Okajima were shut down for a while with tired arms. Kevin Youkilis had a bruised right wrist and you could see him wince on many swings. And big man David Ortiz played through with a bad knee and shoulder.

But the Red Sox held on and won the division.

Among the magic tricks performed by Francona: ending the season with his starting rotation perfectly aligned for the playoffs. Twenty-game winner Josh Beckett was ready to roll as the starting pitcher for the American League Division Series and his sparkling performance set the tone that would carry Boston all the way through to the Promised Land.

And just for good measure, this time the road to the World Series did not lead through the Bronx; the Cleveland Indians—probably the second best team in baseball in 2007—dispatched the Yankees in the ALDS. The Indians would present the greatest challenge to Boston in October.

American League Division Series

ALDS Game 1
at Boston
October 3, 2007

	Score by innings	R	H	E
LA Angels	000 000 000	0	4	0
BOSTON	103 000 00X	4	9	0

PITCHING

	IP	H	R	ER	BB	SO	HR	ERA
LA ANGELS								
Lackey (L 0–1)	6.0	9	4	4	2	4	2	6.00
Santana	2.0	0	0	0	0	2	0	0.00
BOSTON								
Beckett (W 1–0)	9.0	4	0	0	0	8	0	0.00

The line score tells it all: Josh Beckett tossed a four-hit complete game shutout, with eight strikeouts and no walks. He threw 108 pitches, 83 of them for strikes.

After giving up a single to the first batter of the game, Beckett retired the next consecutive nineteen batters, a tie for the third-longest streak in postseason history.

It was the first postseason complete-game shutout for the Red Sox since Luis Tiant baffled the Cincinnati Reds in Game 1 of the 1975 World

Series. And for Beckett, it was his second consecutive October shutout; pitching for the Florida Marlins in Game 6 of the 2003 World Series he had closed down . . . the New York Yankees.

At Fenway, Beckett received a standing ovation from the Red Sox faithful when he came out to the mound for the ninth inning.

"It's a really cool thing to be able to go out there and be the only pitcher that pitches for your team that day," Beckett told us after the game. "After eight innings, I don't think they ever really thought about taking me out. I was going back out there."

The Angels opened with their own ace, 19-game-winner John Lackey. His shutout lasted only one batter; Kevin Youkilis belted a solo home run over the Green Monster in the first inning, which was all the offense Beckett really needed. But just for comfort, in the third inning Big Papi added a two-run shot and Mike Lowell iced the cake with an RBI, driving in Manny Ramírez who had walked and moved to second on a wild pitch.

Youkilis said his wrist was feeling much better. "It's playoff time and adrenaline helps the most," he said.

Beckett took a one-hitter into the sixth inning and never faced a serious challenge. All four Angel hits were singles, and no runner reached third with less than two outs.

The whole package was wrapped up in two hours and twenty-seven minutes and Red Sox Nation went to bed relatively early and quite happy.

	POS	AB	R	H	RBI	BB	SO	LOB	AVG
LA ANGELS									
Figgins	RF, CF	4	0	1	0	0	1	0	.250
Cabrera	SS	4	0	0	0	0	1	1	.000
Guerrero	DH	4	0	2	0	0	0	1	.500
Anderson	LF	4	0	0	0	0	2	3	.000
Izturis	3B	3	0	0	0	0	0	1	.000
Kotchman	1B	3	0	0	0	0	1	0	.000
Kendrick	2B	3	0	1	0	0	0	0	.333
Napoli	C	2	0	0	0	0	1	0	.000
Aybar[a]	PH, RF	1	0	0	0	0	0	1	.000
Willits	CF	2	0	0	0	0	1	0	.000
Morales[b]	PH	1	0	0	0	0	1	1	.000
Mathis	C	0	0	0	0	0	0	0	.000
TOTALS		**31**	**0**	**4**	**0**	**0**	**8**	**8**	

[a]-Grounded into force out for Napoli in 8th.

[b]-Struck out for Willits in 8th.

BOSTON									
Pedroia	2B	4	0	0	0	0	1	0	.000
Youkilis	1B	4	2	2	1	0	1	0	.500
Ortiz	DH	3	1	2	2	1	0	0	.667
Ramírez	LF	3	1	1	0	1	1	1	.333
Ellsbury	LF	0	0	0	0	0	0	0	.000
Lowell	3B	3	0	1	1	0	0	2	.333
Drew	RF	3	0	1	0	0	0	3	.333
Varitek	C	3	0	1	0	0	1	1	.333
Crisp	CF	3	0	0	0	0	0	1	.000
Lugo	SS	3	0	1	0	0	2	0	.333
TOTALS		**29**	**4**	**9**	**4**	**2**	**6**	**8**	

2B: Youkilis (1, Lackey).
HR: Youkilis (1, Lackey), Ortiz (1, Lackey).

ALDS Game 2
at Boston
October 5, 2007

	Score by innings	R	H	E
LA Angels	030 000 000	3	7	0
BOSTON	200 010 003	6	9	0

PITCHING

	IP	H	R	ER	BB	SO	HR	ERA
LA ANGELS								
Escobar	5.0	4	3	3	5	5	0	5.40
Shields	2.0	0	0	0	3	1	0	0.00
Speier (L 0–1)	1.1	1	1	1	0	0	0	6.75
Rodríguez	0.1	1	2	2	1	1	1	54.00
BOSTON								
Matsuzaka	4.2	7	3	3	3	3	0	5.79
López	0.1	0	0	0	0	0	0	0.00
Delcarmen	1.1	0	0	0	0	1	0	0.00
Okajima	1.1	0	0	0	0	2	0	0.00
Papelbon (W 1–0)	1.1	0	0	0	2	1	0	0.00

The first game was a piece of cake; the second was tough as nails. It started on a balmy Friday night at Fenway and ended Saturday morning with Manny being Manny in the best possible way.

Walks played a major role in Boston's victory. Angels pitcher Kelvim Escobar, who averaged less than three bases on balls per nine innings in the regular season, issued five in five frames. There were four more walks by the relievers who followed.

Boston jumped out to a 2–0 lead in the first inning. Kevin Youkilis, a guy who specializes in making pitchers throw strikes, drew a walk. Escobar then gave up a line drive single to David Ortiz. With two outs, Mike Lowell drew another walk to load the bases. Up came J. D. Drew. On the second pitch he saw, he hit a ground ball up the middle to score Youk and Manny.

Daisuke Matsuzaka's first postseason game, though, was less than stellar. Daisuke gave back three runs on a walk, a single, and a pair of doubles in the second inning. Over all, he yielded seven hits and three runs on 96 pitches and was back on the bench with two outs in the fifth inning.

But Boston's bull pen came to the rescue and shut down the Angels for the remainder of the game. Javy López ended the fifth inning without allowing two inherited runners to score, and the Red Sox got four outs each from Manny Delcarmen, Hideki Okajima, and Jonathan Papelbon.

Dustin Pedroia led off the bottom of the fifth with a double and advanced to third on a groundout. Escobar intentionally walked Ortiz to set up the possibility of a double play, but Manny Ramírez emulated Youk: after fouling off three straight pitches, he took the next four balls to draw a walk to load the bases with one out. And then Mike Lowell lifted a fly ball to center field to bring home Pedroia from third with the tying run.

The game remained knotted all the way through to the bottom of the ninth and it was here that Angels manager Mike Scioscia had to make some very difficult choices as the Sox sent up the heart of their relentless batting order.

Julio Lugo set the table with a leadoff line drive single to left. Pedroia grounded out to first base, allowing Lugo to move into scoring position at second.

Scioscia changed pitchers, bringing in his hard-throwing right-handed closer Francisco Rodríguez. K-Rod tried a pickoff move on Lugo but then concentrated on Youkilis at the plate, striking him out on four pitches.

With two outs Scioscia faced the toughest of choices: pitch to David Ortiz or Manny Ramírez. He instructed K-Rod to intentionally walk Ortiz again.

And up comes Manny. He watched the first pitch come in low and outside. And then he swung at the next pitch, a 96-mile-per-hour fastball on the inside of the plate; he kept his hands inside the ball and launched it over the Coke bottles and onto Landsdowne Street.

The three-run homer gave the Red Sox a 6–3 walkoff victory in four hours and five minutes of tight baseball. And hard as it is to believe, it was the first time Manny had hit a walk-off home run as a member of the Red Sox; he picked a great time to check that particular item off his to-do list.

It was Manny's first home run since August 28, when he suffered a strain of his left oblique muscle; he sat out twenty-four games while the Red Sox held on to first place by their fingernails.

He was apparently so pleased with himself that he ended his season-long vow of silence and spoke with the press after the game. "In that moment, I'm just trying to see the ball and trust myself," Ramírez said. "I'm not trying to do too much. I've got a lot of confidence in myself. He's one of the greatest closers in the game and I'm one of the best hitters in the game. You know, he missed his spot and I got good timing on the ball, and that's it."

One of the funnier observations came from David Ortiz, who received a record-setting four walks in the game, including two that were officially intentional. "When a guy hits a ball like that, you might want to pitch to the guy in front of him," Ortiz said.

Mike Lowell, waiting on deck as Ramírez batted, said the swing was unreal. "Oh my God," said Lowell. "I think I was just in amazement before I really realized the game was over. He crushed that ball. It was one of the best bolts I've seen here."

Angels manager Scioscia explained his thinking. "You really pick your poison," he said. "We talked about this all week. Both those guys are terrific. I just think in that situation . . . we're going to take our chances with some matchups. It made sense not to go after David. It didn't work tonight."

It was just the fifth time that a Red Sox player ended a postseason game with a walk-off homer. There was Carlton Fisk's blast against the Reds in the 1975 World Series. Then there was Trot Nixon's against the Athletics in the 2003 ALDS. En route to the World Series championship in 2004, David Ortiz did it twice: against the Angels in the ALDS and against the Yankees in the American League Championship Series.

Suddenly talkative Manny continued. "It feels great," he told reporters. "It's been a long time since I've done something special like that. I haven't been right all year. But, I guess when you don't feel good and you still get hits, that's when you know you are a bad man."

Bad, as in very good.

"It was a great swing," said Red Sox manager Terry Francona. "But I think part of the reason he got a chance to swing was because David's such a good hitter and such a clutch hitter. It's hard to let David beat you. But Manny's such a good hitter behind him, he made them pay."

	POS	AB	R	H	RBI	BB	SO	LOB	AVG
LA ANGELS									
Figgins	CF, RF	5	1	1	1	0	3	3	.222
Cabrera	SS	4	0	1	1	1	0	1	.125
Guerrero	DH	3	0	0	0	0	0	2	.286
Napoli	C	1	0	0	0	0	0	0	.000
Anderson	LF	4	0	2	0	1	0	1	.250
Izturis	3B	5	0	1	0	0	2	5	.125
Kotchman	1B	2	1	0	0	2	0	1	.000
Morales	DH	4	1	1	0	0	1	3	.200
Kendrick	2B	4	0	1	0	0	1	2	.286
Mathis	C	3	0	0	1	0	0	2	.000
Rivera[a]	PH	0	0	0	0	1	0	0	.000
Willits[b]	PR, CF	0	0	0	0	0	0	0	.000
TOTALS		**35**	**3**	**7**	**3**	**5**	**7**	**20**	

[a]-Walked for Mathis in 8th.
[b]-Ran for Rivera in 8th.
2B: Figgins (1, Matsuzaka), Cabrera (1, Matsuzaka), Anderson (1, Matsuzaka).

	POS	AB	R	H	RBI	BB	SO	LOB	AVG
BOSTON									
Pedroia	2B	5	1	1	0	0	0	1	.111
Youkilis	1B	4	1	0	0	1	2	2	.250
Ortiz	DH	1	2	1	0	4	0	0	.750
Ramírez	LF	3	1	1	3	2	1	3	.333
Lowell	3B	2	0	0	1	1	0	3	.200
Drew	RF	4	0	1	2	0	0	2	.286
Varitek	C	4	0	0	0	0	1	2	.143
Crisp	CF	3	0	1	0	1	1	0	.167
Lugo	SS	4	1	1	0	0	2	2	.286
TOTALS		**30**	**6**	**6**	**6**	**9**	**7**	**15**	

2B: Pedroia (1, Escobar).
HR: Ramírez (1, Rodriguez).

ALDS Game 3
at Anaheim
October 7, 2007

	Score by innings	R	H	E
Boston	000 200 070	9	10	0
LA ANGELS	000 000 001	1	8	0

PITCHING

	IP	H	R	ER	BB	SO	HR	ERA
BOSTON								
Schilling (W 1–0)	7.0	6	0	0	1	4	0	0.00
Okajima	1.0	1	0	0	1	0	0	0.00
Gagné	1.0	1	1	1	0	1	0	9.00
LA ANGELS								
Weaver (L 0–1)	5.0	4	2	2	3	5	2	3.60
Shields	2.0	0	1	1	1	3	0	2.25
Speier	0.1	3	4	4	1	0	0	27.00
Oliver	0.2	2	2	2	0	0	0	27.00
Moseley	1.0	1	0	0	0	1	0	0.00

Curt Schilling long ago proved himself to be a Big Game pitcher, and no games are bigger than the ones that come in October. At the age of forty, he no longer relies on heat but instead on guile. And he was about as good as Red Sox Nation could have hoped when he took to the mound in Anaheim.

Schilling tossed seven innings of six-hit ball without giving up a run. On the other side, Jered Weaver was good but not perfect, giving up two runs in five innings.

The Angels threatened in the third inning. With two on and two outs, Vladimir Guerrero walked to load the bases. But Schilling got Reggie Willits to pop out to Jason Varitek in foul territory.

And as often happens in baseball, immediately after the Red Sox wriggled off the hook, they responded with a big inning. David Ortiz led off the fourth inning with a moon shot to right field. And then Manny Ramírez saw eight pitches before he found one he really liked; he hit a long homer onto the artificial mountainside beyond the centerfield fence.

This was the ninth time Ortiz and Ramírez have hit back-to-back home runs since becoming teammates in 2003, and the second time it has happened in the postseason.

After the game Schilling referred to Angels manager Scioscia's comments after Manny beat his team in Boston two days earlier. "Mike put it great," said Schilling. "Pick your poison. There is no way to get either one of those guys out when they're both on."

The next explosion came in the top of the eighth inning. Julio Lugo led off with a walk, and after Justin Speier replaced Scot Shields on the mound, Dustin Pedroia doubled to left. Lugo scored on the double and Pedroia moved on to third on a throw to home. Kevin Youkilis brought him home with a sacrifice fly. Ortiz singled, Ramírez earned a walk, and Mike Lowell doubled. J. D. brought home a run on a fielder's choice. Jason Varitek doubled Lowell home. And Coco Crisp drove in two more runs with a single. A close game suddenly became a rout as the Red Sox scored seven runs to go up 9–0.

The lead gave Terry Francona the opportunity to bring in Eric Gagné in the ninth; he gave up a ground-rule double on a line drive to right field and a wild pitch; the Angels' single run came home on a sacrifice fly. A fly ball to right field ended the game and sent the Red Sox on to the American League Championship with a three-game sweep.

	POS	AB	R	H	RBI	BB	SO	LOB	AVG
BOSTON									
Pedroia	2B	4	1	1	1	1	1	1	.154
Youkilis	1B	4	0	1	1	0	1	2	.250
Ortiz	DH	3	2	2	1	1	1	0	.714
Hinske[a]	PH, DH	1	0	0	0	0	1	1	.000
Ramírez	LF	2	1	1	1	2	0	1	.375
Ellsbury[b]	PR, LF	1	1	0	0	0	0	1	.000
Lowell	3B	4	1	2	1	0	0	1	.333
Drew	RF	4	1	0	1	0	1	3	.182
Varitek	C	4	1	1	1	0	2	2	.182
Crisp	CF	4	0	1	2	0	2	2	.200
Lugo	SS	3	1	1	0	1	0	1	.300
TOTALS		**34**	**9**	**10**	**9**	**5**	**9**	**15**	

[a]-Struck out for Ortiz in 9th.
[b]-Ran for Ramírez in 8th.
2B: Lowell 2 (2, Weaver, Speier), Pedroia (2, Speier), Varitek (1, Oliver).
HR: Ortiz (2, Weaver), Ramírez (2,Weaver).

LA ANGELS									
Figgins	CF	4	0	1	0	0	0	2	.231
Cabrera	SS	4	0	2	0	0	0	2	.250
Guerrero	RF	3	0	0	0	1	0	2	.200
Anderson	LF	1	0	0	0	0	0	1	.222
Willits	LF	2	0	0	0	1	1	3	.000
Morales	1B	4	0	0	0	0	0	2	.111
Izturis	3B	4	1	3	0	0	0	0	.333
Kendrick	2B	3	0	0	1	0	0	2	.200
Rivera	DH	3	0	1	0	0	1	1	.333
Haynes[a]	PH, DH	1	0	0	0	0	1	0	.000
Napoli	C	3	0	1	0	0	2	2	.167
Quinlan[b]	PH	1	0	0	0	0	0	0	.000
TOTALS		**33**	**3**	**8**	**1**	**2**	**5**	**17**	

[a]-Struck out for Rivera in 9th.
[b]-Flied out for Napoli in 9th.
2B: Izturis 2 (2, Schilling, Gagné), Figgins (2, Okajima).

American League Championship Series

ALCS Game 1
at Boston
October 12, 2007

	Score by innings	R	H	E
Cleveland	100 001 010	3	8	0
BOSTON	104 032 00X	10	12	0

PITCHING

	IP	H	R	ER	BB	SO	HR	ERA
CLEVELAND								
Sabathia (L 0–1)	4.1	7	8	8	5	3	0	16.62
Lewis	0.2	3	2	2	0	0	0	27.00
Fultz	0.0	0	0	0	2	0	0	0.00
Mastny	2.0	1	0	0	0	2	0	0.00
Borowski	1.0	1	0	0	1	0	0	0.00

Lewis pitched to two batters in the 6th.
Fultz pitched to two batters in the 6th.

	IP	H	R	ER	BB	SO	HR	ERA
BOSTON								
Beckett (W 1-0)	6.0	4	2	2	0	7	1	3.00
Timlin	1.0	1	0	0	0	1	0	0.00
López	1.0	1	1	1	1	0	0	9.00
Gagné	1.0	2	0	0	1	3	0	0.00

While the Red Sox took care of business in Anaheim, the Cleveland Indians disposed of the New York Yankees in four games. That was, for some fans, the good news; the bad news was that Boston had to face a tough Indians team.

But once again, the Red Sox had their pitching rotation perfectly aligned; a four-day break after the end of the ALDS allowed a banged-up squad to rest. And that meant starting off with the right arm of Josh Beckett.

The Indians put forth their own ace, C. C. Sabathia, the 6' 7" fire-baller who wears his hat off-center. The pregame buildup was that a great postseason pitching matchup was in the offing. That turned out to be half right.

With eight days of rest after his mastery of the Angels, Beckett limited the Indians to just 4 hits and 2 runs, striking out 7 and giving up no walks. The Boston offense put the game out of reach in the sixth inning and Terry Francona was able to give Beckett the rest of the night off after just 80 pitches.

The Indians put the first run on the scoreboard in the first inning. Beckett threw a 96-mile-per-hour fastball that came in right over the plate; Travis Hafner pulled it deep into right field for a solo home run.

But the Sox evened the score in the bottom of the inning with consecutive singles by Kevin Youkilis, David Ortiz, and Manny Ramírez.

Although Sabathia had beaten the Yankees in the opening game of their division series (thank you very much) that had not been a masterful performance; he had given up 3 runs on 4 hits and 6 walks in five innings. Against the Red Sox, his outing was even shorter: he was gone after 4⅓ innings in which he yielded 7 hits, 8 runs, and 5 walks.

This time Ortiz and Ramírez set the table for other hitters in the lineup. Ortiz (2 for 2 plus two walks and a hit by pitch) and Ramírez (2 for 2 with two runs scored and three RBIs) each reached base in all five of their plate appearances.

Boston began to pull away in the third inning. Julio Lugo started it off with a ground-rule double to right field; Dustin Pedroia laid down a sacrifice bunt that moved him to third. Youkilis drew a walk to put runners at the corners, bringing up Big Papi.

Okay, do you pitch to Ortiz or wait for Manny? How about both: Sabathia managed to hit Big Papi in his big kitchen, loading the bases. Up comes Ramírez, showing some great patience; the first two pitches were 96-mile-per-hour strikes, but Ramírez managed to hold off on the next four off-speed pitches and drew an RBI walk.

Mike Lowell, getting more confident with each at bat, hit a double into the rightfield stands bringing home Youkilis and Ortiz. Bobby Kielty, in the game because of his good numbers against Sabathia, was intentionally walked to load the bases. And Jason Varitek brought home the fourth run of the inning on a ground out fielded by the third baseman.

By the end of the third inning, Sabathia had thrown 60 pitches and there was stirring in the Indians bull pen.

Boston tacked on three more in the fifth inning: a walk to Ortiz, a single by Ramírez, and walk to Lowell loaded the bases. Kielty proved Francona's scouts correct when he singled to right field to drive home two runs off Sabathia. Varitek capped off the inning with a run-scoring double.

The ninth and tenth runs of the game came home in the sixth on a bases-loaded walk to eagle-eye Ramírez and a sacrifice fly by Lowell.

Cleveland picked up single runs in the sixth and the eighth. For the ninth inning, with Boston leading 10–3, Francona brought in Eric Gagné to close out the game, which made more than a few Boston fans nervous. And Gagné did not disappoint: he made the last inning very interesting, although in the end did no damage.

With one out the Indians got a line drive single and then a soft line drive double to put runners on second and third. Gagné struck out the fourth batter before walking Casey Blake to load the bases. That brought up Indians center fielder Grady Sizemore, who had hit 24 home runs during the season; Sizemore watched Gagné's first three pitches sail by outside for balls before finally striking out on the sixth pitch to end the game.

At the conclusion of the game, the Red Sox had won the first four games of the postseason, outscoring their opponents in total by 29–7. Things were about to become a lot more difficult.

	POS	AB	R	H	RBI	BB	SO	LOB	AVG
CLEVELAND									
Sizemore	CF	5	0	0	0	0	3	5	.000
Cabrera	2B	3	0	1	2	0	1	0	.333
Hafner	DH	3	1	1	1	1	1	1	.333
Martínez	C	4	0	0	0	0	1	2	.000
Garko	1B	2	0	1	0	0	0	0	.500
Gomez[a]	PH	1	0	0	0	0	1	0	.000
Peralta	SS	4	0	1	0	0	0	2	.250
Lofton	LF	4	0	2	0	0	1	1	.500
Gutiérrez	RF	4	0	0	0	0	3	4	.000
Blake	3B	3	2	2	0	1	0	0	.667
TOTALS		**33**	**3**	**8**	**3**	**2**	**11**	**15**	

[a]-Struck out for Garko in 9th.
2B: Lofton (2, Beckett, Gagné), Blake (2, Beckett, Lopez).
HR: Hafner (1, Beckett).

	POS	AB	R	H	RBI	BB	SO	LOB	AVG
BOSTON									
Pedroia	2B	4	1	1	0	0	1	1	.250
Youkilis	1B	4	3	2	0	1	0	1	.500
Ortiz	DH	2	2	2	0	2	0	0	1.000
Ramírez	LF	2	2	2	3	3	0	0	1.000
Ellsbury[b]	PR, LF	0	0	0	0	0	0	0	.000
Lowell	3B	3	0	1	3	1	0	4	.333
Kielty	RF	2	1	1	2	1	1	0	.500
Drew[a]	PH, RF	2	0	0	0	0	0	4	.000
Varitek	C	5	0	1	2	0	2	6	.200
Crisp	CF	4	0	1	0	0	1	3	.250
Lugo	SS	4	1	1	0	0	0	2	.250
TOTALS		**32**	**10**	**12**	**10**	**8**	**5**	**21**	

[a]-Flied out for Kielty in 6th.
[b]-Ran for Ramírez in 8th.
2B: Lugo (1, Sabathia), Lowell (1, Sabathia), Varitek (1, Lewis), Crisp (1, Mastny), Ortiz (1, Borowski).

ALCS Game 2 at Boston October 13, 2007

	Score by innings	R	H	E
Cleveland	100 311 000 07	13	17	0
BOSTON	003 030 000 00	6	10	0

PITCHING

	IP	H	R	ER	BB	SO	HR	ERA
CLEVELAND								
Carmona	4.0	4	4	4	5	5	0	9.00
Pérez	0.1	3	2	2	0	0	2	54.00

Lewis	2.1	0	0	0	0	1	0	6.00
Betancourt	2.1	1	0	0	0	3	0	0.00
Mastny (W 1-0)	1.0	0	0	0	0	0	0	0.00
Borowski	1.0	2	0	0	0	1	0	0.00
BOSTON								
Schilling	4.2	9	5	5	0	3	2	9.64
Delcarmen	0.2	1	1	1	1	0	0	13.50
Okajima	1.2	1	0	0	1	3	0	0.00
Timlin	1.0	0	0	0	0	0	0	0.00
Papelbon	2.0	1	0	0	1	1	0	0.00
Gagné (L 0–1)	0.1	1	2	2	1	1	0	13.50
López	0.0	2	3	3	1	0	0	36.00
Lester	0.2	2	2	2	0	1	1	27.00

A matchup between Curt Schilling—a proven postseason stud—and twenty-three-year-old phenom Fausto Carmona looked like it had the makings of a tight, well-pitched game. But that's why they play the games: by the end of the fifth inning both pitchers were gone and the score was knotted at 6–6.

Schilling gave up a three-run homer to Jhonny Peralta in the fourth inning, changing a 3–1 Boston lead to a 4–3 deficit. Grady Sizemore added a solo round-tripper in the top of the fifth to make the score 5–3.

The Sox answered back in the bottom of the fifth with a two-run homer by Manny Ramírez into the Boston bull pen in right field; it was Manny's 23rd career postseason home run, putting him first on the all-time list, ahead of former Yankee Bernie Williams.

(In fairness, we need to point out that for most of the history of baseball the postseason consisted of just the World Series. Mickey Mantle had 18 home runs in just the World Series; then again, Mantle got to play in many more Fall Classics than Ramírez, at least thus far.)

And then Mike Lowell put the Sox up by a run, 6–5, with a moon shot off the Sports Authority sign above the Green Monster. It was the fifth time in history that the Red Sox cracked back-to-back homers in the postseason.

That lead, alas, did not last. The Indians immediately tied the game against Manny Delcarmen with a walk, a single, and a fielder's choice.

The Sox came close to winning the game with a walk-off hit in the bottom of the ninth. With two outs, Dustin Pedroia slashed a single against Rafael Betancourt. Jacoby Ellsbury replaced him as a pinch runner; like Dave Roberts in the 2004 ALCS against the Yankees, everyone in the ballpark knew Ellsbury was in the game to steal second . . . and with Kevin Youkilis at the plate that was exactly what he did.

Youkilis put on a clinic at the plate. The first two pitches were low for balls; with the count at 2–2, Youk fouled off the next six pitches. Finally, on the eleventh pitch of the inning Youk found one he liked and lined it to center but Indians center fielder Grady Sizemore made a nice play to save the game and send it into extra innings.

The Indians went ahead . . . and then piled on the insurance runs . . . in the eleventh inning with the go-ahead run knocked in by an old Fenway favorite now wearing the wrong uniform.

After using Delcarmen, Hideki Okajima, Mike Timlin, and Jonathan Papelbon for five scoreless innings of relief, Francona turned to Eric Gagné to start the eleventh. Sizemore singled with one out and Asdrubal Cabrera followed with a walk. The Indians sent up as a pinch hitter lefty Trot Nixon, who had patrolled left field for the Red Sox for nine seasons; Francona pulled Gagné and replaced him with left-hander Javier López.

Nixon poked at a 79-mile-per-hour breaking ball and blooped it into center field just in front of Coco Crisp.

"López is not a very comfortable at bat for left-handers, dropping down submarine," Nixon told reporters. "I was excited to finally get in there at 1:30 in the morning."

The inning got even uglier, including a wild pitch by López that allowed another run, a couple of hits, and after Jon Lester came in as the third reliever of the inning, a three-run homer by Franklin Gutiérrez. The Indians brought home a total of seven runs in the inning; the game sputtered to an end after five hours and fourteen minutes of play. It was Boston's first loss in the 2007 postseason.

	POS	AB	R	H	RBI	BB	SO	LOB	AVG
CLEVELAND									
Sizemore	CF	5	3	3	1	1	0	0	.300
Cabrera	2B	5	1	1	0	1	1	1	.250
Hafner	DH	5	0	2	0	0	0	4	.375
Barfield	PR, DH	0	0	0	0	0	0	0	.000
Nixon[a]	PH, DH	1	0	1	1	0	0	0	1.000
Michaels	PR, DH	0	1	0	0	0	0	0	.000
Martínez	C	4	2	3	1	2	1	0	.375
Garko	1B	6	2	2	1	0	0	5	.375

Peralta	SS	5	3	3	4	1	2	0	.444
Lofton	LF	6	0	1	0	0	0	3	.300
Gutiérrez	RF	6	1	1	4	0	1	2	.100
Blake	3B	6	0	0	0	0	4	1	.222
TOTALS		**49**	**13**	**17**	**12**	**5**	**9**	**16**	

[a]-Singled to center for Barfield in the 11th.
2B: Sizemore (1, Schilling), Martínez (1, Schilling), Peralta (1, Lester).
HR: Peralta (1, Schilling), Sizemore (1, Schilling), Gutiérrez (1, Lester).

BOSTON									
Pedroia	2B	4	1	1	0	1	2	1	.250
Ellsbury[a]	PR	0	0	0	0	0	0	0	.000
Cora	2B	0	0	0	0	0	0	0	.000
Youkilis	1B	4	0	1	0	1	1	3	.375
Ortiz	DH	4	2	1	0	1	0	1	.500
Ramírez	LF	4	1	1	3	1	1	2	.500
Lowell	3B	5	1	2	3	0	1	0	.375
Drew	RF	5	0	2	0	0	0	2	.286
Varitek	C	5	0	0	0	0	2	2	.100
Crisp	CF	5	1	2	0	0	1	0	.333
Lugo	SS	4	0	0	0	1	2	3	.125
TOTALS		**40**	**6**	**10**	**6**	**5**	**10**	**14**	

[a]-Ran for Pedroia in 9th.
HR: Ramírez (1, Pérez), Lowell (1, Pérez).

ALCS Game 3
at Cleveland
October 15, 2007

	Score by innings	R	H	E
Boston	000 000 200	2	7	0
CLEVELAND	020 020 00X	4	6	1

PITCHING

	IP	H	R	ER	BB	SO	HR	ERA
BOSTON								
Matsuzaka (L 0–1)	4.2	6	4	4	2	6	1	7.71
Timlin	1.1	0	0	0	0	2	0	0.00
Okajima	1.1	0	0	0	1	0	0	0.00
Delcarmen	0.2	0	0	0	0	2	0	6.75
CLEVELAND								
Westbrook (W 1–0)	6.2	7	2	2	3	2	1	2.00
Lewis	0.1	0	0	0	0	1	0	5.40
Betancourt	1.0	0	0	0	0	1	0	0.00
Borowski	1.0	0	0	0	0	0	0	0.00

With the league championship knotted at one game apiece, the Red Sox traveled to Cleveland and sent to the mound their "rookie" star Daisuke Matsuzaka to face Jake Westbrook.

Matsuzaka had delivered a solid regular season for Boston but seemed to tire coming down the stretch. His second postseason start turned out to be very similar to his performance in the division series; he threw 101 pitches in just 4⅔ innings, giving up six hits and four runs.

Matsuzaka's frustration on the mound was matched by the Red Sox's aggravation at the plate. When Westbrook pitches well, he's a groundball machine; he induced fourteen outs on the ground and just three in the air, plus two strikeouts in 6⅔ innings. David Ortiz, Coco Crisp, and Manny Ramírez each hit into double plays.

Boston had plenty of chances, including bases loaded with no outs in the second inning; after a shallow fly ball by Jason Varitek, Crisp hit into an inning-ending double play. Boston's only offense came on a two-run homer by Varitek in the seventh inning.

"We've been in worse situations than this and have bounced back and gotten it done," Ortiz said after the game.

	POS	AB	R	H	RBI	BB	SO	LOB	AVG
BOSTON									
Pedroia	2B	4	0	0	0	0	2	1	.167
Youkilis	1B	3	0	1	0	1	1	0	.364
Ortiz	DH	3	0	1	0	1	0	1	.444
Ramírez	LF	3	0	1	0	1	0	2	.444
Lowell	3B	4	0	1	0	0	0	1	.333
Drew	RF	4	1	1	0	0	0	1	.273
Varitek	C	4	1	1	2	0	0	3	.143
Crisp	CF	3	0	0	0	0	1	3	.250
Lugo	SS	3	0	1	0	0	0	0	.182
TOTALS		**31**	**2**	**7**	**2**	**3**	**4**	**12**	

2B: Ortiz (2, Westbrook).
HR: Varitek (1, Westbrook).

	POS	AB	R	H	RBI	BB	SO	LOB	AVG
CLEVELAND									
Sizemore	CF	3	1	0	0	1	0	0	.231
Cabrera	2B	4	0	2	1	0	1	0	.333
Hafner	DH	3	0	0	1	1	1	1	.273
Martínez	C	3	0	1	0	1	1	2	.364

Garko	1B	4	1	1	0	0	2	3	.333
Peralta	SS	4	0	0	0	0	3	2	.308
Lofton	LF	3	1	1	2	0	1	0	.308
Nixon	RF	3	0	0	0	0	1	0	.250
Gutiérrez	RF	0	0	0	0	0	0	0	.100
Blake	3B	3	1	1	0	0	0	0	.250
TOTALS		**30**	**4**	**6**	**4**	**3**	**10**	**8**	

HR: Lofton (1, Matsuzaka).

ALCS Game 4
at Cleveland
October 16, 2007

	Score by innings	R	H	E
Boston	000 003 000	3	8	1
CLEVELAND	000 070 00X	7	9	0

PITCHING

	IP	H	R	ER	BB	SO	HR	ERA
BOSTON								
Wakefield (L 0–1)	4.2	5	5	5	2	7	1	9.64
Delcarmen	0.1	3	2	2	1	1	1	16.20
Lester	3.0	1	0	0	1	4	0	4.91
CLEVELAND								
Byrd (W 1–0)	5.0	6	2	2	0	4	2	3.60
Lewis	2.0	2	1	1	0	0	1	5.06
Betancourt	2.0	0	0	0	0	0	0	0.00

Tim Wakefield has made a solid career baffling opposing hitters with his knuckleball. That worked just fine for the first four innings of the game, but it all came undone in the fifth. The Indians batted for thirty-five minutes and scored seven runs off Tim Wakefield and Manny Delcarmen and the game was put out of reach.

The Red Sox were up against soft-tossing Paul Byrd, who throws mostly breaking pitches in the mid-70s; he doesn't throw the knuckleball, but he uses an old-fashioned full windup—sometimes twice—that can throw off the timing of a hitter. In this game Byrd's funkiness was just enough to keep Boston off-balance; they did not touch him for runs until the sixth inning and they were deep in the hole by then.

The Indians solved Wakefield in the fifth. Casey Blake clobbered a 65-mile-per-hour knuckler over the leftfield wall to make it 1–0. Franklin

Gutiérrez singled to left and Kelly Shoppach was hit by a pitch. Grady Sizemore hit a fielder's-choice grounder to second, making it first and third with one out. It looked as if Wakefield was going to get a critical second out when he induced a foul pop-up by Asdrubal Cabrera, but sure-handed first baseman Kevin Youkilis bobbled and then dropped it.

"Pop fly to Youk, he kind of slipped, then I slipped and ran into him," said Dustin Pedroia after the game. "The ball was bouncing everywhere. If he catches that ball and the runner doesn't go home, maybe we're out of that inning next batter. A lot of things went on and just didn't go our way tonight."

Given an extra out, Cabrera hit a grounder toward the middle that Wakefield got a glove on, only to knock it down for an infield single that made it 2–0; to most eyes it appeared that if Wakefield had gotten to the ball or let it go through to Pedroia it would have been an inning-ending double play.

After striking out Travis Hafner, Wakefield gave up an RBI single to left by Victor Martínez to put Boston down by three. Wakefield went to the bench, replaced by Manny Delcarmen; it was the first time all season that Boston starting pitchers had gone less than five innings in three games in a row.

Delcarmen didn't get the job done; Jhonny Peralta hit a belt-high 96-mile-per-hour fastball over the wall to right for three runs. Old man Kenny Lofton followed it up with a single and then made history with a steal of second—his thirty-fourth in postseason play, passing Rickey Henderson for first place. Blake, who had started off the inning with a home run brought him home with an RBI single and the Red Sox were down 7–0.

The Red Sox finally put on a show in the top of the sixth, with back-to-back-to-back home runs by Youkilis, Ortiz, and Ramírez. The only other team to do that in postseason history was the 1997 Yankees in Game 1 of the ALDS, also against the Indians.

It was impressive, but not enough to win the game, and the Sox went down to defeat 7–3, one game away from elimination in the postseason. In the history of baseball, sixty-five teams have teams have been 1–3 after four games in a best-of-seven series and only ten of those teams have come back to win the series.

That was the bad news. The sorta-good news? The last team to come out of such a deep hole was the 2004 Boston Red Sox who were actually down 0–3 in the ALCS against the Yankees; the miraculous recovery by Boston paved the way for the Red Sox World Championship that year.

"We've got a one-pitch playoff every pitch," said Red Sox captain and catcher Jason Varitek. "We have to go out there with that intensity."

	POS	AB	R	H	RBI	BB	SO	LOB	AVG
BOSTON									
Pedroia	2B	4	0	1	0	0	0	0	.188
Youkilis	1B	4	1	2	1	0	0	0	.400
Ortiz	DH	4	1	1	1	0	1	2	.385
Ramírez	LF	4	1	2	1	0	0	0	.462
Lowell	3B	4	0	0	0	0	0	1	.250
Drew	RF	4	0	1	0	0	1	1	.267
Crisp	CF	4	0	0	0	0	1	2	.188
Mirabelli	C	2	0	0	0	0	1	1	.000
Varitek	C	1	0	1	0	0	0	0	.200
Lugo	SS	3	0	0	0	0	0	0	.143
TOTALS		**34**	**3**	**8**	**3**	**0**	**4**	**7**	

HR: Youkilis (1, Byrd), Ortiz (1, Byrd), Ramírez (2, Lewis).

	POS	AB	R	H	RBI	BB	SO	LOB	AVG
CLEVELAND									
Sizemore	CF	3	1	0	0	2	0	4	.188
Cabrera	2B	5	1	1	1	0	2	4	.294
Hafner	DH	4	0	0	0	0	4	4	.200
Martínez	1B	4	1	1	1	0	0	2	.333
Peralta	SS	4	1	2	3	0	1	0	.353
Lofton	LF	4	1	1	0	0	1	1	.294
Blake	3B	4	1	2	2	0	1	0	.313
Gutiérrez	RF	2	1	1	0	2	1	0	.167
Shoppach	C	3	0	1	0	0	2	3	.333
TOTALS		**33**	**7**	**9**	**7**	**4**	**12**	**18**	

2B: Peralta (2, Wakefield).
HR: Blake (1, Wakefield), Peralta (2, Delcarmen).

ALCS Game 5
at Cleveland
October 18, 2007

	Score by innings	R	H	E
Boston	101 000 230	7	12	1
CLEVELAND	100 000 000	1	6	1

PITCHING

	IP	H	R	ER	BB	SO	HR	ERA
BOSTON								
Beckett (W 2–0)	8.0	5	1	1	1	11	0	1.93
Papelbon	1.0	1	0	0	1	1	0	0.00
CLEVELAND								
Sabathia (L 0–2)	6.0	10	4	4	2	6	1	10.45
Betancourt	1.0	0	0	0	0	1	0	0.00
Pérez	0.1	1	3	1	1	0	0	40.50
Mastny	1.2	1	0	0	2	1	0	0.00

Sabathia pitched to two batters in the 7th.

Their backs up against the wall, one loss away from ending their season, the Red Sox had three not-so-secret weapons in their favor.

First of all, they had Josh Beckett ready to return to the mound. Second, they had Big Papi and other veterans in the clubhouse firing up the troops in a players-only meeting. And third, they knew if they could make it back to the friendly confines of Fenway Park, they could once again enjoy their home field advantage.

The Indians sent out C. C. Sabathia once again, and once again their ace was outdueled. Things started out well when Kevin Youkilis homered to left field in the first inning. With two outs, Manny Ramírez hit a double to left-center and Mike Lowell followed with a single to right, but Ramírez was thrown out at the plate by Indians right fielder Franklin Gutiérrez.

The play at the plate looked large in the bottom of the first after Grady Sizemore led off with a bloop double down the line in left. Asdrubal Cabrera then singled to right, setting up runners at the corners with nobody out. Travis Hafner hit into a 6–3 double play, but Sizemore came in the back door with the tying run. As it turned out, that would be the only run scored by the Indians all night.

For the next seven innings Beckett worked the corners with fastballs in the upper 90s and wicked curveballs that dropped into the strike zone when he needed them.

Boston took back the lead in the third. David Ortiz drew a walk with two outs. Ramírez, the second half of the slugging team, lifted a drive to right-center that landed on the top of the yellow line above the wall before bouncing back into play.

Ortiz came all the way home, but Ramírez was held at first base. Manny and Terry Francona argued that it should have been called a home run, but the umpiring crew held to Jacobs Field ground rules that say a ball must be hit over the yellow line to be a home run.

In the end it was just a footnote, as the Boston offense came back to life. Pedroia led off the sixth with a double to right-center and Youkilis drove him in with a triple that went off the glove of Grady Sizemore. Ortiz hit a sacrifice fly to left to make it 4–1. And the Red Sox went on to score three more runs in the eighth. "When we have the little guys getting on base, it's a totally different situation," Ortiz said after the game. "We had the little guys on base and the middle of the lineup comes up to hit."

Beckett delivered the Red Sox back to Boston, notching his third win and lowering his ERA to 1.17 for this postseason. And he told the press he would be ready to come out of the bull pen in Game 7 if Francona needed him. "I felt good," said Beckett. "Once again, I had great defense and I held them off just long enough for us to put up some runs. It was a team effort. We know what we have to do now: We have to win."

	POS	AB	R	H	RBI	BB	SO	LOB	AVG
BOSTON									
Pedroia	2B	4	1	2	0	1	0	0	.250
Youkilis	1B	4	2	2	3	1	0	1	.421
Ortiz	DH	2	1	1	2	1	1	0	.400
Ramírez	LF	4	0	2	1	1	2	2	.471
Ellsbury	LF	0	0	0	0	0	0	0	.000
Lowell	3B	4	0	1	0	0	1	1	.250
Kielty	RF	3	0	1	0	0	1	3	.400
Drew	RF	1	1	1	0	1	0	0	.313
Varitek	C	4	0	1	0	0	0	2	.211
Crisp	CF	5	1	0	0	0	2	4	.143
Lugo	SS	4	1	1	0	0	1	3	.167
TOTALS		**35**	**7**	**12**	**6**	**5**	**8**	**16**	

2B: Ramírez (1, Sabathia), Pedroia (1, Sabathia), Drew (1, Mastny).
3B: Youkilis (1, Sabathia).
HR: Youkilis (2, Sabathia).

	POS	AB	R	H	RBI	BB	SO	LOB	AVG
CLEVELAND									
Sizemore	CF	4	1	2	0	0	1	0	.250
Cabrera	2B	4	0	1	0	0	2	2	.286
Hafner	DH	4	0	0	0	0	2	1	.158
Martínez	C	4	0	1	0	0	1	0	.316

Garko	1B	4	0	1	0	0	2	1	.313
Peralta	SS	4	0	0	0	0	1	1	.286
Lofton	LF	3	0	0	0	1	0	0	.250
Gutiérrez	RF	3	0	0	0	1	1	3	.133
Blake	3B	3	0	1	0	0	2	2	.316
TOTALS		**33**	**1**	**6**	**0**	**2**	**12**	**10**	

2B: Sizemore (2, Beckett), Garko (1, Papelbon).

ALCS Game 6
at Boston
October 20, 2007

	Score by innings	R	H	E
Cleveland	010 000 100	2	6	2
BOSTON	406 000 02X	12	13	0

PITCHING

	IP	H	R	ER	BB	SO	HR	ERA
CLEVELAND								
Carmona (L 0–2)	2.0	6	7	7	4	2	1	16.50
Pérez	0.1	3	3	2	1	0	0	45.00
Laffey	4.2	1	0	0	1	3	0	0.00
Borowski	1.0	3	2	2	2	0	0	4.50

Carmona pitched to three batters in 3rd.

	IP	H	R	ER	BB	SO	HR	ERA
BOSTON								
Schilling (W 1–0)	7.0	6	2	2	0	5	1	5.40
López	1.0	0	0	0	0	0	0	18.00
Gagné	1.0	0	0	0	0	0	0	7.71

Nothing is easy or a sure thing in the playoffs, but by the end of the first inning in Boston fans had a pretty good feeling about their chances to sing "Sweet Caroline" in a seventh and deciding game.

Big Game Curt finished off a 1–2–3 first inning by striking out Travis Hafner with a three-pitch strikeout. And then we all sat back and watched.

Schilling has pitched five times in his career when his team has faced elimination in the postseason. His record coming into the sixth game of the ALCS was 4–0 with a 1.37 ERA; by the end of the day it was 5–0. And overall, in the postseason Schilling improved to 10–2 with an ERA of 2.25.

Dustin Pedroia led off the first with an infield single to the second baseman, and Kevin Youkilis followed up with another infield hit, this time to short. Fausto Carmona threw three straight balls at 97, 97, and 96 miles per hour to David Ortiz; the big man took the next two pitches for strikes and then let a fourth fastball sail outside to earn a walk.

Things looked a bit sketchy as Manny Ramírez struck out with the bases loaded and Mike Lowell lifted a shallow fly ball to right fielder Trot Nixon. Up to the plate came J. D. Drew, a player who had an unspectacular regular season but was showing signs of heating up as the playoffs arrived. Carmon's fifth pitch, a 97-mile-per-hour heater, came in right over the plate and Drew sent it over the camera well above the wall in center field for a grand slam.

Drew's homer came on the three-year anniversary of Johnny Damon's grand slam in Game 7 of the 2004 ALCS as the Sox completed their historic comeback at Yankee Stadium. "It was a great feeling," said Drew. "More than anything, I was just trying to hit a ball hard up the middle, get a pitch out over the plate that I could handle."

Schilling settled in and held the Indians to just six hits and two runs over seven innings, walking none and striking out five.

On the offense, the Sox pounded Carmona out of the game after just two-plus innings; he yielded 7 runs on 6 hits and 4 walks.

Boston put the game out of reach in the bottom of the third inning, scoring six runs. Back-to-back walks to Ramírez and Lowell opened the inning, followed by an RBI single up the middle by Drew. Carmona was lifted for lefty Rafael Pérez, who got one out.

Jacoby Ellsbury, making his first postseason start, blooped an RBI single into center. Julio Lugo slashed a two-run double down the left-field line. Pedroia drew a walk and then Youkilis hit an RBI single off the wall in left; Youk got caught in a rundown between first and second but second baseman Asdrubal Cabrera's throw hit him on the helmet and Pedroia came home. The score after three innings was 10–1 and thoughts turned toward Game 7.

"We're not comfortable, we're confident," said Ortiz. "This is it. This is where you want to be. [On Sunday], the best team is going to win."

	POS	AB	R	H	RBI	BB	SO	LOB	AVG
CLEVELAND									
Sizemore	CF	4	0	0	0	0	0	3	.208
Cabrera	2B	4	0	0	0	0	0	2	.240
Hafner	DH	4	0	0	0	0	2	2	.130
Martínez	C	4	1	2	1	0	1	0	.348
Garko	1B	4	1	1	0	0	1	1	.300
Peralta	SS	2	0	0	1	0	1	1	.261
Lofton	LF	3	0	0	0	0	0	1	.217
Nixon	RF	3	0	2	0	0	0	0	.429
Blake	3B	3	0	1	0	0	0	1	.318
TOTALS		**31**	**2**	**6**	**2**	**0**	**5**	**11**	

3B: Garko (1, Schilling).
HR: Martínez (1, Schilling).

	POS	AB	R	H	RBI	BB	SO	LOB	AVG
BOSTON									
Pedroia	2B	4	2	2	0	1	0	0	.292
Youkilis	1B	4	2	3	1	1	0	0	.478
Ortiz	DH	4	1	1	0	1	1	3	.368
Hinske	PR, DH	0	1	0	0	0	0	0	.000
Ramírez	LF	2	1	0	1	2	1	3	.421
Crisp	CF	0	0	0	0	0	0	0	.143
Lowell	3B	4	1	2	1	1	0	5	.292
Drew	RF	5	2	3	5	0	1	1	.381
Varitek	C	3	0	0	0	2	0	2	.182
Ellsbury	CF, LF	5	1	1	1	0	1	4	.200
Lugo	SS	4	1	1	2	0	1	0	.182
Cora	SS	0	0	0	0	0	0	0	.000
TOTALS		**35**	**12**	**13**	**11**	**8**	**5**	**18**	

2B: Pedroia (2, Carmona), Lugo (2, Pérez), Ortiz (3, Borowski).
HR: Drew (1, Carmona).

ALCS Game 7
at Boston
October 21, 2007

	Score by innings	R	H	E
Cleveland	000 110 000	2	10	1
BOSTON	111 000 26X	11	15	1

PITCHING

	IP	H	R	ER	BB	SO	HR	ERA
CLEVELAND								
Westbrook (L 1–1)	6.0	9	3	3	1	5	0	3.55
Betancourt	1.2	5	7	6	1	1	1	6.75
Lewis	0.1	1	1	1	0	1	1	6.35

BOSTON								
Matsuzaka (W 1–1)	5.0	6	2	2	0	3	0	5.59
Okajima (H 1)	2.0	3	0	0	0	0	0	0.00
Papelbon (S 1)	2.0	1	0	0	0	1	0	0.00

Okajima pitched to two batters in 8th.

Consider this: Boston's 11–2 victory over Cleveland in the seventh game of the ALCS was a lot closer than the final score would indicate, at least until the eighth inning.

Daisuke Matsuzaka pitched well, holding Cleveland to just two runs and six hits over five innings. Jake Westbrook was almost as good, yielding three runs in six frames.

The difference came when each team's bull pen took the field. For Boston Hideki Okajima and Jonathan Papelbon each pitched two scoreless innings. Cleveland's Betancourt and Lewis gave up eight runs in the seventh and eighth inning.

On offense the Red Sox jumped out of the gate with four singles to score a single run; the inning ended on a J. D. Drew double-play grounder. In the second inning Jason Varitek doubled and moved over to third on Jacoby Ellsbury's single; the captain came home on Julio Lugo's double-play grounder. And in the third Youkilis doubled, moved over to third on an infield out, and came home on a sacrifice fly by Mike Lowell. The score after three innings was 3–0, and that lead would hold up for the rest of the game.

As befits a seventh and deciding game of a playoff series, the middle innings were nail-biters; it was Cleveland that folded, and it happened immediately after starting pitcher Westbrook left the game in the bottom of the seventh inning, replaced by Rafael Betancourt.

The Indians almost tied the game on a strange play in the top of the seventh. Kenny Lofton, still speedy at age forty, reached second on a fielding error by Boston shortstop Julio Lugo. The next batter, Franklin Gutierrez knocked a 1–2 pitch from Hideki Okajima down the third-base line just fair; the ball hit a camera well and bounced back onto the field. It appeared that Lofton could have scored, but Indians third-base coach Joel Skinner put up the stop sign and Lofton skidded to a halt.

"Sometimes that ball caroms right to the shortstop," Boston third baseman Mike Lowell said later. "That's a tough angle. After the fact, maybe you say he has a chance. But I don't think you can second-guess that play."

To the dismay of the Indians, on the very next pitch, Casey Blake hit into a 5–4–3 double play to end the inning.

Boston's rookie outfielder Ellsbury started a seventh inning rally when he reached on a fielding error by Indians third baseman Casey Blake. Julio Lugo bunted him over to third. And then rookie second baseman Dustin Pedroia put one of his big swings on a 95-mile-per-hour fastball and drove the ball into the Monster seats in left field to make it 5–2 Red Sox.

"I hit it good and the wind was kind of blowing it out to center," said Pedroia. "So I was like, 'Geez, don't hit the top of the fence.' Once it went out, I was so excited, I don't even remember running around the bases. It was the biggest at bat of my life, and I'll never forget it."

Okajima, who had already pitched two innings for Boston, started the eighth but gave up singles to the first two batters; in came Papelbon for three quick outs on eight pitches.

In the bottom of the eighth, Boston allowed their fans to start planning for the World Series. They scored six runs on a double by Lowell, single by Drew, double by Varitek, double by Pedroia, and a two-run homer by Youkilis.

"We were down, 3–1, and still felt that we could win," said Pedroia. "There's obviously those three nights you go to bed and you don't sleep. All you think about is trying to win and trying to figure out how we're going to turn this around. We figured it out."

"After our three straight losses, the team kept telling me to get ready to pitch in Game 7," Matsuzaka told the press, through a translator.

	POS	AB	R	H	RBI	BB	SO	LOB	AVG
CLEVELAND									
Sizemore	CF	3	0	1	1	0	1	1	.222
Cabrera	2B	4	0	1	0	0	1	1	.241
Hafner	DH	4	1	1	0	0	2	2	.148
Martínez	C	4	0	0	0	0	0	3	.296
Garko	1B	4	0	1	1	0	0	2	.292
Peralta	SS	4	0	1	0	0	0	1	.259
Lofton	LF	4	0	1	0	0	0	1	.222
Gutiérrez	RF	4	1	2	0	0	0	1	.211
Blake	3B	4	0	2	0	0	0	3	.346
TOTALS		**35**	**2**	**10**	**2**	**0**	**4**	**15**	

2B: Hafner (1, Matsuzaka), Garko (2, Matsuzaka).

BOSTON									
Pedroia	2B	5	3	3	5	0	0	2	.345
Youkilis	1B	5	2	3	2	0	1	0	.500
Ortiz	DH	5	0	0	0	0	2	3	.292
Ramírez	LF	3	0	1	1	1	1	0	.409
Crisp	CF	0	0	0	0	0	0	0	.143
Lowell	3B	3	1	2	1	0	1	0	.333
Drew	RF	4	1	1	1	0	0	4	.360
Varitek	C	4	2	3	0	0	1	0	.269
Ellsbury	CF, LF	3	2	1	0	1	0	1	.250
Lugo	SS	3	0	1	0	0	1	4	.200
TOTALS		**35**	**11**	**15**	**10**	**2**	**7**	**14**	

2B: Varitek 2 (3, Westbrook, Betancourt), Youkilis (1, Westbrook), Lowell (2, Betancourt), Pedroia (3, Betancourt).
HR: Pedroia (1, Betancourt), Youkilis (3, Lewis).

2007 World Series

World Series Game 1
at Boston
October 24, 2007

	Score by innings	R	H	E
Colorado	010 000 000	1	6	0
BOSTON	310 270 00X	13	17	0

PITCHING

	IP	H	R	ER	BB	SO	HR	ERA
COLORADO								
Francis (L)	4.0	10	6	6	3	3	1	13.50
Morales	0.2	6	7	7	1	0	0	94.50
Speier	0.0	0	0	0	3	0	0	0.00
Herges	1.1	0	0	0	1	1	0	0.00
Affeldt	1.0	1	0	0	0	0	0	0.00
Hawkins	1.0	0	0	0	0	2	0	0.00

Speier pitched to one batter in the 5th.
Balk: Morales.

BOSTON								
Beckett (W)	7.0	6	1	1	1	9	0	1.29
Timlin	1.0	0	0	0	0	2	0	0.00
Gagné	1.0	0	0	0	0	1	0	0.00

It was the same old story, but it wasn't boring: the Red Sox dealt their ace, Josh Beckett, and he trumped the Colorado Rockies with ease.

Beckett gave up just 1 run and 6 hits striking out 9 over seven innings.

Beckett won all four of his starts in the postseason, finishing with a 1.20 ERA against the Angels, Indians, and Rockies. Lifetime in the playoffs and World Series, he is 6–2 with a 1.73 ERA.

Third baseman Mike Lowell has been with him for every one of those games; they were teammates for the Florida Marlins before coming to Boston. "It's something special," said Lowell. "I saw it in '03 [with the Marlins]. I thought that was the best three-week stretch I had seen by any pitcher. He's putting a good comparison to that so far this postseason."

The Rockies came to the World Series having won twenty-one out of their previous twenty-two games, including sweeps of Philadelphia and Arizona in the playoffs. Much was made of the fact that the Rockies had to wait eight days after clinching the National League Championship while the Red Sox duked it out with the Indians. That might or might not have made a difference against a pitcher like Beckett who came to the Series at his peak.

In any case Beckett made a statement in the first inning: He struck out the side on fifteen pitches, all of them in the range of 95 to 97 miles per hour.

And then the Boston bats came to the plate. Dustin Pedroia, who said his home run in the seventh inning of the seventh game of the ALCS had been the biggest at bat in his rookie career, swung at the second pitch he saw from Rockies pitcher Jeff Francis and parked it in leftfield seats for a leadoff round-tripper. The Red Sox never trailed again in the game.

Pedroia became only the second player in World Series history to lead off the first inning of Game 1 with a homer, joining Don Buford of the 1969 Orioles in the record book.

The Sox scored twice more in the first inning on a double by Youkilis, RBI single by Ramírez, single by Varitek, and a run-scoring line drive double by J. D. Drew.

The Rockies got one run back—their only run in the game—in the top of the second, on a pair of doubles by Garrett Atkins and Troy Tulowitski. But Boston took back their three-run lead in the bottom of that inning when David Ortiz hit a two-run double to center field, driving in Youkilis who reached base on a walk.

Two more Boston runs crossed the plate in the fourth inning when Varitek hit a ground-rule double to left, bringing home David Ortiz (single) and Manny Ramírez (double).

And the Red Sox put the game out of reach in the fifth when they scored seven runs. The following all happened with two outs in the inning: double by Youkilis, double by Ortiz, single by Ramírez, double by Lowell, walk by Varitek, single by Drew, and then three consecutive run-scoring walks (Lugo, Ellsbury, and Pedroia). Thirteen batters came to the plate, and the Colorado Rockies learned—if they didn't know it coming into the game—that the Boston lineup was relentless.

The Sox set a World Series record with nine doubles in the game. Beckett sat down after seven innings and ninety-three pitches and Mike Timlin and Eric Gagné each threw an inning of hitless, scoreless ball to close out the game.

"Maybe twenty years down the road, they'll be mentioning guys that do good things in October and saying it looks like a Beckett postseason," said Lowell after the game. "That's as dominating as he's been. I'm just really happy that he's been on my team the last two postseasons, because I'd rather not face him."

	POS	AB	R	H	RBI	BB	SO	LOB	AVG
COLORADO									
Taveras	CF	4	0	0	0	0	2	1	.000
Matsui	2B	4	0	1	0	0	1	0	.250
Holliday	LF	4	0	0	0	0	2	1	.000
Helton	1B	4	0	2	0	0	1	0	.500
Atkins	3B	4	1	1	0	0	1	2	.250
Hawpe	RF	4	0	0	0	0	4	2	.000
Tulowitzki	SS	3	0	2	1	0	0	0	.667
Torrealba	C	3	0	0	0	0	1	2	.000
Spilborghs	DH	2	0	0	0	0	0	1	.000
TOTALS		**32**	**1**	**6**	**1**	**1**	**12**	**9**	

2B: Atkins (1, Beckett), Tulowitzki 2 (2, Beckett, Beckett), Helton (1, Beckett).

	POS	AB	R	H	RBI	BB	SO	LOB	AVG
BOSTON									
Pedroia	2B	5	1	1	2	1	0	2	.200
Youkilis	1B	5	3	2	1	1	1	3	.400
Ortiz	DH	5	2	3	2	0	0	1	.600
Hinske[a]	PH,DH	1	0	0	0	0	1	0	.000
Ramírez	LF	4	3	3	2	1	0	0	.750

Crisp	CF	1	0	0	0	0	0	0	.000
Lowell	3B	3	1	1	0	2	0	3	.333
Varitek	C	4	1	2	2	1	2	1	.500
Drew	RF	5	1	2	2	0	1	2	.400
Lugo	SS	4	0	3	1	1	0	2	.750
Cora	SS	0	0	0	0	0	0	0	.000
Ellsbury	CF,LF	4	1	0	1	1	1	3	.000
TOTALS		**41**	**13**	**17**	**13**	**8**	**6**	**17**	

[a]-Struck out for Ortiz in the 8th.
2B: Youkilis 2 (2, Francis, Morales), Drew (1, Francis), Ortiz 2 (2, Francis, Morales), Ramírez (1, Francis), Varitek (1, Francis), Lowell (1, Morales).
HR: Pedroia (1, Francis).

World Series Game 2 at Boston October 25, 2007

	Score by innings	R	H	E
Colorado	100 000 000	1	5	0
BOSTON	000 110 00X	2	6	1

PITCHING

	IP	H	R	ER	BB	SO	HR	ERA
COLORADO								
Jiménez (L)	4.2	3	2	2	5	2	0	3.86
Affeldt	0.0	0	0	0	1	0	0	0.00
Herges	1.0	1	0	0	1	0	0	0.00
Fuentes	2.0	1	0	0	0	1	0	0.00
Corpas	0.1	1	0	0	0	0	0	0.00

Affeldt pitched to one batter in the 5th.

	IP	H	R	ER	BB	SO	HR	ERA
BOSTON								
Schilling (W)	5.1	4	1	1	2	4	0	1.69
Okajima (H 1)	2.1	0	0	0	0	4	0	0.00
Papelbon (S 1)	1.1	1	0	0	0	2	0	0.00

Game 2 of the World Series was as tight as a drum, with warhorse Curt Schilling turning over a one-run lead to Boston's premier bull pen team of Hideki Okajima (2⅓ innings, no hits and no runs) and Jonathan Papelbon (1⅓ innings, one hit, and no runs).

A win is a win is a win, though. The last game of the year played at Boston was one that kept fans awake until the final pitch. And it included a brilliant piece of coaching that eliminated a potential tying run for Colorado.

The game began a bit shaky, as Schilling hit the first batter of the game, Willy Taveras; it was a glancing blow off the hand—if it hit him at all—but Taveras put on an Academy Award–level hand shaking exhibition. After an out Matt Holliday singled to deep third and both runners moved up a base on a rare throwing error by Boston third baseman Mike Lowell. Taveras came home with a run on Todd Helton's fielder's-choice grounder to first.

The Rockies hung on to a 1–0 lead into the fourth inning on the strong pitching of rookie Ubaldo Jiménez; his fastball approached 100 miles per hour at times. In the third inning he escaped a jam after walking Dustin Pedroia and Kevin Youkilis with two outs; David Ortiz hit a shot down the right-field line that landed just a foot or so on the foul side of Pesky's Pole.

Boston tied the game in the fourth inning after Lowell walked and showed some aggressive and smart baserunning as he crossed over to third on J. D. Drew's single. He came home on a sacrifice fly by Jason Varitek.

"Sometimes you get that spin where you stay inside the ball, and I saw it go a little bit towards center and I figured, 1–0, one out, I was going to go," said Lowell. "I was figuring a perfect throw was what it would take. He made as close to a perfect throw as there was and I was fortunate to get in there."

And then it was Lowell once again, driving in the second (and ultimately the winning) run in the fifth inning. With two outs David Ortiz drew another walk and then Manny Ramírez moved him to second with a hard groundball single into left. Up came Lowell, and down the leftfield line went an RBI double. The score after five would be the same as it was at the end of the game: 2–1 Boston.

Schilling lasted one out into the sixth inning; after giving up a single and a walk he was replaced by lefty Hideki Okajima who became the first Japanese-born pitcher to appear in a World Series game. "Last year, I pitched in the Japanese World Series, and I have some experience in a big stage like this, so I was confident out there," Okajima said through a translator. "I felt real good out there."

After 2⅓ perfect innings, in came Papelbon who gave up a groundball single to Matt Holliday. There were two outs in the inning, the potential tying run on base, and Todd Helton at bat.

From the Red Sox dugout, bench coach Brad Mills flashed a sign to catcher Jason Varitek, who relayed it to Papelbon on the mound. Mills said after the game that Boston's advance scouting had uncovered the fact that Holliday usually runs on first pitches when he tries to steal a base; instead of throwing home, Papelbon wheeled and fired a strike to Youkilis at first and Holliday was picked off base easily.

It was Papelbon's first pickoff of a runner in his major league career and one of those elements of inside baseball that wins games and World Series. The inning, and the last threat of the night by the Rockies, was over.

"This was the Pap-ajima Show tonight," said Schilling. "That was just phenomenal to watch. Okajima was perfect, absolutely perfect every single pitch."

Schilling got the win and is now 11–2 with a 2.23 ERA for his career in the postseason; in the World Series he is 4–1 with a 2.06 ERA.

	POS	AB	R	H	RBI	BB	SO	LOB	AVG
COLORADO									
Taveras	CF	3	1	0	0	0	1	1	.000
Matsui	2B	4	0	0	0	0	2	1	.125
Holliday	LF	4	0	4	0	0	0	0	.500
Helton	1B	3	0	0	1	1	1	2	.286
Atkins	3B	4	0	0	0	0	0	4	.125
Hawpe	RF	4	0	1	0	0	2	3	.125
Tulowitzki	SS	2	0	0	0	1	1	1	.400
Torrealba	C	2	0	0	0	0	0	1	.000
Spilborghs	DH	3	0	0	0	0	3	1	.000
TOTALS		**29**	**1**	**5**	**1**	**2**	**10**	**14**	
BOSTON									
Pedroia	2B	4	0	1	0	1	0	1	.222
Youkilis	1B	3	0	0	0	2	0	1	.250
Ortiz	DH	3	1	0	0	1	1	4	.375
Ramírez	LF	4	0	1	0	0	0	0	.500
Lowell	3B	3	1	1	1	1	0	0	.333
Drew	RF	2	0	2	0	1	0	0	.571
Varitek	C	3	0	0	1	0	2	5	.286
Ellsbury	CF	3	0	1	0	1	0	0	.143
Lugo	SS	3	0	0	0	0	0	2	.429
TOTALS		**28**	**2**	**6**	**2**	**7**	**3**	**13**	

2B: Lowell (2, Jiménez).

World Series Game 3 at Colorado
October 27, 2007

	Score by innings	R	H	E
BOSTON	006 000 031	10	15	1
Colorado	000 002 300	5	11	0

PITCHING

	IP	H	R	ER	BB	SO	HR	ERA
BOSTON								
Matsuzaka (W)	5.1	3	2	2	3	5	0	3.38
López	0.0	2	0	0	0	0	0	0.00
Timlin (H 1)	0.2	2	2	2	0	0	0	10.80
Okajima (H 2)	1.0	2	1	1	0	2	1	2.70
Delcarmen	0.2	1	0	0	1	0	0	0.00
Papelbon (S 2)	1.1	1	0	0	0	0	0	0.00

López pitched to two batters in the 6th.
Timlin pitched to two batters in the 7th.

	IP	H	R	ER	BB	SO	HR	ERA
COLORADO								
Fogg (L)	2.2	10	6	6	2	2	0	20.25
Morales	2.1	1	0	0	0	1	0	21.00
Affeldt	1.0	0	0	0	0	1	0	0.00
Herges	1.0	0	0	0	0	3	0	0.00
Fuentes	1.0	3	3	3	1	0	0	9.00
Hawkins	1.0	1	1	1	0	0	0	4.50

Three years to the day after they broke their eighty-six-year drought to win the 2004 World Series, the Red Sox moved within one more win of a new set of rings. They scored early, and late; in the middle the Rockies clawed back to within a run.

Daisuke Matsuzaka pitched one of his better games in the second half of his long "rookie" season in the major leagues, giving up just three hits and two runs in 5⅓ innings.

Playing in a National League park for the first time in the postseason, manager Terry Francona had to choose amongst three stars for two positions. It's an enviable position; Francona gave David Ortiz a glove at first base and kept Mike Lowell in position at third base, sitting Kevin Youkilis for the start of the game.

Removing Youk also resulted in a shuffling of the top of Boston's lineup; speedy rookie Jacoby Ellsbury was slotted in the leadoff spot, followed by Boston's other rookie star Dustin Pedroia. It worked pretty well, too—the pair were seven for ten between them, including three doubles for Ellsbury. They set the table all night long.

Boston built up a 6–0 lead in the third inning. Ellsbury led off with a line drive double and moved over to third when Pedroia laid down a safe bunt hit. Rockies manager Clint Hurdle had the same difficult choice faced by teams all year long: pitch to David Ortiz or Manny Ramírez?

Ortiz turned around Josh Fogg's first pitch, doubling on a line drive to right scoring Ellsbury. With runners now on second and third, Ramírez was intentionally walked; that didn't work out either, as Mike Lowell singled into left field to score Pedroia and Ortiz. After a pop-up by J. D. Drew, Jason Varitek singled to left fielder Matt Holliday; Ramírez rounded the corner at third base (tossing off his helmet and then kicking it as he ran) and was thrown out at the plate on a very close call.

In a National League game, a manager would very much like to have the number eight batter make the third out of the inning so that a weak-hitting pitcher would lead off the next frame. But Fogg was unable to put away Julio Lugo, walking him on four straight pitches.

And so Matsuzaka came up to the plate with bases loaded and two outs. He had been up to bat just four times in the regular season during interleague play and he was hitless in his brief career as a major leaguer. But he swung at the first pitch he saw, a 78-mile-per-hour breaking ball, hitting a grounder through the left side of the infield for a two-run single.

Ellsbury, the tenth batter, struck his second double of the inning, bringing home Lugo with the sixth run. In doing so he joined Matt Williams of Arizona (Game 6 of the 2001 World Series against the Yankees) as the only players to hold that particular record.

In the bottom of the sixth, Francona gave Ortiz the rest of the night off; Youkilis came in as a defensive (and offensive) replacement at first base. And the manager was also ready with a quick hook for Matsuzaka, which he used after the pitcher yielded back-to-back walks with one out.

Reliever Javier López faced the next two batters and gave up run-scoring singles to each of them. Mike Timlin came in and Ryan Spilborghs cracked a line drive deep into center field but Ellsbury got to it just in front of the wall. Pinch hitter Jeff Baker worked Timlin for six pitches before slashing a liner that looked like it would be a damaging hit. But Red Sox shortstop Julio Lugo showed his ups and timed his leap perfectly to grab the ball for the third out. The score after six innings was 6–2.

"That might have saved the game right there, Lugo's play," said Lowell. "I didn't think he had a chance. That ball looked like it kept rising. He got up there, and we were all pumped when he came down with it."

Timlin stayed in the game to begin the seventh. The first batter, Kazuo Matsui, laid down a safe bunt hit to third and promptly stole second base. Troy Tulowitski followed up with a single to center, putting runners at the corners.

Francona removed Timlin and replaced him with Hideki Okajima who had performed so reliably for most of the season and all of the postseason. But slugger Matt Holliday swung at Okajima's first pitch, a changeup over the plate, and parked it over the wall in center field. Suddenly the game was no laugher; Okajima got the next three outs but the score was Boston 6, Colorado 5.

"Oki has been great for us all year," Lowell said. "I don't think he lets previous at bats change his focus and change his approach. He goes after hitters and did a great job again today. After that big home run, we just needed to get out of the inning with the lead and see if we can tack on a few more."

That's exactly what they did, as the new top of the order came through again. With one out Lugo drew a walk and defensive substitution Coco Crisp followed up with a soft line drive single. Up came Ellsbury; he doubled to right field, scoring Lugo. Then Pedroia nearly duplicated that hit, doubling home Crisp and Ellsbury. Three quick runs, and Boston led by four.

The icing on the cake came in the ninth. Mike Lowell led off with a line drive single. Alex Cora sacrificed him over to second, and with Jason Varitek at the plate Lowell stole third base. A fly ball to center by Varitek brought home the tenth run.

	POS	AB	R	H	RBI	BB	SO	LOB	AVG
BOSTON									
Ellsbury	CF, RF	5	2	4	2	0	0	0	.417
Pedroia	2B	5	1	3	2	0	0	2	.357
Papelbon	P	0	0	0	0	0	0	0	.000
Ortiz	1B	4	1	1	1	0	2	2	.333
Youkilis	1B	1	0	0	0	0	0	1	.222

Ramírez	LF	4	0	0	0	1	1	3	.333
Lowell	3B	5	2	2	2	0	1	2	.364
Drew	RF	4	0	1	0	0	1	2	.455
Okajima	P	0	0	0	0	0	0	0	.000
Delcarmen	P	0	0	0	0	0	0	0	.000
Cora	2B	0	0	0	0	0	0	0	.000
Varitek	C	4	1	1	1	0	1	1	.273
Lugo	SS	3	2	1	0	2	0	1	.400
Matsuzaka	P	3	0	1	2	0	1	2	.333
López	P	0	0	0	0	0	0	0	.000
Timlin	P	0	0	0	0	0	0	0	.000
Crisp	CF	1	1	1	0	0	0	0	.500
TOTALS		**39**	**10**	**15**	**10**	**3**	**7**	**16**	

2B: Lugo (1, Fogg), Ellsbury 3 (3, Fogg, Fogg, Fuentes), Ortiz (3, Fogg), Drew (2, Morales), Pedroia (1, Fuentes).

COLORADO									
Matsui	2B	5	1	3	0	0	1	2	.308
Tulowitzki	SS	4	1	1	0	1	1	3	.333
Holliday	LF	5	1	1	3	0	0	3	.385
Helton	1B	4	1	1	0	1	1	1	.273
Atkins	3B	2	1	0	0	2	1	1	.100
Hawpe	RF	5	0	2	1	0	2	3	.231
Torrealba	C	5	0	2	1	0	0	3	.200
Sullivan	CF	2	0	0	0	0	0	2	.000
Spilborghs[b]	PH,CF	2	0	0	0	0	0	2	.000
Fogg	P	0	0	0	0	0	0	0	.000
Morales	P	1	0	0	0	0	1	0	.000
Smith[a]	PH	1	0	1	0	0	0	0	1.000
Affeldt	P	0	0	0	0	0	0	0	.000
Baker[c]	PH	1	0	0	0	0	0	2	.000
Herges	P	0	0	0	0	0	0	0	.000
Fuentes	P	0	0	0	0	0	0	0	.000
Taveras[d]	PH	1	0	0	0	0	0	0	.000
Hawkins	P	0	0	0	0	0	0	0	.000
TOTALS		**38**	**5**	**11**	**5**	**4**	**7**	**22**	

[a]-Singled for Morales in 5th.
[b]-Flied out for Sullivan in 6th.
[c]-Lined out for Affeldt in 6th.
[d]-Lined out for Fuentes in 8th.
3B: Hawpe (1, Papelbon).
HR: Holliday (1, Okajima).

World Series Game 4 at Colorado
October 28, 2007

	Score by innings	R	H	E
Boston	100 010 110	4	9	0
COLORADO	000 000 120	3	7	0

PITCHING

	IP	H	R	ER	BB	SO	HR	ERA
BOSTON								
Lester (W)	5.2	3	0	0	3	3	0	0.00
Delcarmen (H 1)	0.2	2	1	1	0	1	1	6.75
Timlin (H 2)	0.2	0	0	0	0	2	0	7.71
Okajima (H 3)	0.1	2	2	2	0	0	1	7.36
Papelbon (S 3)	1.2	0	0	0	0	1	0	0.00
COLORADO								
Cook (L)	6.0	6	3	3	0	2	1	4.50
Affeldt	1.0	1	0	0	0	1	0	0.00
Fuentes	0.2	2	1	1	1	0	1	9.82
Corpas	1.1	0	0	0	0	1	0	0.00

Cook pitched to one batter in the 7th.

Winning the World Series shouldn't be easy. After all, it took the Red Sox eighty-six years to get to hang a banner in 2004. And it took all nine innings of Game 4 in 2007 for Boston to win again.

It also required a great story of personal courage. One year earlier, young starter Jon Lester was undergoing chemotherapy treatments for anaplastic large cell lymphoma, a rare form of cancer. Lester was carefully brought back through the minor leagues and onto the Red Sox roster. And he got the start because longtime Boston stalwart Tim Wakefield took himself out of the rotation before the World Series because of shoulder problems.

Lester made the most of his opportunity and threw 5⅔ shutout innings, earning the win in his first start in a postseason game. "Words can't describe it," said Lester. "It really hasn't sunk in. Maybe it will sink in when we go ride around Boston with the trophy. This is the one you work for ever since you first picked up a baseball. This is what you dream of and this is what you work towards all year."

The Sox scored just enough runs—one each in the first, fifth, seventh, and eighth—and then held on for dear life as the Rockies came within a run of tying the game. The heroes of the final game of the Series included the usual gang: David Ortiz, Jason Varitek, and Mike Lowell as well as youngsters Jacoby Ellsbury and Lester. And the eventual winning run came courtesy of a cameo appearance by a bit player who came off the bench.

Once again, the Red Sox scored early. Jacoby Ellsbury, who had four hits in Game 3, led off the final game with a double and moved to third on a groundout by Pedroia; he scored on a single to right by Ortiz.

Rockies pitcher Aaron Cook, making his first start in more than two months because of a muscle strain, kept the Red Sox from scoring again for the next four innings. In the fifth, though, Lowell hit a leadoff double to center and then slid home head first after a single to right by Varitek.

Lowell hit a solo homer in the top of the seventh to give Boston a 3–0 lead. But in the bottom of that inning, Brad Hawpe answered with a shot of his own off Boston's Manny Delcarmen.

In the top of the eighth inning, Francona sent up Bobby Kielty as a pinch hitter for Mike Timlin. It was Kielty's only appearance at the plate in the World Series—the first of his career—and he made the most of it. He swung at the first pitch he saw from reliever Brian Fuentes and put it over the leftfield wall for a home run.

"You have to have horses," said Red Sox right-hander Curt Schilling. "You have to have Papelbons, you have to have Becketts, you have to have Mannys, you have to have Davids, but when you have Jon Lester winning it and Bobby Kielty hitting the game-winning homer, it just speaks to the depth of the club."

The Red Sox were in a commanding position, up three games to none, but Terry Francona pulled no punches in trying to end the Series in Game 4. Although Hideki Okajima and Jonathan Papelbon had both pitched the day before, they were at the ready in the bull pen.

Okajima came in to start the bottom of the eighth inning and he may have been out of gas. With one out he gave up a single to Todd Helton and five pitches later he left a fat pitch right over the plate for Garret Atkins; the result: a two-run homer that cut the score to 4–3.

In came Jonathan Papelbon for the final five outs of the game: 23 pitches, 18 strikes, 0 hits, 0 runs, and his 3rd save in the World Series. In fact his ERA for seven postseason appearances including the Series was a nice, even set of goose eggs: 0.00.

"It got a little dicey there after Atkins hit the home run," said Lowell, "but Pap's been there all year for us. There's no better guy to have in that situation than him."

Papelbon climbed the ladder on pinch hitter Seth Smith to strike him out on a 95-mile-per-hour fastball. He tossed his glove high in the air and beckoned Varitek—and the rest of the team—to join him on the mound in celebration of Boston's second World Series championship in four seasons.

Mike Lowell was selected as World Series MVP, a salute to his hot hitting and steady play at third base. Not that anyone in Boston wanted to see a Game 5, but if there had been one, the starting pitcher was scheduled to be Josh Beckett who would have had a very good chance of becoming the first pitcher in history to win five starts in one postseason.

	POS	AB	R	H	RBI	BB	SO	LOB	AVG
BOSTON									
Ellsbury	CF, LF	4	1	2	0	0	1	2	.438
Pedroia	2B	4	0	0	0	0	0	2	.278
Ortiz	1B	3	0	1	1	1	0	0	.333
Crisp[b]	PR, CF	0	0	0	0	0	0	0	.500
Ramírez	LF	4	0	0	0	0	1	2	.250
Okajima	P	0	0	0	0	0	0	0	.000
Papelbon	P	0	0	0	0	0	0	0	.000
Lowell	3B	4	2	2	1	0	0	0	.400
Drew	RF	4	0	0	0	0	1	1	.333
Varitek	C	4	0	2	1	0	0	0	.333
Lugo	SS	3	0	1	0	0	0	1	.385
Lester	P	2	0	0	0	0	1	2	.000
Delcarmen	P	0	0	0	0	0	0	0	.000
Timlin	P	0	0	0	0	0	0	0	.000
Kielty[a]	PH	1	1	1	1	0	0	0	1.000
Youkilis	1B	0	0	0	0	0	0	0	.222
TOTALS		**33**	**4**	**9**	**4**	**1**	**4**	**10**	

[a]-Kielty homered for Timlin in the 8th.
[b]-Crisp ran for Ortiz in the 8th.
2B: Ellsbury (4, Cook), Lowell (3, Cook).
HR: Lowell (1, Cook), Kielty (1, Fuentes).

	POS	AB	R	H	RBI	BB	SO	LOB	AVG
COLORADO									
Matsui	2B	4	0	1	0	0	1	2	.294
Corpas	P	0	0	0	0	0	0	0	.000
Smith[b]	PH	1	0	0	0	0	1	0	.500
Tulowitzki	SS	4	0	0	0	0	3	3	.231
Holliday	LF	4	0	0	0	0	1	1	.294
Helton	1B	4	1	2	0	0	0	0	.333
Atkins	3B	3	1	1	2	1	0	1	.154
Spilborghs	CF	3	0	0	0	1	1	2	.000
Hawpe	RF	3	1	1	1	1	0	1	.250
Torrealba	C	4	0	0	0	0	0	2	.143

Cook	P	2	0	1	0	0	0	0	.500
Affeldt	P	0	0	0	0	0	0	0	.000
Sullivan[a]	PH	1	0	1	0	0	0	0	.333
Fuentes	P	0	0	0	0	0	0	0	.000
Carroll	2B	1	0	0	0	0	0	0	.000
TOTALS		**34**	**3**	**7**	**3**	**3**	**7**	**12**	

[a]-Singled to center for Affeldt in the 7th.
[b]-Struck out for Corpas in the 9th.
2B: Helton (2, Lester), Matsui (1, Lester).
HR: Hawpe (1, Delcarmen), Atkins (1, Okajima).

2007 Playoffs Composite Stats

American League Divisional Series, American League Championship Series, World Series totals

Boston Red Sox Batting (Ranked by at bats)

PLAYER	POS	AVG	OBP	G	AB	R	H	2B	3B	HR	RBI	BB	SO
Dustin Pedroia	2B	.283	.348	14	60	12	17*	6	0	2	10	6	7
Jason Varitek	C	.269	.310	14	52	6	14	5	0	1	10	3	14*
J. D. Drew	RF	.314	.352	14	51	7	16	3	0	1	11	2	6
Mike Lowell	3B	.353	.410	14	51	10	18	7*	0	2	15	6	4
Kevin Youkilis	1B	.475*	.475	14	49	16*	19	4	1*	4*	10	9	8
Julio Lugo	SS	.271	.327	14	48	7	13	3	0	0	3	5	9
David Ortiz	DH,1B	.370	.508*	14	46	16*	17*	6	0	3	10	14	9
Manny Ramírez	LF	.348	.508*	14	46	11	16	2	0	4*	16*	16*	9
Coco Crisp	CF	.182	.206	13	33	3	6	1	0	0	2	1	9
Jacoby Ellsbury	OF	.360	.429	11	25	8	9	4	0	0	4	3	3
Bobby Kielty	PH,OF	.500	.571	3	6	2	3	0	0	1	3	1	2
Daisuke Matsuzaka	P	.333	.333	4	3	0	1	0	0	0	2	0	1
Jon Lester	P	.000	.000	3	2	0	0	0	0	0	0	0	1
Eric Hinske	PH	.000	.000	3	2	1	0	0	0	0	0	0	2
Doug Mirabelli	C	.000	.000	1	2	0	0	0	0	0	0	0	1
Alex Cora	SS	.000	.000	4	0	0	0	0	0	0	0	0	0
TOTALS		**.313**	**.392**	**14**	**476**	**99**	**149**	**41**	**1**	**18**	**96**	**66**	**85**

*Team leaders with more than 25 AB.

Boston Red Sox Pitching (Ranked by IP)

PLAYER	W	L	SV	ERA	IP	G	GS	CG	SHO
Josh Beckett	4	0	0	1.20	30.0	4	4	1	1
Curt Schilling	3	0	0	3.00	24.0	4	4	0	0
Daisuke Matsuzaka	2	1	0	5.03	19.2	4	4	0	0

Hideki Okajima	0	0	0	2.45	11.0	8	0	0	0
Jonathan Papelbon	1	0	4	0.00	10.2	7	0	0	0
Jon Lester	1	0	0	1.93	9.1	3	1	0	0
Mike Timlin	0	0	0	3.18	5.2	6	0	0	0
Tim Wakefield	0	1	0	9.64	4.2	1	1	0	0
Manny Delcarmen	0	0	0	8.31	4.1	6	0	0	0
Eric Gagné	0	1	0	6.23	4.1	5	0	0	0
Javier López	0	0	0	15.43	2.1	5	0	0	0

Boston Red Sox Pitching (Extended)

PLAYER	H	R	ER	HR	BB	SO	WHIP	OPP AVG
Josh Beckett	19	4	4	1	2	35	0.70	.200
Curt Schilling	25	8	8	3	3	16	1.17	.302
Daisuke Matsuzaka	22	11	11	1	8	17	1.53	.348
Hideki Okajima	9	3	3	2	3	11	1.09	.267
Jonathan Papelbon	5	0	0	0	4	7	0.84	.220
Jon Lester	6	2	0	1	4	8	1.07	.263
Mike Timlin	3	2	2	0	0	7	0.53	.150
Tim Wakefield	5	5	5	1	2	7	1.50	.364
Manny Delcarmen	7	4	4	2	3	5	0.60	.458
Eric Gagné	4	3	3	0	2	6	0.40	.316
Javier López	5	4	4	0	2	0	1.33	.500

Pickoffs: Papelbon 1.
Wild pitches: Beckett 2, Matsuzaka 3, Gagné 1, López 1.

2007 World Series Composite Stats

Boston Red Sox Batting (Ranked by hits)

PLAYER	POS	AVG	G	AB	R	H	TB	2B	3B	HR	RBI
Jacoby Ellsbury	OF	.438	4	16	4	7	11	4	0	0	3
Mike Lowell	3B	.400	4	15	6	6	12	0	0	1	4
J. D. Drew	RF	.333	4	15	1	5	7	0	0	0	2
Julio Lugo	SS	.385	4	13	2	5	6	1	0	0	1
Dustin Pedroia	2B	.278	4	18	2	5	9	1	0	1	4
David Ortiz	DH,1B	.333	4	15	4	5	8	3	0	0	4
Jason Varitek	C	.333	4	15	2	5	6	1	0	0	5
Manny Ramírez	LF	.250	4	16	3	4	5	1	0	0	2
Kevin Youkilis	1B	.222	4	9	3	2	4	2	0	0	1
Coco Crisp	CF	.000	3	2	1	1	0	0	0	0	0
Bobby Kielty	PH	1.000	1	1	1	1	4	0	0	1	1
Daisuke Matsuzaka	P	.333	1	3	0	1	1	0	0	0	2
Eric Hinske	PH	.000	1	1	0	0	0	0	0	0	0
Jon Lester	P	.000	1	2	0	0	0	0	0	0	0
Alex Cora	PH	.000	0	0	0	0	0	0	0	0	0
TOTALS		**.333**		**141**	**29**	**47**	**73**	**13**	**0**	**3**	**29**

Boston Red Sox Extended Batting (Ranked by hits)

PLAYER	SH	SF	HP	IBB	SO	SB	CS	DP	E	SLG	OBP
Jacoby Ellsbury	0	0	0	0	2	1	0	0	0	.688	.500
Mike Lowell	0	0	0	0	1	1	0	0	1	.800	.500
J. D. Drew	1	0	1	0	3	0	0	0	1	.467	.412
Julio Lugo	0	0	0	0	0	0	0	1	0	.462	.500
Dustin Pedroia	0	0	0	0	0	0	0	1	0	.500	.350
David Ortiz	0	0	0	1	3	0	0	0	0	.533	.412
Jason Varitek	0	2	0	0	5	0	0	0	0	.400	.33
Manny Ramírez	0	0	0	2	2	0	0	1	0	.313	.33
Kevin Youkilis	0	0	0	0	1	0	0	0	0	.444	.417
Coco Crisp	0	0	0	0	0	0	0	0	0	.500	.500
Bobby Kielty	0	0	0	0	0	0	0	0	0	4.000	1.000
Daisuke Matsuzaka	0	0	0	0	1	0	0	0	0	.333	.333
Eric Hinske	0	0	0	0	1	0	0	0	0	.000	.000
Jon Lester	0	0	0	0	1	0	0	0	0	.000	.000
Mike Timlin	0	0	0	0	0	0	0	0	0	.000	.000
Alex Cora	1	0	0	0	0	0	0	0	0	.000	.000
TOTALS	**2**	**2**	**1**	**3**	**20**	**2**	**0**	**3**	**2**		

Boston Red Sox World Series Pitching (Ranked by innings pitched)

PLAYER	R/L	W	L	ERA	G	GS	CG	GF	SHO	SV
Josh Beckett	R	1	0	1.29	1	1	0	0	0	0
Jon Lester	L	1	0	0.00	1	1	0	0	0	0
Daisuke Matsuzaka	R	1	0	3.38	1	1	0	0	0	0
Curt Schilling	R	1	0	1.69	1	1	0	0	0	0
Jonathan Papelbon	R	0	0	0.00	3	0	0	3	0	3
Hideki Okajima	L	0	0	7.36	3	0	0	0	0	0
Mike Timlin	R	0	0	7.71	3	0	0	0	0	0
Manny Delcarmen	R	0	0	6.75	2	0	0	0	0	0
Eric Gagné	R	0	0	0.00	1	0	0	1	0	0
Javier López	L	0	0	—	1	0	0	0	0	0

Boston Red Sox World Series Pitching (Extended)

PLAYER	IP	H	R	ER	HR	BB	IBB	SO	WP	BK	OPP AVG
Josh Beckett	7.0	6	1	1	0	1	0	9	0	0	.259
Jon Lester	5.2	3	0	0	0	3	0	3	0	0	.261
Daisuke Matsuzaka	5.1	3	2	2	0	3	0	5	0	0	.304
Curt Schilling	5.1	4	1	1	0	2	0	4	0	0	.333
Jonathan Papelbon	4.1	2	0	0	0	0	0	3	0	0	.143
Hideki Okajima	3.2	4	3	3	2	0	0	6	0	0	.267
Mike Timlin	2.1	2	2	2	0	0	0	4	0	0	.222
Manny Delcarmen	1.1	3	1	1	1	1	0	1	0	0	.500
Eric Gagné	1.0	0	0	0	0	0	0	1	0	0	.000
Javier López	0.0	2	0	0	0	0	0	0	0	0	1.00

My Catfish Hunter impersonation, probably from my rookie year in 1975.

Photo courtesy Los Angeles Angels of Anaheim Baseball Club

CHAPTER THIRTY-TWO

Days of My Baseball Life

As the World Turns

At the end of a long day with my coauthor, Corey Sandler, he startled me with a question: "If you hadn't had success as a professional baseball player, would you today be an accountant in Fall River, Massachusetts?"

You know, I just might have been. When I was a kid, I had worked for my uncle, who was an accountant. I don't know if I ever would have gotten out of Somerset, where I grew up.

Things happened so quickly after I graduated from high school. I was seventeen years old when I was drafted by the Washington Senators; I had to decide whether to sign with them or go to college.

I went down to a school in Florida, but that didn't work out, and in the meantime my chance to sign with the Senators had passed. In those days, though, they had a secondary draft, and in January 1971, I was drafted by the Angels as their eighth and last pick. This time, I signed.

I've been fortunate that since graduating from high school, with the exception of that short time in Florida, I've never really had to decide on anything but baseball. The most serious decision I had to make came when I was done playing. I always thought I would be a coach or a manager. I never expected to be a broadcaster. But I have now been in the booth for more years than I was on the field.

Picking Up a Bat

Do I wake up now and miss playing? No—I really don't. Failure was very hard for me to deal with. And even success was hard for me, because I didn't know how long it was going to last. I was not a superstar player. Every day was a trial for me.

Once I retired, it was nice not to get up every morning and wonder what today was going to be like: Am I going to be pissed? Am I going to be good? Am I going to be happy? I really don't miss that.

I don't need to whack the ball around anymore or execute a double play. I did that enough. I was doing that from the time I was in Little League to the time I finished playing Major League Baseball. I have taken enough swings. I knew I wasn't going to get any better.

I faced the guys I had to face. This generation is facing the guys it has to face.

People have also asked me, "Since you have retired, have you ever gotten into the batting cage against one of today's pitchers?" And the answer is "no." Or, more specifically, "Have you ever wondered what it would be like to stand in against Pedro Martínez?" And the answer to that is, "I prefer not to wonder about that."

I can watch a pitcher and pretty much figure out my chances of getting a hit off of him. And I also can see how he could get me out. A top pitcher like Martínez at his peak could have walked up to me and announced, "I am going to throw you five straight changeups," and I probably wouldn't hit them. But I also think I could have made contact with his fastball. That doesn't mean I would get a hit. But I know I could handle it.

I don't know if my injuries had something to do with the way I feel. My last few years in the major leagues were not fun. I didn't play very much because of bad knees, and I kept breaking down. It was get the knee fixed, go try it, get it fixed again, and go try it again. It was frustrating and it was almost a relief for me to not to have to deal with it anymore.

It's not like I had to leave the game because I was a lousy player. And I didn't leave because of age. I just couldn't do it anymore. So I think that made it a little bit easier for me.

My Seven Home Runs

I have such an advantage over Barry Bonds, Sammy Sosa, Mark McGwire, David Ortiz, Manny Ramírez, and the other great home-run hitters of our time. I can recall almost every one of my homers, all seven of them.

Home Run 1

May 19, 1975, at Cleveland

California Angels 12, Cleveland Indians 5

It was the fourth inning, two on and two out. Jim Perry came in as a reliever with the Angels ahead 5–3. Perry was a former Cy Young winner in his seventeenth season in the majors and I was six weeks into my major league career.

I pulled the pitch, and the ball just barely cleared the fence. I was flying around the bases and I didn't know it was gone until I was at second base. I had never hit a homer, and I was running it out like it was going to be a triple. I never got into a home-run trot.

On that one swing, everything worked right. I hit the right pitch on the right part of the bat. Frank Robinson was the Cleveland manager, and he said if Remy can hit a home run off Perry, he can't pitch for me anymore. The next day Perry was released from the Indians. He played a few more games for Oakland that season, but then he was finished.

Home Run 2

May 17, 1977, at Anaheim

California Angels 6, Boston Red Sox 2

Two years later, I hit my second home run, this one off Ferguson Jenkins, leading off the fifth inning in a game where we beat Boston. Something was working right; 1977 was my home-run season. I hit four that year.

Home Run 3

July 3, 1977, at Anaheim

California Angels 6, Oakland Athletics 4

Seven weeks later, I homered off Mike Norris in the third inning, scoring Thad Bosley and knocking Norris out of the game. We won that game, too.

Home Run 4

August 12, 1977, at New York

New York Yankees 10, California Angels 1

We had just finished a series in Boston and moved on to New York for a doubleheader. My first at bat was against Catfish Hunter. Yankee Stadium has the short porch in right field, and it went out good. And I said to myself, "Wow, I'm 1 for 1 with a home run."

Every other time I came up to bat that day, I tried to hit a home run. I never tried to do that in my life, and I certainly shouldn't have. I didn't get another hit in that game, and only one hit in the second game of the doubleheader. And we lost both games.

Home Run 5

August 26, 1977, at Detroit

California Angels 7, Detroit Tigers 4

I was obviously on a tear. Two weeks later at Detroit, I hit a lead-off homer off Jack Morris. And then in the eleventh inning, I led off with a single and scored the go-ahead run on a Bobby Bonds home run.

Home Run 6

August 5, 1978, at Milwaukee

Boston Red Sox 8, Milwaukee Brewers 1

I guess it wasn't much of a streak; my next four-bagger took almost a year to come. My first home run for Boston came off Eduardo Rodríguez in the third inning with two outs, scoring Butch Hobson.

Home Run 7

August 20, 1978, at Oakland

Boston Red Sox 4, Oakland Athletics 2

Matt Keough was said to throw a spitball, and I think that's what he threw me. I swung wildly and missed the pitch, but the umpire behind home plate, Durwood Merrill, called it a foul tip. Everybody in the ballpark, including me, thought I had struck out, but Merrill said it was a foul ball. I was already walking back to the dugout.

By the time I got back to home plate, Keough was screaming and yelling at the umpire. He was going crazy.

He throws the next pitch in, and I hit a home run. It was just hilarious.

You know they say, "Don't give power hitters a second chance." Here I am, a guy who almost never hits home runs. I got a chance when I should have been out, and I hit a home run off him, scoring Butch Hobson and Rick Burleson.

That was the last home run I ever hit, and it should never have happened.

The Greatest Game

On October 2, 1978, one of the greatest games in the history of baseball was played. It was a perfect game. Perfect, except we lost.

On that beautiful October afternoon, there was a one-game playoff in Boston to decide the division championship of the American League East. It was the Red Sox against the Yankees, the two best teams that year. It couldn't have been a better matchup.

The Yankee starter was Ron Guidry, who was 25–3 with a 1.74 ERA and on his way to winning the Cy Young Award unanimously, finishing second to Boston's Jim Rice in the voting for Most Valuable Player in the American League. Mike Torrez started for Boston.

In the seventh inning Bucky Dent hit an improbable three-run homer to put the Yankees ahead by a run. And then came the bottom of the ninth.

With one out and one on, I hit a Goose Gossage fastball on a line drive to right field. Lou Piniella couldn't see the ball in the late afternoon sun. "I knew it was headed towards me," he told sportswriter Peter Gammons. "I just had to wait for it to come into sight and react like a hockey goalie."

The ball landed just in front of Piniella, and he just held his glove out there and grabbed it. "If it had gone by me," he told Gammons, "it would've rolled to the bull pen, Remy would've had an inside-the-park homer, and he would forever be remembered as the man who ended the Curse. Instead, I got lucky."

Carl Yastrzemski made the final out. We lost the game by one run, and the Yankees went on to the Series.

In my opinion I would have had a triple. I don't think I would have had an inside-the-park home run, but Burleson would have scored. We would have been tied, I would have been on third with one out, and we would have had Rice and Yastrzemski coming up behind me.

Looking back I can see how Piniella's play was pure luck. When I hit the ball, I knew he wasn't going to catch it; I had a pretty good idea the ball was going to drop in. What I didn't know was that he had lost the ball in the sun. All he did was stick his glove out, and the ball bounced right in. That held Burleson at second and me at first base.

Had the ball been one inch to his left, it would have gone by him, Burleson would have scored, I would have been on third base, and there might be a monument to me at Fenway Park. That's how crazy that inning was.

We had come to the ballpark with our bags packed to go to Kansas City had we won. It was crushing, a lousy way to go into the off-season. But then you start the next season and you move on.

When I retired, I thought about it more. Gee, that was a great game to play in, a great atmosphere. And then I realize that was as close as I got to being in the World Series. That stings.

The Dirt Dawgs

I love to watch a great hitter launch a home run. I love to watch a great center fielder make a terrific catch. I'm thrilled to watch a shortstop go deep into the hole to make a great play. And I love to watch a good runner go from first to third on a single.

But what I love most of all are guys who like to play. I like to watch guys charging the ball. I like to watch guys who give the same effort when they are down by ten runs as when they are ahead by ten runs. I like to see guys get upset when they are not playing well.

I can't stand guys who mail it in. It just doesn't sit well with me. The only thing you can control in the game is effort. You can't control anything else. Once the ball leaves your bat, somebody is either going to catch it or not. I want to see guys who play hard all the time: run the bases hard, break up double plays, throw to the right bases, guys who are fundamentally sound.

Some of my favorite players have been guys who didn't have the best ability, but they had the most heart. There are a lot of times I would rather pay to see a lesser player than a so-called superstar.

These are the *dirt dawgs:* guys who are relentless, an infielder who will dive for every ground ball to keep it in the infield.

I've already said a few times how difficult baseball is to play every day, for 30 spring training games and 162 regular season games. It is mentally and physically draining. When a guy consistently gives maximum effort, he's someone I really appreciate watching.

I loved Pete Rose as a player. He was so competitive. He didn't want to lose. He didn't want to be embarrassed. This guy played every single day like it was the last game he was going to play. Can every player look in the mirror and say, "I got the most out of myself in this brief career"?

Former Red Sox Trot Nixon was a guy who could not live with himself when he didn't do well. Jason Varitek is another example. I can't help liking them because of the way they play the game.

When fans go to the ballpark, they look for great moments. He wants to see home runs. She may want to see superstars have a great day. And they both may hope to see Curt Schilling or Josh Beckett or Daisuke Matsuzaka mow down the opposition with outstanding stuff. I love to watch that stuff, too. But I also love to watch a player who is going to battle every single day for his team and for himself.

Speaking for myself, I may not have had the greatest stats. I may not have made the most money. But I can live with myself knowing that I had the opportunity to play on the big stage, and I did it as best as I possibly could every single day.

Rem Dawg Remembers

Jerry Remy

I tried to get the best out of what I had. I didn't have great ability by any measure, but I worked very hard, and I'm very proud of the fact that I played eleven years in the majors and made an All-Star team.

I could run—that was my best attribute—so I used that to my advantage.

I know that I left nothing behind. When I left the game, there was nothing that I felt I didn't accomplish. I did what I wanted to do, and I did it the way I wanted to do it.

Appendix: Jerry Remy

Jerry Remy, *Gerald Peter Remy*

Bats *Left,* **Throws** *Right*

Height *5' 9",* **Weight** *165 lb.*

Born *November 8, 1952, in Fall River, Massachusetts*

Major League Debut *April 7, 1975*

Major League Hitting Stats

Year	Team	Games	AB	Hits	2B	3B	HR	TB	BB	K
1975	Angels	147	569	147	17	5	1	177	45	55
1976	Angels	143	502	132	14	3	0	152	38	43
1977	Angels	154	575	145	19	10	4	196	59	59
1978	Red Sox	148	583	162	24	6	2	204	40	55
1979	Red Sox	80	306	91	11	2	0	106	26	25
1980	Red Sox	63	230	72	7	2	0	83	10	14
1981	Red Sox	88	358	110	9	1	0	121	36	30
1982	Red Sox	155	636	178	22	3	0	206	55	77
1983	Red Sox	146	592	163	16	5	0	189	40	35
1984	Red Sox	30	104	26	1	1	0	29	7	11
Career Totals		**154**	**4455**	**1226**	**140**	**38**	**7**	**1463**	**356**	**404**

AB: at bats, TB: total bases, BB: walks, K: strikeouts.

Major League Hitting Stats (Productivity)

Year	Team	AB	BA	R	RBI	On-base percentage (OBP)	Slugging percentage (SLG)	On-base plus slugging (OPS)
1975	Angels	569	.258	82	46	.311	.311	.622
1976	Angels	502	.263	64	28	.313	.303	.615
1977	Angels	575	.252	74	44	.322	.341	.663
1978	Red Sox	583	.278	87	44	.321	.350	.671
1979	Red Sox	306	.297	49	29	.350	.346	.697
1980	Red Sox	230	.313	24	9	.339	.361	.700
1981	Red Sox	358	.307	55	31	.368	.338	.706
1982	Red Sox	636	.280	89	47	.337	.324	.661
1983	Red Sox	592	.275	73	43	.320	.319	.639
1984	Red Sox	104	.250	8	8	.297	.279	.576
Career Totals		**4455**	**.275**	**605**	**329**	**.327**	**.328**	**.656**

BA: batting average, R: runs scored, RBI: runs batted in.

Major League Hitting Stats (Extended)

Year	Team	SF	SH	HBP	IBB	GIDP	TPA	XBH
1975	Angels	3	12	0	1	15	629	23
1976	Angels	4	13	0	1	5	557	17
1977	Angels	4	19	2	2	9	659	33
1978	Red Sox	6	14	0	0	13	643	32
1979	Red Sox	2	6	0	1	2	340	13
1980	Red Sox	2	7	0	0	6	249	9
1981	Red Sox	3	13	0	2	6	410	10
1982	Red Sox	5	18	2	1	14	716	25
1983	Red Sox	3	12	0	2	12	647	21
1984	Red Sox	0	2	0	0	1	113	2
Career Totals		**32**	**116**	**4**	**10**	**83**	**4963**	**185**

SF: sacrifice flies; SH: sacrifice hits; HBP: hit by pitch; IBB: intentional walk; GIDP: grounded into double play; TPA: total plate appearances; XBH: extra base hits.

Common Hitting Ratios

Year	Team	At bats per home run (AB/HR)	At bats per strikeout (AB/K)	At bats per RBI (AB/RBI)
1975	Angels	569	10.3	12.4
1976	Angels	—	11.7	17.9
1977	Angels	143.8	9.7	13.1
1978	Red Sox	291.5	10.6	13.2
1979	Red Sox	—	12.2	10.6
1980	Red Sox	—	16.4	25.6
1981	Red Sox	—	11.9	11.5
1982	Red Sox	—	8.3	13.5
1983	Red Sox	—	16.9	13.8
1984	Red Sox	—	9.5	13
Career Totals		**636.4**	**11**	**13.5**

Baserunning

Year	Team	Stolen bases	Caught stealing	Stolen base percentage
1975	Angels	34	21	.618
1976	Angels	35	16	.686
1977	Angels	41	17	.707
1978	Red Sox	30	13	.698
1979	Red Sox	14	9	.609
1980	Red Sox	14	6	.700
1981	Red Sox	9	2	.818
1982	Red Sox	16	9	.640
1983	Red Sox	11	3	.786
1984	Red Sox	4	3	.571
Career Totals		**208**	**99**	**.678**

Fielding Stats

Year	Team	Pos	G	Total chances	PO	A	E	DP	Fielding percentage
1975	Angels	2B	147	777	336	427	14	111	.982
1976	Angels	2B	133	701	279	406	16	77	.977
1977	Angels	2B	152	746	307	420	19	90	.975
	Angels	3B	1	0	0	0	0	0	—
1978	Red Sox	2B	140	784	327	444	13	114	.983
	Red Sox	SS	1	3	1	2	0	0	1.000
1979	Red Sox	2B	76	363	147	205	11	43	.970
1980	Red Sox	2B	60	305	109	189	7	30	.977
	Red Sox	OF	1	0	0	0	0	0	—
1981	Red Sox	2B	87	441	162	272	7	58	.984
1982	Red Sox	2B	154	735	290	432	13	104	.982
1983	Red Sox	2B	144	678	295	376	7	104	.990
1984	Red Sox	2B	24	113	40	70	3	13	.973
Career Totals			**1120**	**5646**	**2293**	**3243**	**110**	**744**	**.981**

Pos: position; G: games; PO: putouts; A: assists; E: errors; DP: double plays.

Minor League Stats

Year	Team	Lg	Age	Org	Level	G	AB	R	H	2B	3B	HR	RBI	BA	SLG
1971	Magic Valley	Pio	18	Cal	Rookie	32	104	25	32	5	3	0	6	.308	.413
1972	Stockton	Cal	19	Cal	A+	133	532	59	141	18	3	4	43	.265	.333
1973	Quad Cities	Midw	20	Cal	A	117	478	66	160	23	10	4	36	.335	.450
1974	El Paso	Tex	21	Cal	AA	91	394	74	133	34	5	4	46	.338	.450
1974	Salt Lake	PCL	21	Cal	AAA	48	195	33	57	6	5	0	21	.292	.374

Lg: league, Org: major league affiliation, G: games, AB: at bats, R: runs, H: hits, BA: batting average, SLG: slugging average.

Index

Note: Page references in **bold** indicate World Series roster listings.

T

About the Authors

JERRY REMY has been the color analyst for Boston Red Sox television broadcasts since 1988. He played ten years at second base in the major leagues for the California Angels and the Boston Red Sox, compiling a .275 lifetime batting average. He can be reached through his Web site at www.theremyreport.com or directly by e-mail at jerry@theremyreport.com.

COREY SANDLER is the author of more than 150 books on sports, business, history, and travel. A former newsman for the Associated Press and Gannett Newspapers, he lives in Nantucket, Massachusetts. He can be reached through his Web site at www.econoguide.com or directly by e-mail at csandler@econoguide.com.